PRAISE FOR *WILDCRAFTED SEEDS AND GRAINS*

"Pascal Baudar's books keep getting better. He is an intrepid experimentalist and original thinker whose ideas about ways of using foraged food are deepening over time with his accumulated experience. With *Wildcrafted Seeds and Grains*, once again, I am wowed."

—Sandor Ellix Katz, author of *The Art of Fermentation*, *Wild Fermentation*, and other titles

"Pascal Baudar is one of the great foraging visionaries and wild food teachers in the world, and his latest book will inspire foragers, foodies, and seekers alike for years to come. From the first pages, we are presented with perspective-shifting knowledge, and it's likely you will find yourself scanning the backyard, weedy edgelands, and wild places for the smallest offerings from the plants, tucked under leaves and folded into husks. Sharing his expertise in foraging, preservation, and culinary artistry, Baudar reveals one of the most ancient forms of flavor, beauty, and sustenance that we often overlook in the culinary and foraging worlds: wild grains and seeds. Guiding the reader through straightforward methods of gathering and extracting seeds from common and invasive plants to ways of preserving and incorporating them into meals, *Wildcrafted Seeds and Grains* is an essential addition to every forager, cook, and food lover's bookshelf."

—Tara Lanich-LaBrie, author of *Foraged and Grown*

"In *Wildcrafted Seeds and Grains*, Pascal Bauder transcribes the time-honored practice of seed saving to the page and teaches you how to see whatever wilderness you've got near you for the diverse seed store it is. Here, yet again, Baudar demonstrates just how deep his knowledge of wild foods is and just how delicious those foods can be."

—David Zilber, chef; coauthor of *The Noma Guide to Fermentation*

"A new book by Pascal Baudar is always cause for excitement and—even better—anticipation: 'What am I going to learn?' Pascal's work is rigorous in its research, practical in application, and, in a culinary realm where appropriation is rife, it is authentic. Focusing on seeds and grains was a natural step for him, since he seems to have explored almost everything else wild. I can't wait to apply what I learn from *Wildcrafted Seeds and Grains*, and I am immensely grateful that Pascal continues to explore beyond-conventional ingredients with his particular brand of curiosity, creativity, and generosity of spirit."

—Marie Viljoen, author of *Forage, Harvest, Feast*

"The indefatigable Pascal Baudar has done it again. As industrial agriculture constantly reduces the number and variety of grains and seeds on which we subsist, Pascal teaches us to forage completely forgotten species on our own."

—Ken Albala, food historian; chef; author of *Opulent Nosh*

"As a perpetually curious chef and forager, I have always found Mr. Baudar's writing both revelatory and relevant. I have gleaned from his past experiments such knowledge as creating vinegar with the help of fruit flies, and I can now add to that list using a common blender as a grain thresher. His sense of wonder is eclipsed only by his passion for experimentation."

—Evan Mallett, chef; author of *Black Trumpet*

Wildcrafted Seeds and Grains

Also by Pascal Baudar

The New Wildcrafted Cuisine:
Exploring the Exotic Gastronomy of Local Terroir

The Wildcrafting Brewer:
Creating Unique Drinks and Boozy Concoctions
from Nature's Ingredients

Wildcrafted Fermentation:
Exploring, Transforming, and Preserving
the Wild Flavors of Your Local Terroir

Wildcrafted Vinegars:
Making and Using Unique Acetic Acid Ferments
for Quick Pickles, Hot Sauces, Soups,
Salad Dressings, Pastes, Mustards, and More

Wildcrafted Seeds and Grains

An Introduction to Extracting, Preparing, Storing, and Cooking with Common Wild Varieties

PASCAL BAUDAR

Chelsea Green Publishing
White River Junction, Vermont
London, UK

First published in 2025 by Chelsea Green Publishing | PO Box 4529 | White River Junction, VT 05001 | West Wing, Somerset House, Strand | London, WC2R 1LA, UK | www.chelseagreen.com
A Division of Rizzoli International Publications, Inc. | 49 West 27th Street | New York, NY 10001 | www.rizzoliusa.com

Publisher: Charles Miers
Deputy Publisher: Matthew Derr
Developmental Editor: Natalie Wallace
Assistant Editor: Yardena Carmi
Copy Editor: Buzz Poole
Proofreader: Karen Wise
Indexer: Shana Milkie
Designer: Melissa Jacobson

ISBN 978-1-64502-272-5 (paperback) | ISBN 978-1-64502-273-2 (ebook)
Library of Congress Control Number: 2025029385 (print) | 2025029386 (ebook)

Our Commitment to Green Publishing
Chelsea Green sees publishing as a tool for cultural change and ecological stewardship. We strive to align our book manufacturing practices with our editorial mission and to reduce the impact of our business enterprise in the environment. We print our books using vegetable-based inks whenever possible. This book may cost slightly more because it was printed on paper from responsibly managed forests, and we hope you'll agree that it's worth it. *Wildcrafted Seeds and Grains* was printed on paper supplied by Versa that is certified by the Forest Stewardship Council.®

Authorized EU representative for product safety and compliance
Mondadori Libri S.p.A. | www.mondadori.it
via Gian Battista Vico 42 | Milan, Italy 20123

Printed in the United States of America.
10 9 8 7 6 5 4 3 2 1 25 26 27 28 29

Deep gratitude to
Gloria Putnam for offering
such a beautiful and
inspiring workspace in
the pristine mountains of
Southern California

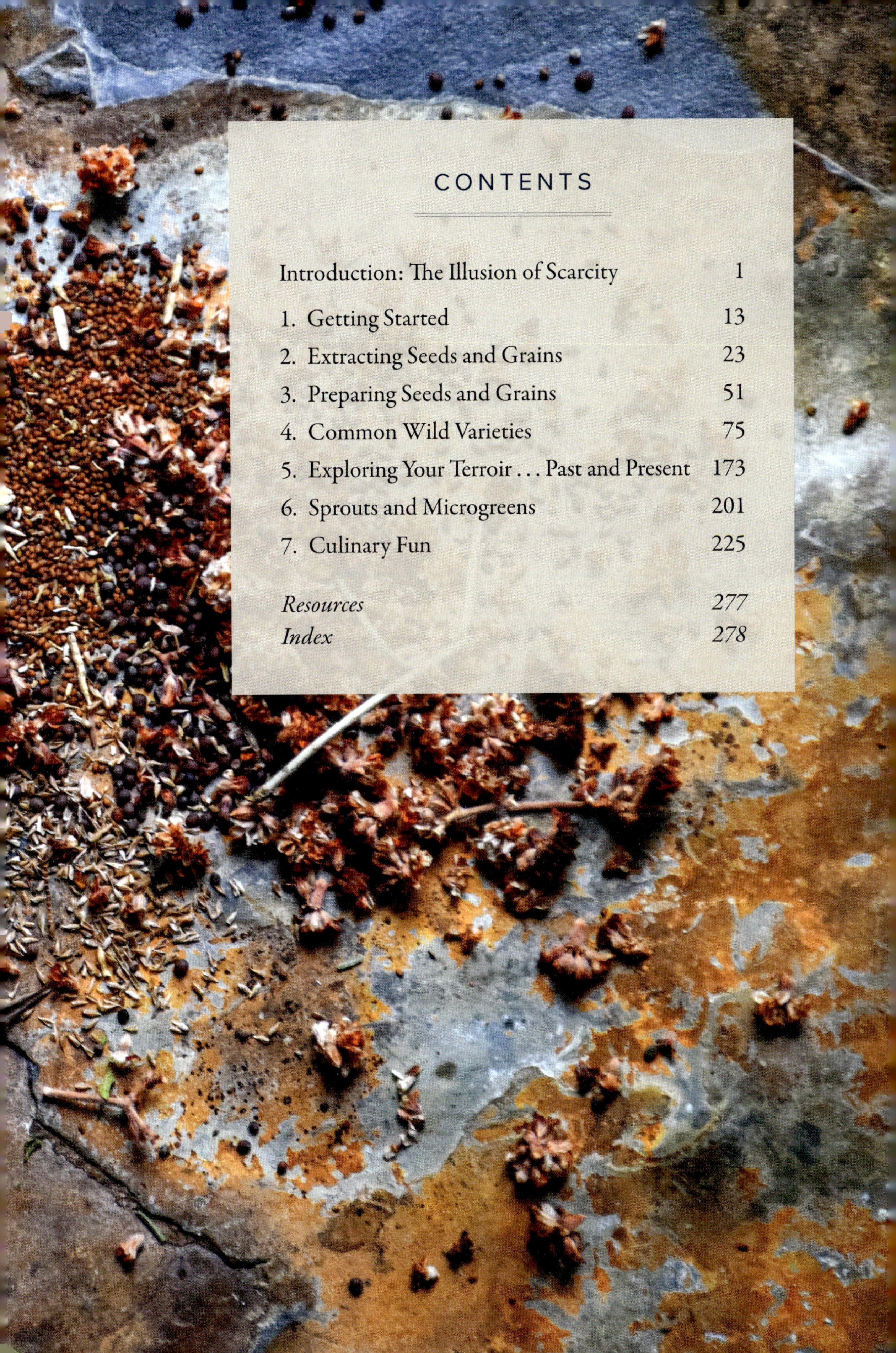

CONTENTS

INTRODUCTION

The Illusion of Scarcity

In my foraging classes and workshops, I often tell my students the following: "We are surrounded by edible plants. Without knowledge of these plants, they remain invisible to us. However, once we learn to identify and use them, they reveal themselves abundantly all around us."

This is especially true for edible wild seeds and grains. They surround us in late summer or fall, depending on where you live, yet they often go unnoticed. For example, after a harsh summer in Southern California, the hills around Los Angeles are covered with dried plants, which most people see as nothing more than dead vegetation prone to exacerbating fires. What many miss is that these seemingly "dead" plants are loaded with edible seeds and grains that our ancestors would have collected and used in numerous culinary applications as an added source of nutrition. A region like Southern California offers around 120 edible wild seeds and grains, none of which are available at the local supermarket. Forgotten knowledge keeps these plants hidden from most people's view.

I've long wanted to write this book in order to help people realize that, wherever they live, they are always surrounded by food. Seeds and grains are especially important because they are packed with essential nutrients, including healthy fats, fiber, and protein, making them a great source of sustained energy. Seeds, like flax and chia (wild or commercial), are particularly rich in omega-3 fatty acids. And let's not forget flavor! Some seeds, once toasted or roasted, release their natural oils, often giving them a warm, nutty taste that nicely complements a variety of dishes.

All these factors prompted me to start researching edible wild seeds and grains over ten years ago, when I was working on my first book, *The New Wildcrafted Cuisine*. As a forager, this subject has fascinated me, mainly because so much of this knowledge has been lost. Colonization, industrialization, and the rise of modern agriculture contributed to the eradication of Indigenous cultures, along with their knowledge and practices. Much of my work involves researching and experimenting with various methods of extraction and preparation once I find a new edible seed or grain, as there is often no historical documentation available on how they might have been processed.

We know these seeds and grains were eaten in the past through archaeological research, mentions in ethnobotany books, and the discovery of caches in ancient pots, but much of the information about processing methods and culinary uses has been lost, especially when it comes to wild seeds and grains associated with Europe and other parts of the Old World. The early rise of agriculture in those regions reduced the need for foraging, causing the knowledge about what was edible to disappear.

Diversity, Health, and Freedom of Choice

When I began to tackle this subject, my first obstacle was the sheer number of edible seeds and grains that exist in the world. We're not talking a few hundred; we are talking thousands, and possibly tens of thousands. It would probably take more than one lifetime of research to cover them all in a book.

In Southern California alone, I've collected over ninety edible wild seeds and grains, and I find more each year. Many of them are non-native and sometimes invasive. For instance, the hills around Los Angeles are covered with various non-native species of mustards (*Brassica* spp.), common wild oat (*Avena fatua*), cheatgrass (*Bromus tectorum*), great brome (*Bromus diandrus*), wild radish (*Raphanus raphanistrum*), and countless other plants bearing edible seeds and grains. Many of these are cultivated in other countries, but locally, they're viewed as "weeds"—unwanted and unused.

The county's typical approach is to spray them with chemicals like glyphosate, which poisons the environment, or to engage in "habitat restoration," which means these resources are simply removed and discarded. In some cases, we might call this "food waste." It's sad that, in a city where some people cannot afford healthy organic food, the concept of utilizing these resources doesn't exist.

We seem content with the illusion of abundance provided by modern civilization, but we don't grasp the true diversity nature offers us—and what we are missing. In my earlier books, I used the example of potatoes: at a store, you might find four or five varieties, which seems plentiful enough. But worldwide, there are over 4,000 varieties of potatoes.

Do you know how many grains and seeds you can find in a regular supermarket in America? Typically, you'll find five to eight different types of grains, including wheat, corn, rice, oats, quinoa, barley, bulgur, and farro. For seeds, you'll find four to six types, such as sesame, sunflower, chia, flax, and pumpkin. That's it!

Where I live, out of the approximately 120 edible seeds and grains that can be found in the environment, *none* of them are available at a typical supermarket, or even in a health food–type store, which usually has a wider selection. Even the chia seeds you buy in stores (*Salvia hispanica*) are not the same as the chia seeds that grow abundantly in the desert (*Salvia columbariae*). The reason is, of course, money. *Salvia hispanica* is commonly sold due to its broader commercial cultivation and higher yield.

In our current food system, we are offered what seems an abundance, but the reality is that our choices are extremely limited. Modern agriculture prioritizes quantity and financial gain over diversity and nutrition. The focus is on plants that are easy to grow and can feed a lot of people, meaning they are profitable.

Our ancestors knew much better. When I was researching the edible grains and seeds of Europe, I found a gold mine of information in the studies of bog bodies and their stomach contents. If you're not familiar with them, bog bodies are naturally preserved human bodies that have been found in peat bogs across Europe, especially in countries like Denmark, Germany, Ireland, and the UK. Many of these bodies date back thousands of years, and some of them appear to have been victims of ritualistic killings or sacrifice.

The interesting part is that, in some cases, due to their remarkable preservation, archaeologists and scientists were able to study the stomach contents of these bodies. It was discovered that many of them ate gruel as their last meal.

Now, agriculture was introduced in Europe during the Neolithic period, around 6000 to 4000 BCE, and many of the bodies studied were from around 2000 BCE. So, you would think that a gruel made at that time would be composed of whatever grains or seeds were commonly cultivated—such as barley, wheat, or rye—but in many cases, the gruel also contained a substantial amount of "weed seeds," which, of course, were edible wild seeds. The combination of wild and cultivated plants suggests a varied diet that still relied on foraging alongside farming practices.

From a forager's perspective, it is quite clear that the main reason those people added edible wild seeds to their diet was diversity: many of those seeds were nutrient rich and added extra flavor and texture to culinary preparations.

This should be a lesson to us today, as many contemporary or so-called "lifestyle" diseases are linked to poor nutrition. While bread is now often made with refined wheat flour alone, in ancient times it was common for bread to be made with a mix of different grains and seeds, including wild ones. The diversity would have significantly boosted the nutritional value of that bread.

Quantity Versus Diversity

When I started writing this book, I was fixated on quantity—how much I could harvest of any given plant in a reasonable amount of time. Perhaps it was because I used to teach survival skills and mistakenly saw foraging seeds and grains as a survival activity worth doing only if the harvest was decent.

Two years later, I've realized that foraging seeds and grains is not about survival; it's truly about diversity. The reality is that some grains and seeds are difficult to harvest, while others are extremely easy. For instance, collecting and extracting common wild oat is not easy and may not be worth the effort for some. Meanwhile, seeds from mustards, like black mustard (*Brassica nigra*) or tumbleweed mustard (*Sisymbrium altissimum*), are super easy to collect in large quantities—up to 4 cups (1 L) in one hour. That's abundance!

So why collect those hard-to-process grains and seeds?

As you collect seeds and grains throughout the year, you build a diverse pantry. You may end up with large quantities of some and small amounts of others, and that's okay. Chances are you're not in a survival situation, and even if you were, there are plenty of other things to forage, such as roots, berries, and nuts, depending on your location and the time of year.

Foraging seeds and grains can be time-consuming and labor-intensive, but the resulting diversity is crucial. It ensures a broad spectrum of nutrients, flavors, and preparations that enrich our diets. Wild seeds and grains often have higher protein, fiber, and mineral contents than their domesticated counterparts, and working with wild edible grains and seeds, even the challenging ones, touches every aspect of the culinary arts—from diversity and nutrition to aesthetics.

One of my favorite grains is great brome. I use it in many recipes—ferments, salsas, porridges, and more—and I extract it by hand for my classes. Although there are quicker extraction methods, you can't beat hand extraction if you want a truly beautiful grain. Great brome is one of the most invasive plants in my area, and I love how I can harvest these grains to enhance the aesthetics of my recipes. If you're a chef or an experienced cook, you know how important the look of a dish is in the experience of eating.

A New Foraging Dimension

If you are already an experienced forager, grains and seeds will open a new foraging "dimension" for you—and I know a few things about foraging dimensions. Aside from harvesting wild edibles, I also forage a wide variety of materials to create pottery: wild clays to form the objects; rocks and ashes to make glazes; fibers to make the cordage for some of my pots; and even interesting sticks to make teapot handles, spoons, ladles, and so on.

When I first got involved with this creative endeavor, I realized that there are various dimensions in which you can explore the landscape. For example, when I started foraging, I only looked for very common edible wild plants such as lamb's-quarter (*Chenopodium album*), dandelion (*Taraxacum officinale*), wild mustard, and so on, because those plants were all I knew. That was my "dimension," and it informed how I interacted with the land.

Then I started making wild brews, lacto-ferments, and vinegars and I recognized I was working on another level—searching for yeast and bacteria. The fascinating part is that each time I learned a new skill, I would look at the same old landscape in a brand-new way and find it exciting all over again, as if I was a complete newbie forager. It's quite exhilarating!

Making pottery added even more dimension. I was able to venture in the same landscape I'd been interacting with for over twenty years and find something new and exciting—clay, stones, fibers, and so much more.

Well, guess what? Seeds and grains opened another new dimension for me. When I was new to foraging, this dimension was completely invisible because I simply didn't know enough to see it, but as I accumulated knowledge over the years, it slowly opened to me.

That's the beauty of learning new skills; it keeps things exciting. The more I learn and explore the possibilities the land offers, the more I realize I don't know much. It's very humbling, but I have to tell you, from that place of humility I've gained an incredible appreciation for what nature offers. It's truly limitless.

I'm at a point where I must select the foraging dimension I want to inhabit for the day; otherwise, it becomes too much and too confusing. I have clay days, mushroom days, seed and grain days, and so on. I try to stick to the chosen activity, although I'm always open to a nice opportunity—I won't pass a beautiful cluster of oyster mushrooms even if I'm looking for fibers.

How to Approach This Book

This book is a summary of my research and experiences with wild seeds and grains, covering methods and techniques that have been useful to me, though you may find better ones. In contrast to my other books, which take more of a culinary deep dive, this book is really an introduction to this type of foraging. I've intentionally profiled plants that are very common pretty much anywhere in the world. It's a good way to get started.

Chapter 1 orients you with some basic terminology, equipment, and precautions. Chapters 2 and 3 walk you through techniques for seed and grain extraction and processing, offering methods for reducing antinutrients and making your harvest palatable. In chapter 4, you'll encounter many of the most common wild varieties around the world, learning how to identify, extract, process, and cook with them. Chapter 5 is an exciting exploration of our ancestors' use of wild seeds and grains, along with a present-day glimpse into my Southern California landscape, which will give you an idea of the possibilities in your own local environment. In chapter 6, you'll discover how to grow nutrient-dense sprouts and microgreens from your wild harvest, and in chapter 7 you'll find thirty-five of my favorite recipes that incorporate wild seeds and grains.

With a bit of experience dealing with the most common wild edible seeds and grains, you'll gain the confidence to look for others in your locality and discover how you can extract, process, and use them. By all means, share your discoveries with the world on social media, in foraging groups, and so on. That way, we can all improve, as there is still so much to learn about this subject. This book only scratches the surface.

Finding Edible Grains and Seeds in Your Area

We are very lucky to be living in this incredible information age. When I started foraging, knowledge was still mostly transferred orally from one human to another. Sure, there were books, but they were often quite basic and lacked high-quality photos.

Although nothing can really beat human connection and that sort of information exchange, these days we have a vast array of tools that can help us identify plants and understand their uses, including apps for identification, the internet and AI tools for information on historical uses and wild food processing, and social media facilitates the sharing of knowledge with fellow foragers from all over the world.

It's quite incredible, the changes I've seen in my lifetime.

So, let me give you some pointers on how I find and research new seeds and grains. The same rule that applies to foraging plants or mushrooms applies to foraging seeds and grains: you need to be able to identify the seed or grain and the plant it came from, then establish that it is indeed edible. You will find poisonous seeds—poison hemlock (*Conium maculatum*), jimsonweed (*Datura stramonium*), etc.—or deadly fungal infections (ergot, for example) connected to seeds and grains; thus, you need to gain certainty before consuming them.

As of 2024 (and if you're reading this in 2124, this information will be very outdated), the tools I've found incredibly helpful are plant identification apps. They're not perfect, but they're definitely useful. My go-to app, which is free to download, is called iNaturalist.

Here are some of the best plant identification apps available at no cost:

iNaturalist: great for identifying plants, animals, and fungi with AI recognition and community support.

Seek by iNaturalist: beginner-friendly and does not require an account. It identifies plants using your phone camera and works offline.

PlantNet: uses photo recognition to identify wild plants, backed by a large scientific community.

Flora Incognita: developed by scientists and uses AI to identify wild plants with detailed species information available offline.

iPhones also have a built-in feature that can help identify plants directly from your photos.

That said, you can't rely solely on apps to identify plants, especially when plants are going to seed and lack leaves or flowers, which are crucial for accurate identification. To forage wild seeds and grains, you'll need to ID the plants first when they're still flowering and have leaves, then go back later in the year when the plants are going to seed.

Apps are super useful, but they can be wrong. My rule is to use at least three different methods of identification before consuming a plant. When my app suggests a plant name, I usually enter it in an image search and compare various photographs to ensure they match the plant I have. Once I feel confident that the identification is correct, I deepen my search using phrases like "[plant name] identification features" or "How to ID [plant name]?" to verify the specific identifying characteristics.

If I'm still not completely certain that an identification is correct, my next step is to post a picture of the plant in plant identification groups. Unfortunately, you might get incorrect IDs from people who aren't very knowledgeable, but over time, you'll learn to recognize the individuals you can trust, such as trained botanists and experienced foraging experts.

If you're still uncertain, reach out directly to trusted individuals. In the past, I collected plants I couldn't identify and brought them to my teachers during wild food classes. Nowadays, I can simply message trusted contacts with a picture of the plant or even send a quick video for confirmation.

There are many other options for identifying plants, including:

Field guides and books: Use regional field guides dedicated to plants, wildflowers, trees, or other flora. Many guides include illustrations, photos, and keys to help you identify plants based on features like leaf shape, flower color, and habitat.

Local botanical gardens and nature centers: Many botanical gardens and nature centers offer plant identification services. You can bring samples or photos and get assistance from staff or volunteers.

Herbarium visits: Herbariums, often found at universities or museums, are excellent resources with extensive plant collections. Experts there can help identify unknown specimens.

Once you are fully confident in the plant's identity, then you can explore its edibility, if you're still uncertain about that. I usually start with an online search using questions like "Is [plant name] edible?" or "[plant name] edibility." If multiple sources confirm that it is edible, it's a good sign. However, if you find only one or two sources, be cautious, as they could be inaccurate.

If the search results indicate that the plant might be edible, I then consult reliable sources such as trusted books, field guides, reputable websites, or social media groups specifically focused on edible plants.

Here are a couple of websites I trust:

Plants For A Future (PFAF): This database has information on thousands of plants, including details on their edibility, medicinal uses, and other properties. www.pfaf.org

Native American Ethnobotany: Good for North America, this detailed database documents the traditional uses of plants by Native American tribes, including edibility, medicinal uses, and cultural significance. This resource is valuable for understanding the historical and traditional uses of native plants. http://naeb.brit.org

The key is to make sure you've identified a plant and confirmed its edibility before you proceed to collect the grains and seeds. Don't assume that if a plant is edible, the seeds or grains will be. For example, while apples are edible, the seeds contain amygdalin, a compound that can release cyanide when chewed or digested. In small quantities, the seeds are unlikely to cause harm, but consuming large amounts could be dangerous.

Finally, once you know that the seeds or grains of a plant are edible, then you can search for recipes or experiment and come up with your own recipes. The latter is the fun part.

Because so much information has been lost, it's not always an easy process when you're dealing with edible wild seeds and grains. You sometimes have to dig really deep and spend days, or weeks, researching archaeological findings, consulting books, or even connecting with scientists. For example, I learned a lot about the European Neolithic diet by connecting with archaeologists and purchasing books about bog bodies, as well as downloading online documents about archaeological findings from the excavation of places such as Must Farm, also called the "British Pompeii," which is a remarkably preserved Neolithic village.

As a disclaimer, you should note that the information in this book is based on my personal research, knowledge, and experience with edible wild grains and seeds over the last twenty years. While I have made every effort to identify and describe these seeds as accurately as possible, some might require specific processing methods, such as cooking or parching, to ensure their safety (e.g., some buttercup [*Ranunculus*] seeds). Additionally, scientific understanding of plant edibility can evolve, and seeds considered edible today may be reevaluated in the future.

Thus, I cannot guarantee the safety of any plant, seed, or grain described in this book. Proper identification and preparation are critical. As always with foraging, the responsibility for determining the edibility, safety, and suitability of any wild plant, mushroom, fruit, berry, seed, or grain rests entirely with you.

By using this book, you acknowledge and accept that the author and publisher are not liable for any harm, illness, or injury that might result from the consumption or misuse of the wild plants, seeds, and grains described herein. Foraging and consuming wild plants always involves a degree of risk. Proceed with caution and responsibility . . . and have fun!

On Foraging

Foraging can be done for good or evil; it can help the environment or intensify sustainability issues. Over the years, I've learned to streamline my activities so as to minimize my impact on nature. It's been a learning curve with trials and errors. But now I believe foraging can be done in such a way as to help your local environment, both by removing non-native plants—around 90 percent of what I pick—and sustainably harvesting or growing the native plants you need. At this point I've pretty much planted all the

native plants I use in this book in much larger quantities than I'll ever use, mostly on private lands owned by friends.

You don't need to be a fanatic tree hugger to see that our planet faces real problems, such as pollution, climate change (naturally occurring or not), human population expansion, loss of natural habitat, species extinctions, and much more. At this point in our evolution, we absolutely need to be part of the solution, and this responsibility even applies to the simple activity of harvesting wild plants. We must take care when we pick wild plants, keeping in mind environmental health and integrity.

Picking seeds and grains for food, drink, and medicine reconnects us with nature. It is a sacred link that, as a species, we all share. We are here because our ancestors had a very intimate relationship with nature, knew which plants to use for food and medicine, and, in many instances, knew

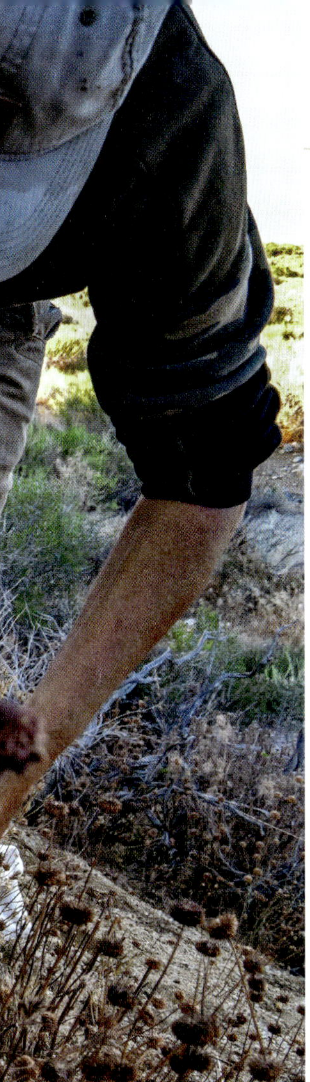

Photo courtesy of Nicolas Snyder

how to sustainably interact with their wild environment. No matter where we live, it's part of our cultural DNA.

I don't think the impulse to save nature by protecting it at all costs with a look-don't-touch mentality will work. Growing up in Belgium, my love for nature came through a deep interaction with my wild surroundings. If you truly love something, you will take care of it and make sure it's still there for generations to come.

When I was a kid, raising animals, growing food in our garden, and picking wild berries, nuts, and plants were normal parts of life. The knowledge was kept by the elders, who would pass it on to the next generation. In many modernized countries, this cycle of transferring knowledge has been lost. Very valuable and nutritious food plants such as dandelion, mallow, and others are looked upon as "weeds," and TV commercials gladly promote the use of toxic chemicals to destroy them. The people I've seen trashing the wilderness are the product of our current society: if you don't know or understand the value of something, you simply won't care for it.

Respect the environment, learn which plants are rare or illegal to pick, don't forage plants in protected areas (natural preserves and the like), work with native plant nurseries, and educate yourself on how to grow native plants and remove non-native ones. Forage the right way!

If you take from nature, work with her and make sure you always plant more than you'll ever harvest so future generations will have the same creative opportunities you do—or more.

CHAPTER 1

Getting Started

This chapter is designed to provide you with the basics of foraging and working with wild seeds and grains. We begin by looking at the difference between seeds, nuts, and grains—terms that are often used interchangeably but mean different things. Understanding what makes a grain a grain, or why a nut isn't always just a seed, will help you feel more confident as you begin collecting and processing these wild foods. While this book focuses mainly on seeds and grains, it's useful to understand where nuts fit in, even if we won't spend much time on them.

We'll also go over the practical side of things—how to harvest, clean, and store what you collect. You'll learn what husks and chaff are, why they matter, and how to remove them using simple tools and techniques. I've included a basic list of equipment to get you started, along with some tips for properly drying and storing your harvests.

Lastly, we'll learn how to identify the most common diseases that affect seeds and grains so you can forage safely. Whether you're brand new to this or need a refresher, this chapter lays the groundwork for everything that follows.

Seeds, Nuts, and Grains

To make it simple, seeds, nuts, and grains are all plant parts that are often used as a source of food. While they share some similarities that can make them difficult to differentiate, they do have distinct characteristics.

Seeds are the reproductive structures of plants that contain the embryo of a future plant, along with the nutrients it needs to germinate and grow into a new plant. They can be either edible or nonedible and come in various shapes and sizes. Examples of edible seeds include chia seeds, sunflower seeds, lamb's-quarter seeds, pumpkin seeds, curly dock (*Rumex crispus*) seeds, and sesame seeds—but there are many more.

Nuts are a type of seed that is surrounded by a hard shell or fruit that does not open on its own. Examples of nuts include acorns, walnuts, pecans, almonds, and cashews. In this book, I skip the nuts and concentrate on seeds and grains.

Grains are the edible fruits or kernels of cereal crops (or their wild ancestors), such as wild barley (*Hordeum spontaneum*), wheat, corn, regular rice, and wild oats.

One of the main differences between these three plant parts is their composition. Nuts are typically higher in fat and protein than seeds and grains, while seeds can be high in fat and protein but also contain fiber and other nutrients. Grains are mainly a source of carbohydrates and fiber.

Another difference is their culinary use. All three can be used in baking, but nuts are often eaten as a snack, either raw or roasted; seeds are often used as flavoring or a source of oil; and grains are used in side dishes or processed into breads, pastas, and breakfast cereals.

Even with these distinctions, it can still be tricky to categorize plant parts. For example, American wild rice (*Zizania* spp.) is technically a seed rather than a grain. It comes from aquatic grasses that grow in marshes and other shallow water. While it is commonly referred to as "wild rice," it is not directly related to the rice found in stores (*Oryza sativa*). Apparently, great brome produces seeds, but I've always called them grains because they simply fit the nutrient profile (carbohydrates and fiber), and they look like grains. So, there you go!

Most of the time, we'll get it right, and that's good enough for this book.

Of Husk and Chaff

Before we get into collecting and processing wild seeds and grains, it helps to understand two terms that come up a lot: *husk* and *chaff*. These are common terms in farming, but they are very useful in foraging, too. They help us keep things simple and avoid technical words such as *pericarp*, *endosperm*, and *bran*.

Both *husk* and *chaff* refer to the outer layers that surround a seed or grain, but they're used a bit differently. Husk is the tough, often fibrous outer shell that encases and protects grains and some seeds, such as corn, wheat, and sesame. The term *hull* is sometimes used interchangeably with *husk*. In many cases, the husk doesn't need to be removed before you use the grain or seed.

Chaff, on the other hand, is the lighter, dry, flaky material that sticks to cereal grains like wheat, wild barley, and wild oats. It usually includes small, scaly protective casings and other lightweight plant parts that are not edible but are somewhat easy to separate with winnowing—a process that uses airflow to blow away the lighter material from the heavier seeds or grains, whether by tossing the seeds or grains into the air on a windy day, using a fan, or gently blowing.

Note that when you're working with wild or farmed grasses—including wheat, barley, rye, and rice—the grain is covered by several thin, dry layers (technically called *glumes*, *lemmas*, and *paleas*). These layers form a dry husk around the grain, but once they're removed and floating around, people often refer to them as chaff. It can be a little confusing!

To keep things simple and clear in the book, the terms *husk* and *hull* refer to the tougher, more fibrous outer layer that's attached to the grain, and *chaff* refers to the lighter, loose material that easily can be removed with airflow.

Removing chaff is usually necessary, since it's light and gets in the way, but removing the husk is not always a priority. It depends on the grain and how you plan to use it. In traditional grinding, people often crushed the whole grain—husk and all—using stone tools. The flour was then sifted if they wanted a finer texture, but many ancient breads and flatbreads were made with coarse flour that still contained bits of husk.

Collection and Processing Equipment

To collect, clean, and process wild grains and seeds, you'll need a few basic tools. You'll find more equipment suggestions in the chapters that follow, but here is a brief list to get you started.

Collection Equipment

Gloves: Protect your hands from thorns, sharp edges, or irritating plants. In Southern California, gloves are especially useful for foraging seeds like chia, thistle sage (*Salvia carduacea*), and some mustard seeds.

Bags or baskets: Use breathable bags, such as paper bags, or baskets to collect seeds and grains. These containers allow air circulation, which prevents mold. Plastic bags also work, but you'll need to empty them as soon as you get home to prevent rotting.

Scissors or pruning shears: For cutting stems and branches easily.

Handheld sickle or knife: Useful for cutting stems or seedpods if you intend to forage a large quantity of grains.

Cleaning and Processing Equipment

Sieve or strainer: To separate seeds and grains from chaff and other debris. Having sieves with various mesh sizes is essential—you can never have too many. I've collected a large assortment over the years, some with holes just big enough for tiny wild amaranth seeds to fall through.

Mortar and pestle: For small-scale processing to remove seeds from husks or break open hard seedpods, such as wild radish (*Raphanus raphanistrum*).

Winnowing basket or large bowl: To help separate seeds and grains from lighter debris using airflow.

The perfect sieve for processing mustard seeds. Notice how the chaff stayed in the sieve but the seeds went through.

Screens or trays: For drying seeds and grains evenly.

Cloth or tarp: For spreading out grains for drying (if you don't use screens or trays) or threshing.

Bowls: Trust me, you'll need bowls of all sizes for winnowing and otherwise processing your grains and seeds.

Airtight containers: For storing cleaned and dried grains and seeds. Personally, I use glass jars or plastic containers, and sometimes paper bags.

Optional Equipment

Fan: For additional drying or assisting with winnowing. There is a decent amount of wind in the mountains where I live, so I've never needed to use a fan.

Desiccant packs: To keep stored grains and seeds dry. I don't use them since I usually eat my foraged grains within a year, but they are an option for long-term storage.

Notebook, pen, and labeling supplies: To keep track of different batches and types of seeds and grains. Also good for labeling bags, jars, and containers for storage. While many people use phones to record and take photos, I also like using pen and paper.

Drying and Storage

Obviously, after you spend a bunch of time foraging seeds and grains, you want to make sure your harvest does not spoil. I learned this lesson the hard way. The first time I collected black mustard seeds, I stored the fresh seeds in a closed jar, and within a week, the contents were moldy and rotten. It was quite a frustrating experience.

Properly storing grains and seeds is crucial to maintaining their freshness and nutritional value and preventing spoilage. It's heartbreaking to spend hours collecting something only to lose it due to improper storage.

If there's one basic piece of advice I can give you, it is this: dry your seeds or grains before storing them in a closed jar or similar container by spreading them out on a clean, flat surface that allows for good air circulation. You can use a fine mesh screen, a plate, baking sheets lined with parchment paper, or a clean cloth spread out on a table. Place the seeds or grains in a warm, dry area away from direct sunlight, ideally at a temperature of around 70°F (21°C). Stir them occasionally to ensure even drying and to prevent mold growth. Once they are completely dry, you can store them in airtight jars to keep them fresh.

Drying seeds and grains takes about one to two weeks. I usually do a visual and tactile inspection to see if they appear dry and feel hard. You can even try breaking a larger grain or seed with a knife or your fingernail; if it snaps cleanly, it is dry. If you have a large quantity, weighing them at the start and during the drying process can also help; when they stop losing weight, they are likely dry.

That's my basic procedure, but let's go into greater detail for those of you who intend to store seeds or grains for longer than a year and for different purposes, such as planting, sprouting, and growing microgreens.

Cool and dry environment: Store grains and seeds in a cool, dry place. The ideal temperature is below 60°F (15°C), and the humidity should be low to prevent mold and insect infestations. Living in California, it's hard for me to meet that temperature criterion. It hasn't been too much of a problem, but I store oil-rich seeds (sunflower, mustard, etc.) in the fridge. The lower temperature helps slow down the degradation of oils, preventing rancidity and extending the shelf life of the seeds. I do the same thing with oil-rich nuts such as acorns or walnuts.

Airtight containers: Use airtight containers such as glass jars, metal canisters, or food-grade plastic containers to protect against moisture and pests.

Labeling: Clearly label containers with the type of grain or seed and the date of storage to keep track of freshness.

Freezing: For longer-term storage, freezing seeds or grains can significantly extend the shelf life to several years. Freezing also protects against insect infestations, making it a reliable method for long-term preservation.

In summary, make sure your seeds are dry before you store them in closed containers. Label and store the containers in a cool, dry place, preferably below 60°F (15°C). I've never had any trouble with my harvest lasting up to a year at room temperature, even with the warmer storage conditions in Southern California. However, if I want to extend the shelf life beyond a year for some of my seeds or grains, I store them in the refrigerator or freezer.

Storing Sprouted Grains and Seeds

In chapter 6, we'll learn about sprouting wild grains and seeds, so let's talk about proper storage for sprouts and microgreens.

Make sure the sprouts or microgreens are completely dry before storing to prevent mold growth. To ensure safety and freshness, discard any that smell bad, look slimy, or have discoloration. Store them in the refrigerator in an airtight container or a resealable plastic bag. As an extra step for microgreens, I usually place them between damp paper towels to create a humid environment that prevents early wilting. Your sprouts/microgreens should stay fresh for up to a week.

Fungal Infections: Ergot and Smut

When foraging wild grains and seeds, it is crucial to be aware of potentially toxic fungal infections. On the positive side, they are pretty easy to spot if you know what to look for. Two common fungal diseases are ergot and smut, both of which produce dark fungal spores in the heads and grains of infected plants.

Ergot is a fungal infection caused by fungi from the genus *Claviceps*. The most well-known species is *Claviceps purpurea*, which primarily infects the grains of rye, both wild and domesticated. The fungus forms a hard, black mass called a sclerotium, which contains toxic chemicals that can cause ergotism in humans and animals if ingested. Ergotism, also known as "St. Anthony's Fire," can lead to severe symptoms, including convulsions, hallucinations, and gangrene.

Smut is a fungal disease that affects grains and grasses, replacing their seeds with dark, powdery spores. It is caused by a variety of species in the

Ergot fungus on rye. *Photo by Martina Berg / Shotshop.com*

Ustilaginaceae family, each affecting different host crops. For instance, *Ustilago hordei* causes a type of smut disease on oats and barley wherein the grain heads stay mostly intact but are filled with black fungal spores. *Tilletia laevis* causes a similar type of smut in wheat. Another kind of smut, produced by *Ustilago nuda* on barley and *Ustilago tritici* on wheat, causes the grain heads to open up and release the black spores more freely into the air. *Ustilago bullata* generally affects grasses in the *Bromus* genus, commonly known as brome grasses.

These spores can spread to other healthy plants through rain or wind. Unlike ergot, smut is usually not toxic to humans or animals (aside from possible allergies), but it can change the flavor of the infected grain.

While they aren't as common as ergot and smut, here are a few other toxic fungal infections to look out for:

Aflatoxins: Produced by the fungi *Aspergillus flavus* and *Aspergillus parasiticus*, aflatoxins are highly toxic and can grow on a variety of crops, including wild grains and seeds, especially in warm and humid conditions. Look for greenish-yellow mold growth on the grains or seeds.

Fusarium head blight (Scab): Caused by the *Fusarium* species, it usually affects wheat, barley, and corn, but also some wild grass species. This fungal infection can be harmful to humans and animals, causing nausea, vomiting, and immunosuppression. Look for whitish or sometimes pinkish fluffy fungal growth on seed heads.

Before you freak out about foraging grains and seeds, keep in mind that all kinds of fungal infections, including toxic ones, can show up on cultivated plants, fruits, and berries as well. There is no need to panic; just remember the importance of inspecting plants for signs of fungal contamination. They're usually quite obvious. If a plant looks suspicious, don't forage it.

CHAPTER 2

Extracting Seeds and Grains

Extraction: it's the main reason why your local supermarket doesn't offer the thousands of edible wild grains and seeds available in nature. Simply put, many wild seeds and grains are not very easy to extract, and there is no machinery that can do it speedily; therefore, nobody can make a quick buck off these plants. This is pretty much the history of agriculture in a nutshell: if it's not easy to produce and profit from, and if it can't feed a lot of people rapidly, then it's not worth it from a business perspective. But as we've seen, the reality is that people didn't stop foraging for wild seeds and grains until modern times.

When I first started foraging seeds and grains, the slow and sometimes laborious collection and extraction bothered me. But over time, I dropped the capitalistic focus on speed and profit, finally realizing how foraging these plants is about dietary diversity. By collecting the various edible seeds and grains in your local environment throughout the year, you can put together an incredible pantry. Some seeds and grains, such as wild oats, are hard to extract, especially when compared with their cultivated counterparts, while others, such as wild barley, tumble mustard, and nettle (*Urtica* spp.) are much easier to collect.

There are endless potential methods for extracting seeds and grains, and hopefully the text that follows will inspire you to invent your own methods based on your local terroir and plants.

Some of the methods I use are:

Hand extraction: That's right—use your fingers! Sometimes you don't have a choice, and that's alright.

Shake and gather: Place a large, non-porous bag over the top of the plant, gently tip the plant to the side, and shake to dislodge the seeds. This works well with some wild amaranth species.

Natural seed release: Hang the mature plants upside down over a bowl and allow the seeds to fall naturally as they dry.

Rolling pin method: Use a rolling pin to separate grains from their husks.

Traditional threshing: Threshing is the process of separating grains or seeds from the stalks and husks of harvested plants. It involves beating or rubbing the harvested plant material to loosen the edible parts from the inedible chaff. There are many different methods, including hand threshing, mechanical threshing, flail threshing, and animal treading.

Stick method: This is one method that approximates traditional threshing. All you need is a stick and a basket or similar container. You get my drift.

Comb threshing: Use a comb to gently rake through the seed heads of plants like Indian ricegrass (*Eriocoma hymenoides*). This action removes the seeds efficiently, and you can collect them in a bowl as they fall away from the plant.

Hand rubbing: Hold a bunch of seeds or grains between your hands and press them while making a circular motion. This action effectively separates the seeds from the chaff and husk.

Bag threshing: Place mustard branches and seedpods in a plastic bag, then dance on the bag to separate the seeds from the chaff. Cut a hole in the bottom of the bag and shake, allowing the seeds to fall through a sieve into a bowl.

Flame winnowing: Set the seed-containing tops of the plants on fire to burn away the chaff and husk, leaving the grains behind. This method takes advantage of the different combustion properties—the lighter chaff and husk burn away quickly, while the heavier grains remain intact for collection.

Stone grinder: Use a hand stone grinder (*molcajete*) to gently move the grains between the stone surfaces, effectively removing the husk without crushing the grains.

Basket and paddle threshing: This traditional method works well for collecting seeds from chia, thistle sage, and similar plants. Using a paddle, seed beater, or gloved hand, strike the mature seed heads so the seeds fly off into a large basket or box placed nearby. This technique allows you to gather a large number of seeds quickly without pulling the plants.

Vitamix threshing: This may be the best extraction method for the appropriate grains and seeds—it was a game-changing discovery for me.

Let's examine some of these methods in more detail.

Extracting thistle sage seeds in the local desert using the basket and paddle (or glove) threshing technique.

HAND EXTRACTION

This method of extraction involves using your fingers to separate grains from their husks or chaff. As such, you can use hand extraction only for grains that are large enough to be manipulated in this way. The husk is sometimes inedible and needs to be removed before the inner part can be eaten or processed. This is true for many grains, like wild oats and great brome.

When I set out to write this book, one of my first questions was: is hand extraction even worth it? It sounded terribly inefficient. For example, working with wild oat grains for a couple of hours, you'll be lucky to extract ¼ cup (70 g).

Yet these days, I use hand extraction for my favorite grain, great brome. Despite trying various methods, I prefer hand extraction because it preserves the aesthetic quality of these beautiful grains. In fact, one high-end restaurant that I supplied with wild edibles had a staff member spend an entire day extracting great brome grains to be used in one of their dishes. Typically, I boil the grains for around 60 minutes, after which removing the husk and chaff becomes much easier (see page 90).

There are other grains I extract by hand if I need a small quantity to make a dish for a class. Such is the case for wild oat grains, which I add to my ferments. Not too long ago, I removed milk thistle seeds from the dried flowers by hand so I could toast them and serve them the next day to my students as part of a dish.

If you are determined to build a wild food pantry that includes edible seeds and grains, you'll find that hand extraction is a worthwhile activity that significantly broadens the diversity and aesthetic qualities of your offerings.

Extracting wild ingredients by hand can set you apart and make you a standout. For example, one of my favorite foraged ingredients is lerps sugar—a sweet, crunchy, honeydew-like substance produced by psyllids. Collecting lerps is incredibly time-consuming, but offering it to my students gives them a truly unique and memorable experience. It's like serving caviar instead of burgers, if you get my drift. That kind of detail makes people remember you.

On a deeper, personal level, I find the slow process of hand-extracting grains to be quite enjoyable and meditative. It offers an escape from a world focused on speed and profit. It's perfectly fine to be a grain anarchist, breaking the rules and striving for a fulfilling connection to your environment.

SHAKE AND GATHER

If you need a quick snack when you're foraging for seeds—or, in my case, when I need to gather a small quantity for a class demonstration—this straightforward method works wonders. It's particularly effective for plants in the mint family, such as wild chia, amaranth (*Amaranthus* spp.), thistle sage, black sage (*Salvia mellifera*), white sage (*Salvia apiana*), and others. These plants have seed heads that naturally release seeds with a gentle shake, making them ideal candidates for this super simple collection technique.

Materials

Paper or plastic bag: a paper bag works well for absorbing moisture, while a plastic bag is more durable.

Method

1. Identify plants that are ready to release their seeds. Look for mature seed heads that appear dry and seeds that have started to loosen naturally.
2. Open your bag wide enough to allow the seed heads to fit comfortably inside. It's important that the bag is large enough to catch the seeds without spilling them.
3. Hold the bag under the seed head and gently shake the plant, allowing the seeds to fall directly into the bag. If the seeds are stubborn and don't fall easily, use your hand to gently tap the stem or seed head, encouraging the seeds to drop. Move systematically through the area where the plants are abundant, repeating this process for each plant to gather the amount you need.
4. Once you have collected the seeds, inspect them for any debris or unwanted material. Gently blow or sift through the seeds to remove excess chaff and ensure they are clean. It's important to ensure they are fully dry before storing to avoid spoilage (see Drying and Storage, page 18).

NATURAL SEED RELEASE

This method is an easy way to extract seeds from plants like miner's lettuce (*Claytonia perfoliata*), chickweed (*Stellaria media*), and others that naturally release their seeds as they dry and die. I've also successfully used this technique with watercress (*Nasturtium officinale*), which I foraged in bunches when the seedpods turned brown and began to open. It also worked well with Palmer amaranth (*Amaranthus palmeri*), which appeared in my garden last year. It's a useful method for many plants.

Materials

Sharp scissors or garden shears to collect the plants (if necessary)
Large box or bowl for collection and another bowl for sifted seeds
Sieve or fine mesh screen

Method

1. It is crucial to collect the plants when they are mature with seeds ready to be released. This means that the seeds are fully developed and viable. Harvest the plants by carefully cutting them and placing them in a large box or bowl. It is important to choose a container that is large enough to accommodate the plants without overcrowding, as this will facilitate better air circulation and even drying.
2. Place the box or bowl in a dry place, but out of direct sunlight. Direct sunlight can cause the plants to dry too quickly, which can impede their seed release. A dry, shaded area is ideal.
3. Gently stir the contents of the box or bowl at least twice daily, using your hands to mix the plant material for a minute or so each time. This regular stirring is essential, as it helps the plants dry slowly and evenly and encourages the seeds to separate from the plants. Depending on the ambient humidity and temperature, the plants will dry out after several days, and the seeds will naturally fall to the bottom of the container. In Southern California, it may take 3 to 5 days for the plants to dry completely. If you live in a humid area, you may need to use a dehydrator on a very low temperature.
4. Once the plants are completely dry, gently shake the dried mass to release any remaining seeds, then remove. Pour the remaining material through an appropriately sized sieve, transferring the seeds to a new bowl while leaving behind the smaller pieces of dried plant material and twigs. Any remaining undesired plant material can usually be removed by gently blowing on the seeds.

Collect the plants when they are mature with seeds ready to be released.

Place the harvested plants in a box or bowl that is large enough to accommodate the plant material without overcrowding.

Stir the contents of the box or bowl at least twice daily to allow slow, even drying and encourage seed separation.

Remove the dried plant mass and sieve the remaining contents into a new bowl.

Even after sifting, the seeds will be mixed with tiny bits of dried plant, chaff, and other undesirable plant material.

Gently blow on the seeds to remove the chaff. The seeds are now ready for final drying and storage.

CABELA'S

TWIST AND GATHER

This method is most effective for plants with seedpods that can be physically broken open to release their contents. It can be an extremely effective technique for some mustard plants or plants from the same family (Brassicaciae), such as wild or feral arugula. I've been able to collect up to 3 cups (450 g) of seeds per hour with my local tumble mustard and tansy mustard (*Descurainia pinnata*). That's true abundance!

This method is similar to the shake and gather method, but in this case, instead of shaking the seed heads, we actually twist quite aggressively because we're dealing with seedpods. By twisting back and forth, we break the pods and release the seeds.

Materials

2 bowls
Gloves
Sieve or fine mesh screen

Method

1. Begin by setting up a large bowl underneath the plant you are harvesting so it catches the seeds as they fall. Ensure the bowl is wide enough to cover the area under the seedpods to maximize seed collection.
2. After uprooting or breaking the dried plant, grab the stems and run your hand slowly upward along the plants to gather the seedpods into a tight bunch. By creating a compact group of seedpods, you can apply the twisting motion more effectively, breaking multiple pods simultaneously. Be sure to wear gloves during this process, as seedpods can be sharp.
5. When the seedpods are gathered into a tight bunch, firmly grasp them and twist back and forth aggressively. The twisting action should be strong enough to break open the pods, allowing the seeds inside to fall into the bowl below. The lighter chaff will fall on top or around the edges of the bowl. This natural separation makes it easy to remove the unwanted plant material when you're finished. You'll still need a sieve to remove any small debris.
4. Ensure the seeds are fully dry before storing to avoid spoilage (see Drying and Storage, page 18).

FLAT STONE EXTRACTION

This traditional method is an effective way to remove grains from tough husks, like those of wild oats. I have also found it to work well for feral wheat and barley I foraged while in Colorado. Consider this option if you struggle to remove husks from your grains. It may not be perfect, but it is faster than hand extraction. Nearly every culture on the planet has a version of these tools. You can forage for these yourself—you'll need a somewhat flat stone and another stone to use as a grinder—or you can purchase them online. In the Mexican stores, they are called *metates* (flat stones) and *manos* (grinding stones or handstones). In Europe, they are known as quern-stones and handstones.

Materials

Flat stone

Handstone, which can be round, cylindrical, or rectangular

Method

1. Place your grains on the flat stone.
2. Gently move the handstone back and forth over the grains, applying light pressure to separate the husks from the grains. The back-and-forth motion is essential for this process. As you push the handstone over the grains, the friction loosens most of the husks. The gentle pressure carefully removes the husks without crushing the grains. You can then remove the husks by hand or by winnowing.
3. Ensure the seeds are fully dry before storing to avoid spoilage (see Drying and Storage, page 18).

Note that this method is not suitable for seeds, which are usually more fragile than grains. For seeds, I often use a stone mortar and pestle (*molcajete*) and gently move the pestle in a circular motion to remove the husks.

Rolling Pin Method

As an alternative to the flat stone method, you can use a rolling pin to extract grains from their husks. Place the grains on a flat surface such as a cutting board. Apply firm pressure and roll the pin back and forth over the grains. This motion crushes the grains slightly, which helps force the husks to break open and separate from the grains. Continue pressing and rolling until most of the husks are adequately broken, then separate the grains from the husk fragments with your hands or by winnowing. This method is effective, but it can result in some grain breakage.

TRADITIONAL THRESHING AND THE STICK METHOD

Threshing is the process of separating grains or seeds from the stalks and husks of harvested plants. It involves beating or rubbing the plant material to loosen the edible parts from the inedible chaff.

It is speculated that in the early days of agriculture, people likely used sticks to beat out the grains or beat the bundles on the ground to collect the grains. Traditional threshing methods were developed over time, often

incorporating homemade tools to more efficiently separate the grains from their husks. Here are a couple of examples:

Flail threshing: A flail (two wooden sticks connected by a flexible joint) is used to beat the bundles and release the grains.

Animal treading: Animals like oxen, sheep, or horses walk over the harvested plants to crush and separate the grains. This was often done on high ground so the wind could blow away the chaff, leaving the grain behind.

The stick method is a simplified version of traditional flail threshing. For the small quantities of grains and seeds I collect, I use a sturdy stick instead of a flail to "beat" the plants. It's somewhat effective for processing some wild grains and seeds, like mustard seeds.

Materials

Stick
Large bowl

Method

1. Collect plants that have mature seeds or grains.
2. Put the plants in a bowl wide enough to accommodate the plant material and deep enough to prevent the seeds from scattering.
3. Using a sturdy stick, beat the plants inside the bowl. This helps to separate the seeds or grains from their husks or pods. No need to go crazy; the beating should be controlled, ensuring that the seeds are dislodged without causing damage to the grains, seeds, or your bowl.
4. After the plants have been thoroughly beaten, the grains or seeds will settle at the bottom of the bowl, while the husks and other plant material will remain on top. You can further winnow or sift the contents to separate the seeds from the chaff.
5. Once the grains or seeds are separated, collect them for further processing or storage. As usual, ensure they are completely dry before storing to prevent spoilage (see Drying and Storage, page 18).

COMB THRESHING

This is a helpful method for certain difficult-to-extract seeds. For instance, Indian ricegrass—detailed on page 193—is quite common in the desert by me. The brown and tan seeds resemble tiny grains of rice, each about the size of a sesame seed. Each seed is encased in a thin, papery layer and has a long, hairlike tail called an awn. These seeds grow in clusters at the top of the grass, giving the plant a feathery appearance.

The challenge is that the seeds can be difficult to dislodge. I've tried using a stick to beat them, rubbing them between my hands, and various other methods. The most effective techniques I've found are using a comb to remove the seeds right after harvesting or waiting a few months until the seeds loosen, then employing the bag threshing method (page 41). With the comb threshing method, the trick is to find a comb that will grab the seeds but allow the stalks to pass through. Here is how it works, using Indian ricegrass as an example.

Materials

Sickle or shears
Large paper or plastic bag
Comb
Bowl
Sieve

Method

1. Cut the Indian ricegrass when the seeds are ripe, typically in late summer or early fall. The seeds should be brown or tan and still attached to the seed heads. Use a sharp sickle or shears to cut the grass stalks at their base.
2. Gather the cut grass into bundles, put them in the bag, and transport them home for further processing. Spread the bundles out in a dry, well-ventilated area and allow them to dry for about a week. This drying period helps the seeds to naturally loosen from the stalks, making them easier to dislodge during the combing process.
3. After the grass has dried, select a comb with teeth spaced just right for harvesting the seeds. The teeth should be close enough to catch the seeds but wide enough to let the stalks pass through easily.
4. Begin the combing process by holding a bundle of dried grass over a bowl and using a gentle but steady motion to pass the comb through the seed heads. Start at the base of the seed cluster and move downward, allowing the teeth of the comb to catch and pull the seeds from the stalks. As you comb, the seeds should fall into the bowl.
5. Once you've combed through all the grass bundles, you'll likely have a mix of seeds and some chaff. Gently blow on the chaff or use a sieve to separate it from the seeds. After cleaning, the seeds are ready for drying and storage.

HAND RUBBING

This method works well for separating seeds from chaff and can also be used for grains that are relatively easy to extract. It's particularly effective with seeds like lamb's-quarter, white sweet clover (*Melilotus albus*) and broadleaf plantain (*Plantago major*), and I've also used it for feral grains—commercial grains found in the wild—such as wheat, barley, and rye. When it comes to grains, though, I recommend wearing gloves, as the spiky awns can be rough on bare hands.

I prefer to use my Vitamix (see page 47) to process wild grains such as wild oats, wild barley, and great brome. It's a highly efficient method that quickly separates grains from chaff with minimal effort. If you have access to electricity, this is a great option, as it requires much less physical work and can handle larger batches in a shorter time.

However, in situations where you don't have access to a blender, or if you prefer to work manually, hand rubbing is a reliable and effective method. It's also cost-effective since it doesn't require any special equipment, making it a great option for foraging or survival situations where simplicity and accessibility are key.

Materials

Gloves
Two bowls

Method

1. Start by removing the seeds, still enclosed in their chaff, from the stalks and placing them in a large bowl. Make sure they're dry; this will make it easier to separate the seeds from the chaff.
2. Take a handful of the seeds and rub them between your palms in a circular motion, applying gentle pressure. This action will begin to break the seeds free from their coverings. As you rub, the seeds and chaff will both fall into the bowl. This step may take a few minutes, depending on the amount you're working with.
3. Once most of the seeds have been separated from their coverings, it's time to winnow. Gently blow across the top of the mixture to let the lighter chaff fly off, leaving mostly seeds behind. On a windy day, you can pour the mixture from one bowl to another, letting the wind carry away the chaff.
4. After winnowing, you may still find some seeds with chaff clinging to them. If so, repeat the rubbing and winnowing steps as necessary until you have mostly clean seeds. If you're working with a large batch, the whole process may take 10 to 15 minutes. For feral grains, I find this method quite efficient, usually taking less than 3 minutes per handful.
5. Ensure the seeds are fully dry before storing to avoid spoilage (see Drying and Storage, page 18).

Grab the tops of the branches containing the seed-pods. I like to grab as much as I can as quickly as possible. Don't be like me—wear gloves!

Twist the branches to break them, then immediately cram them into your bag.

Do a little stomp dance on the bag. This helps break down the pods and release all the seeds.

Tip the bag at an angle and shake it. Cut a hole in the bottom where the seeds have accumulated.

Position a strainer and bowl below the opening, then gently shake the bag so the seeds and chaff fall into the strainer.

Collect the seeds that pass through the strainer and fall into the bowl.

BAG THRESHING

This is a fantastic method for collecting seeds from plants in the mustard family. It makes the job so easy, and you'll be amazed at the number of seeds you can collect. This is my preferred method for extracting seeds from shortpod mustard (*Hirschfeldia incana*), black mustard, feral arugula (*Eruca sativa*), and the like.

This foraging takes place when the plants have gone to seed and are thoroughly dried. In Southern California, this period is from late July to early September. For quality seeds, don't wait too long. And be sure to wear gloves, to protect your hands from the prickly dry seedpods.

My process is quick and easy because I don't like spending too much time in the relentless sun.

Material

Gloves
Plastic or paper bag
Strainer
Bowl

Method

1. Grab a bunch of the dry plant tops containing the seeds pods, then twist the branches to break them and immediately cram them into a bag. My local mustard plants are so abundant that it usually doesn't take more than 5 to 10 minutes to fill a bag with the dried branches and seedpods.
2. Once home, close the bag and place it on the ground. Now, you can have some fun with a little stomp dance on the bag. This helps break down the pods and release all the seeds. There's no need to dance for long; usually, 5 to 10 seconds is enough.
3. Tip the bag at an angle and shake it vigorously.
4. Using scissors, cut a hole in the bottom corner of the bag where the seeds have accumulated.
5. Position the strainer and bowl below the opening so the seeds can fall through while the larger chaff remains inside the bag.
6. Gently shake the bag to encourage the seeds and smaller chaff to fall into the strainer.
7. Collect the seeds that pass through into the bowl.
8. Once the seeds are collected, ensure they are completely dry before storing to prevent spoilage (see Drying and Storage, page 18).

A variation of this method is to use a tarp instead of a bag. Lay the tarp on the ground and spread the dried plants with seedpods on top. Fold the tarp on top of the plants and step on it, pressing down or "dancing" to help release the seeds. Unfold the tarp and remove any excess plant material. Then, fold the tarp at an angle to easily pour the seeds into a large bowl. To finish, you can use a strainer to separate the remaining small debris from the seeds.

FLAME WINNOWING

This method is definitely not a new one, and similar processes can be found across many cultures and continents. In North America, some Indigenous communities practiced controlled burning of grasslands in late summer or fall. After the fire passed, they would gather the heavier seeds that remained on the scorched earth, making harvesting easier and more efficient.

Of course, we're not farmers. As foragers, we don't want to get in trouble by starting large fires! But the concept is highly effective for collecting some grains and seeds. It works beautifully to burn away the chaff from seed or grain heads like Indian ricegrass and wild barley. This process works because the seeds or grains can withstand the fire, while the lighter chaff burns away. You'll end up with slightly burned seeds or grains, but parching grains often adds flavor. It's not a bad thing.

Material

Large heat-resistant bowl
Kitchen torch or lighter
Sieve

Method

1. Place the dry seed or grain heads in a heat-resistant bowl.
2. Ignite the plant material. As it burns, shake and stir the contents to ensure an even burn. Be cautious not to let the fire get too intense or burn for too long—just enough to burn off the chaff. It takes some practice. This method works best when the grains or seeds are not fully dried and still have some moisture. Avoid burning a large batch to prevent the fire from getting too big and damaging the grains.
3. Once the chaff is gone and the fire burns out, you'll have (mostly) seeds or grains left behind. Use a sieve to remove any burned bits. Sometimes, as with wild barley grains, you may still need to rub the burned chaff or grains between your hands for a better result.
4. Ensure the seeds or grains are fully dry before storing to avoid spoilage (see Drying and Storage, page 18).

Native Americans have a similar, more effective method involving a woven basket and embers. Dry seed heads, such as those from wild grasses, are placed in the basket. Instead of lighting the material on fire, hot embers or coals are added to the basket with the plants. The heat from the embers burns away the light chaff that covers the seeds.

To spread the heat evenly, the basket is shaken or tossed, moving the embers through the seeds. This burns off the chaff while keeping the seeds safe from scorching. Once the chaff is gone, the seeds are cleaned by removing any ash or leftover debris. This method is efficient and ensures clean, undamaged seeds.

THE ROLLING STONE

I have a weird hobby on the side: I like to collect round stones. But there is a good reason for it. They can be quite useful for extracting seeds and grains.

The rolling stone is a method I use when I need to extract seeds and grains from somewhat messy combinations of raw materials, including seedpods, dried stems, chaff, and other debris that can be difficult to separate by hand. I place these mixed materials into a stone grinder and use a rounded stone to roll over the contents. By holding the grinder with both hands, I roll the round stone back and forth, applying enough pressure to break down the chaff and pods while keeping the seeds or grains intact. The weight of the stone is crucial—it needs to be heavy enough to crush the outer layers but light enough to avoid damaging the seeds. That's why I collect round stones of various sizes and weights.

This method works particularly well with lamb's-quarter, some amaranth species, brassica seedpods like wild arugula or black mustard, and others where the rolling action efficiently separates the seeds from the tough pods and surrounding debris.

After the rolling, I sieve the crushed content into a bowl and winnow it in the wind to remove the remaining chaff and debris, leaving the clean seeds or grains behind. The rolling stone is another valuable tool in my seed and grain extraction method toolbox.

POUNDING METHOD

Sometimes seedpods can be really tough, like those of wild radish. They're so hard that it's difficult to break them open by hand to extract the seeds. Even using a heavy rolling stone won't do the job.

My solution is to place a few pods, about five or six, in my stone grinder and crush them using a pestle. It takes some practice, but you'll quickly learn how much force to apply to break down the pods without damaging the seeds. It's a bit tedious since you have to separate the seeds from the debris each time.

However, the most effective method I've found for extracting wild radish seeds is using a Vitamix (see page 47). I place a cup or two of dried seedpods in the blender and run it on the lowest setting for 5 to 10 minutes. This efficiently removes the seeds without crushing them.

Afterward, I transfer the content to a sieve with holes just the right size for the seeds, and voilà! It's a simple process if you have a Vitamix and the right sieve. Other food processors might work too, but I haven't tested them.

THUMB GRINDER

Sometimes it's easy to remove the outer chaff from a grain, but the husk can be tougher to get off—especially with wild oats. Since I make pottery, I made a special grinder with a thumb groove on the side. It's designed to remove husks and chaff from grains like wild oats, and it's also great for finishing up after the Flame Winnowing method (page 42).

This tool is straightforward to use and gives you good control over the pressure. Place a small number of grains (especially after burning) on the rough, ridged surface inside, then press down with your thumb. Move the grains back and forth to rub off the husk. This method works well for small batches—for example, when I want to add some grains to a ferment. However, it can be a bit rough on your thumb, so it's best for occasional use.

STONE OR CERAMIC GRINDER

A stone or ceramic grinder with a pestle is great for processing seeds and grains. It's easier on your thumb and lets you work with larger amounts. The rough surface helps remove husks and chaff without damaging the seeds.

This tool is perfect for tough seeds with chaff, like lamb's-quarter, bulrush (*Schoenoplectus* spp.), and wild amaranth. I often use it to break down wild radish or tall evening primrose (*Oenothera elata*) seedpods, and also for grains like wild rye.

Method

1. Place seeds, pods, or grains into the grinder bowl. Using the pestle, press down on the contents of the bowl. Instead of grinding, gently rub and crush to loosen the husk and chaff from the seeds. With practice, you'll get a feel for the right amount of pressure for different types of seeds. The rough surface helps to rub away the husk and chaff while keeping the seeds intact.
2. Use a sieve or winnow the mixture to fully separate the seeds from any remaining chaff.

THE GAME CHANGER: VITAMIX THRESHING

While writing this book, I've continued to experiment with various methods of extraction. The methods we've covered work well for extracting most seeds and grains, but I was still having issues extracting certain ones efficiently, both in terms of ease and quantity.

One day, as I was about to use my stone grinder to break down some wild radish pods and extract the seeds for sprouting, I decided to do a quick test with my Vitamix. For reference, I use a classic Vitamix 5200 blender with a 64-ounce/2.0-liter container. I bought it "certified reconditioned" from the company in 2022 for $265. It has variable speed control with 10 different settings.

I threw a handful of radish seedpods into the blender and turned the control knob between 1 and 2—basically, a very low speed. I placed the cover on the blender and let it run for about 5 minutes while I was busy doing something else. When I came back and looked, *wow*! Most of the seedpods had broken, and the extracted seeds were almost completely intact. I decided to give it another 5 minutes, and the results were fantastic. Nearly all the seedpods were broken, and the seeds were fully extracted.

I was so impressed that I decided to try another test, this time with one of the most difficult grains to extract unless you do it by hand after cooking it: great brome grains. I tossed a handful of unthreshed grains into the container, turned the speed knob to 2, and let it go for about 20 minutes.

To be honest, I didn't have much hope that the blending action would remove the chaff from the grains, but I'm a dreamer. And sometimes crazy experiments are worth it, because . . . *it worked*!

After 20 minutes, the container had a mixture of dust, debris, stem pieces, chaff, and what appeared to be grains at the bottom. Intrigued, I poured the contents into a bowl, went outside, and blew on it to remove the chaff and debris. I was completely shocked—the grains were superbly separated from the chaff! I immediately thought, *This is a game changer for foraging grains*!

I began experimenting with various plants, such as cheatgrass, Canada wild rye (*Elymus canadensis*), wild oats, and wild barley. The results were again spectacular, with minimal effort on my part—the machine did most of the work. The only thing I had to do afterward was winnow the contents in the wind or blow gently to remove the debris. When it comes to grain extraction, I'm pretty much sold on using this method.

The method works well for certain seeds, too. Yesterday, I used it to extract mint seeds. I placed the dried flower heads into the Vitamix, and it worked wonders, separating the tiny seeds within a couple of minutes at speed 2. Winnowing afterward was a breeze. The same thing happened with lamb's-quarter seeds.

Tips and Pointers

Can you use another type of blender? Possibly, but I've looked at what's available on the market similar to Vitamix, and you won't find anything of the same quality much cheaper. Plus, Vitamix gives you excellent speed control and a tamper tool that's extremely useful for grain extraction.

The tamper is a long, sturdy stick that fits through the blender lid and stops short of the blades. It's essential for keeping the mixture moving when it sticks to the sides or when air pockets form, especially with thick foods like nut butters, smoothies, ice cream, or, in my case, wild plant-based cheese ingredients. But when we are dealing with grains, the tamper is super helpful for pushing down the spikes, or ears (seed heads), and other materials.

For example, say I wanted to extract some Indian ricegrass grains. I start with bunches of grass containing the grains, which are tough to extract. I cut the grass into smaller parts, place them in the container, close the top, set the knob to speed 2 (low speed), and use the tamper to push the stems and seed heads toward the blades.

It takes 2 to 3 minutes of pushing down the materials with the tamper for the blades to break down the stems enough that I don't need to use the tamper anymore. After another 10 minutes, I have beautiful grains removed from the chaff and just need to winnow the content. Without the tamper, this task would have been much harder.

There's still a lot of experimentation to do with this method, and if you decide to use it, you'll need to figure out the timing for different grains (or even seeds in some cases). Here are my pointers for the local grains I've tried so far:

Great brome: 20 minutes at speed 2
Canada wild rye: 10 minutes at speed 2
Wild oats: 20 minutes at speed 2
Wild barley: 15 to 20 minutes at speed 1.5
Cheatgrass: 15 minutes at speed 1.5

Note that the speed is always around 1 or 2. I wouldn't advise going higher unless you have some specific plant material that requires it, because higher speeds could damage the grains.

Add the unthreshed grains to the Vitamix container and set the speed to 1 or 2. Start the blender and use the tamper if needed to guide the grains toward the blades. After 2 to 3 minutes, the grains should begin churning on their own as the blades turn.

After 20 minutes, you'll have fine dust, loose chaff, and grains settled at the bottom.

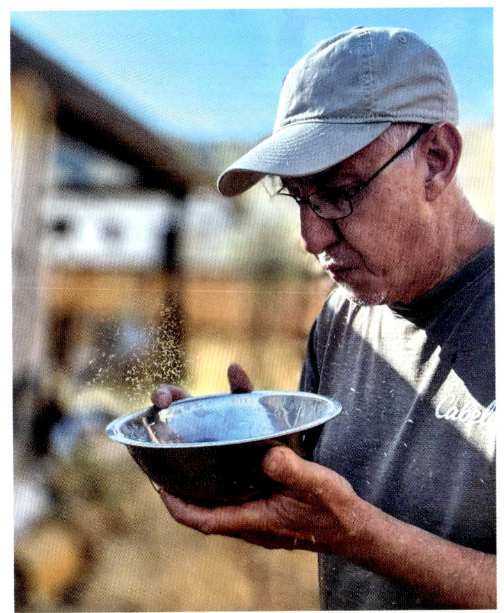

Remove the dust and loose chaff by gently blowing or using wind winnowing.

And there you have it! I successfully extracted beautiful wild barley grains, which are usually very difficult to separate.

Nothing is perfect, and that applies to this extraction method as well.

Although the grains generally look fine, when it comes to cooking, they may not appear as aesthetically pleasing as the results of gentler methods.

Specifically, I'm referring to my favorite—great brome grains. They are beautiful and relatively easy to extract by hand after cooking for 60 minutes, resembling perfect, beautiful red rice grains.

When I cooked the Vitamix-extracted brome grains, they didn't have the same exact appearance. Some of the grains had opened, and they didn't look as attractive as those extracted by hand. The difference was tiny, but I could see it. That said, they still work perfectly in many recipes, such as when used as an addition to kimchi and other ferments. However, if I want to showcase their beauty in a wild-food dish, I continue to extract them by hand.

I didn't notice any difference in quality with my wild oats or barley grains between this extraction method and others.

A Note of Caution

I have a strong reaction to the small hairs on wild oat awns (the hairy part surrounding the grains). Awns can irritate the skin, causing itching or a rash. The fine hairs and dust can also cause respiratory irritation or allergic reactions, especially if you're sensitive to grasses or grains.

When I extract grains using the Vitamix method, I wear a mask and do it outside. I also make sure I'm not in the wind path while winnowing processed oats in particular.

So, use common sense and caution when dealing with your local plants, grains, and seeds.

There are, of course, other methods for extracting seeds and grains, and I'm sure you will come up with your own as you start to work with the wild edibles you find in your own environment, but hopefully this chapter will get you started.

CHAPTER 3

Preparing Seeds and Grains

Now that we know the basics of collecting and extracting wild seeds and grains, it's time for the next step: preparing them.

By "preparation," I mean transforming these raw ingredients into something you'd actually want to eat—something tasty, nutritious, and versatile. Granted, a lot of seeds and grains don't have much flavor to start with, but you'll be surprised how simple methods like parching, roasting, or fermenting can turn something boring into an exciting ingredient.

How you prepare your grains and seeds depends on several factors: the type of grains or seeds you're working with, your culinary goals, and what tools or resources you have at your disposal. For instance, some seeds and grains, like curly dock, smilo grass (*Stipa miliacea*), Indian ricegrass, or wild barley, are perfect for grinding into flours. These flours can be used to make bread, thick soups, or rustic baked goods like crackers or flatbreads. They often impart unique flavors that add a distinctive character to your recipes.

Other grains, like wild oats or great brome, can be added to ferments like kimchi and sauerkraut. They absorb the tangy flavors of the brine while also contributing nutrients. If you enjoy experimenting in the kitchen, fermented grains by themselves open up a world of possibilities, too.

Another classic option is making porridge or gruel. This method has stood the test of time because it's simple, nourishing, and filled with creative possibilities. With the addition of nuts, berries, and other wild foods, the combinations are endless. You can make it savory or sweet, depending on the grains and your mood, and it's a great way to work with harder grains that need a little extra cooking time to become tender.

Feeling creative? Certain grains and seeds can also be used to make beverages. For example, roasted barley tea is enjoyed in many cultures for its toasty flavor. Or you could try experimenting with a lightly fermented grain "beer" or a nutrient-packed smoothie with ground seeds for an earthy twist.

And let's not forget sprouting. As you'll read in chapter 6, many grains and seeds can be sprouted or grown as microgreens, unlocking even more nutrition and flavor. Sprouting turns hard, dry grains into something fresh and vibrant, perfect in salads and stir-fries, or as a topping for soups. It's an easy way to breathe new life into your grains and seeds.

But before we dive into these exciting possibilities, we need to cover the basics of preparation. How do you turn your grains and seeds into fine flours? What's the best way to make them soft and palatable? And how do you handle antinutrients, like tannins and phytic acid, to maximize their nutritional value and make them easier to digest? These can be important steps to get your grains and seeds from raw to ready to eat.

In this chapter, I'll guide you through the tools and techniques I've developed to prepare grains and seeds. These methods are shaped by my environment—what I like to call my terroir—and years of trial and error.

Your approach will likely vary depending on where you live and what resources you have, but that's the beauty of working with wild foods: it's all about adaptation and creativity. My hope is that this chapter gives you a solid foundation for preparing your own grains and seeds and sparks some new ideas along the way.

By the end of this chapter, you'll be equipped to turn your grains and seeds into delicious, wholesome ingredients for your meals. Whether you're baking fresh bread with wild flours, crafting hearty porridges, fermenting grains into flavorful dishes, or sprouting seeds for fresh greens, there's a world of possibilities waiting for you.

Antinutrients in Grains and Seeds

Antinutrients are natural substances in plants that can make it harder for our bodies to absorb some of their important nutrients. These substances help plants protect themselves from being eaten by insects or succumbing to diseases. This makes sense from a plant's perspective, but the reality is that when we eat plants without proper preparation, antinutrients stop our bodies from getting all the good stuff, like vitamins and minerals. Even when we think we're eating healthy foods, we might not be getting all the nutrients we need.

How does this work? To put it simply, antinutrients attach themselves to vitamins like B12 and minerals like calcium, iron, and zinc in our food. When this happens, our bodies can't absorb these vitamins and minerals well. For example, if antinutrients attach to iron, it makes it harder for our body to use that iron. This can cause us to have low levels of these important nutrients, even if we eat foods that are high in those nutrients.

This information is important for foragers to know, especially when it comes to seeds and grains. When I first started foraging, many of my teachers were survivalists, and the notion of nutrition was not on their radar. Wild plants were often just listed as edible or not. Not knowing any better, I ended up with a nice kidney stone after my first two years of exploring and eating wild food. Unknowingly, I was consuming a high-oxalate diet, and based on my genetics, this was a recipe for disaster.

To be more specific, one of my favorite edible wild plants, curly dock, contains several antinutrients, including oxalates and tannins. Oxalates can bind with calcium in the digestive system, forming a compound the body cannot easily absorb. So, even though curly dock is high in calcium, the oxalates prevent our bodies from getting the full benefit of that calcium, which is important for our bones and teeth.

Oxalates can also bind with calcium in the kidneys to form crystals, which can lead to the development of kidney stones, as in my case. Eating high-oxalate foods in large amounts can increase the risk of forming these painful stones, especially if you are prone to them. Tannins, another type of antinutrient in curly dock, can interfere with the absorption of iron. Tannins bind to iron, making it harder for the body to absorb this mineral, which is essential for carrying oxygen in our blood.

But knowledge is power! Antinutrients are nothing to freak out about. On the contrary, once you're armed with the knowledge of what they are, you can learn how to prepare food to reduce their effects. So, let's examine the most common antinutrients we, as foragers, should be aware of.

Goitrogens: Found in cruciferous vegetables like broccoli, cabbage, and kale and present in many plants from the mustard family, such as black or garlic mustard and wild radish, goitrogens can interfere with iodine uptake, potentially affecting thyroid function.

Lectins: Found in wild or commercial grains and legumes, lectins can affect the lining of the gastrointestinal tract and interfere with the absorption of nutrients.

Oxalates (oxalic acid): Found in lamb's-quarter, curly dock, various sorrels, purslane (*Portulaca oleracea*), wild amaranth, stinging nettles (late growing stage), and wild rhubarb, among other wild plants, and also present in foods like spinach, beet greens, and rhubarb, oxalates can bind to calcium and form insoluble compounds, reducing calcium absorption.

Phytates (phytic acid): Found in legumes and many wild edible plants, such as wild rice, amaranth, lamb's-quarter, and purslane, phytic acid can bind to minerals like iron, zinc, calcium, and magnesium, making them less available for absorption.

Protease inhibitors: Found in soybeans, legumes, and some grains, protease inhibitors can make it harder for your body to digest proteins by blocking the enzymes that break them down.

Saponins: Found in legumes, some grains, and wild seeds like lamb's-quarter and amaranth, saponins can bind to proteins and minerals, making them harder for your body to use.

Tannins: Found in wild food like acorns, black walnuts (*Juglans nigra*), and sorrel (*Rumex* spp.), and also in tea, coffee, wine, and some fruits, in large quantities, tannins can make it harder for your body to absorb iron and can block digestion.

Note that you don't have to take all this information from a negative perspective. There are also good sides to some of these substances. For example, tannins can help keep fermented foods crunchy, act as natural preservatives, and add depth and complexity to drinks like wine and wild beers.

Ultimately, what matters most is paying attention to the amount of food you consume that is higher in certain antinutrients and how often you consume such food. Within the context of this book, we need to pay close attention to these substances because grains and seeds often have higher levels of antinutrients than other plants and plant parts such as vegetables and fruits. This difference is partly because grains and seeds are designed to protect the plant's genetic material, so they produce more of these compounds for defense and preservation. Therefore, it's a good idea to use preparation methods that reduce these antinutrients in grains and seeds to maximize their nutritional benefits and minimize potential harm from overconsumption.

This is nothing new, by the way. Once I became aware of the antinutrients present in some of my favorite wild foods, I started researching how our ancestors used to cook and prepare these foods. Guess what? From generation to generation, they passed on the knowledge of how to prepare these foods properly to minimize the negative effects. For example, curly dock and lamb's-quarter were often boiled or blanched first, with the water changed before eating. These simple cooking techniques help leach out oxalates, making the plants safer to eat.

Here are some of the basic preparation methods that help unlock the full nutritional potential of wild grains and seeds, making them healthier and safer for you to eat.

Soaking and rinsing: Soaking grains and seeds in water for several hours, or overnight, helps to reduce phytates and other antinutrients. Frequent rinsing can also reduce or remove saponin in seeds like quinoa and lamb's-quarter.

Cooking: Boiling, steaming, or baking grains and seeds can reduce antinutrients that interfere with protein digestion and cause stomach discomfort.

Fermenting: Fermentation engages beneficial bacteria and yeast to break down the antinutrients in grains and seeds. For example, making sourdough bread from fermented grain dough greatly reduces phytate levels. Fermentation also generates probiotics, which improve gut health and help your body better absorb nutrients.

Sprouting: Sprouting activates enzymes that break down antinutrients like phytates and lectins. Sprouting also boosts vitamin levels and makes proteins easier to digest, making the grains and seeds more nutritious and easier for your body to use. For more information on sprouting wild seeds and grains, see chapter 6.

Now that you have all this information, there is no need to be an extremist about it. When you know the rules, it's okay to break them from time to time.

Managing Oxalic Acid

When I've shared some of my experiments and recipes on social media, a few people have raised concerns about oxalic acid in grains. While it isn't harmful in small amounts, consuming too much oxalic acid can interfere with calcium absorption and contribute to the formation of kidney stones in some people, like myself. As a forager, understanding how to reduce oxalic acid can make these seeds and grains safer and more enjoyable to eat, especially for regular consumption. The methods mentioned above all work, and you can also combine them. For example, you can soak grains or seeds before adding them to a batch of kimchi, where the fermentation process will further lower oxalic acid content. Adding a small amount of vinegar or lemon juice to the soaking water can also help break down oxalic acid. As is so often the case, looking at how cultures have traditionally prepared dishes also offers insight. Dishes often combine seeds and grains with calcium-rich foods to bind oxalates, reducing their absorption in the body. For example, tahini is mixed with yogurt in Middle Eastern cuisines, while amaranth porridge is commonly paired with milk. Poppy seed dumplings served with sour cream are another example. Other good potential pairings include bone broth and leafy greens low in oxalates and high in calcium (such as mallow, watercress, arugula, and cooked mustard greens).

For example, eating bread or crackers made with wild flours from time to time or adding some unprocessed tasty seeds as a topping on hummus will not make a real difference to your health. But, overall, you'll notice that many of my recipes include some form of soaking, cooking, fermentation, or sprouting.

Boiling Grains and Seeds

This simple method can turn grains or seeds you thought were unsuitable into something edible. When I first started to explore wild seeds and grains, boiling them was a game changer. In fact, it's how I discovered that my local cheatgrass and great brome could be eaten. Boiling has also helped me make seeds I thought were too hard, like narrowleaf plantain (*Plantago lanceolata*), edible.

For me, boiling has become an essential test for determining whether a seed or grain is worth eating. Take great brome grains, for example. When I first experimented with them, I found them tough and bland. I tried grinding them into flour, soaking them, and even boiling them briefly, but none of those methods worked well. Finally, I tried boiling them as I would wheat—for 50 to 60 minutes—and that did the trick. After an hour of boiling, the grains turned soft and plump like cooked rice grains, and reddish.

Basic Procedure for Boiling Grains and Seeds

1. Rinse your wild seeds or grains under cold water to clean them.
2. Place 1 cup (250 ml) of the seeds or grains in a pot, followed by 3 cups (750 ml) of water. Bring to a boil, then lower the heat to a simmer.
3. Cover the pot and let it cook for 50 to 60 minutes, or until the grains are tender but still chewy.
4. Drain any extra water and use the grains however you like.

Culinary Uses

Boiled grains and seeds are quite versatile. I often use them in wild food ferments or toss them into salads. They're also great in soups and stews. Wild barley, oats, or rice can add a hearty texture. For salads, toss them with herbs and dressings to make a wild-style tabbouleh. They're an excellent filling for stuffed vegetables like peppers and zucchini. One of my favorite uses is adding them to plant-based burgers or patties for texture.

Boiling might seem basic, but it opens up so many possibilities with wild grains and seeds.

Soaking Grains and Seeds

This method is mostly applicable to grains, but it can be useful for some seeds, too, as we'll see later in the chapter. Soaking has many benefits, rendering grains easier to cook and healthier to eat. Here's why it's worth the effort.

Faster cooking: If you intend to cook your grains instead of using them raw, soaking softens the outer layer so they cook faster, saving you time and energy in the kitchen. Soaking also starts the breakdown of starches and proteins, making them gentler on your stomach.

Reduction of antinutrients: As mentioned above, soaking reduces phytic acid, tannins, and enzyme blockers in grains and seeds.

Taste enhancement: Soaking reduces bitterness and mellows out strong flavors, making some seeds and grains more enjoyable to eat.

I mostly soak my grains when I intend to make flours or add them to ferments or salads. This makes the grains softer and more palatable. My method is simple: I soak them overnight, check the texture in the morning, and if I'm happy with the result, I add them to my salads or kimchis and sauerkrauts.

Soaking grains before adding them to ferments like kimchi or sauerkraut isn't strictly necessary (since they will soften during fermentation), but I often add them to a premade ferment before a class, and in that case, soaking make sense.

Keep in mind, soaking doesn't work well for all grains—great brome and cheatgrass don't respond well—but it's perfect for grains like wild oats, wild barley, proso millet (*Panicum miliaceum*), einkorn (*Triticum monococcum*), and similar varieties.

Basic Procedure for Soaking Grains and Seeds

1. Rinse your grains under cold water to clean them.
2. Put the grains in a bowl or jar and cover with water until it is 2 to 3 inches (5–8 cm) above the grains. It is a good idea to cover the container with plastic wrap or a lid.

3. Optional: Add ½ to 1 teaspoon (2.5–5 ml) of vinegar or lemon juice per pint jar (500 ml) to help reduce tannins and phytic acid.
4. Soak overnight at room temperature or in the fridge. For smaller grains, 4 to 6 hours might be sufficient. I personally prefer using the fridge, as the cold temperature inhibits unwanted bacterial growth and prevents fermentation, if it's not desired.
5. After soaking, drain and rinse the grains. Use them right away or refrigerate for up to 2 days.

Culinary Uses

I use my soaked grains in many different ways.

Salads: Toss soaked grains (if tender enough) into salads or grain salads like tabbouleh for a nice chewy texture.
Baking: Add them to bread, muffins, or crackers for extra flavor and texture.
Soups and stews: Use soaked grains to make soups and stews thicker and heartier.
Stuffings: Soaked grains are a great addition to stuffed vegetables.
Ferments: Add soaked grains to kimchi, sauerkraut, or other ferments. They absorb the flavors well and contribute to the nutrition of your ferment. Soaked grains also contain natural sugars and starches that feed fermentation microbes.

Parching, Toasting, and Roasting

When I started to explore the culinary uses of wild grains and seeds across different cultures, I noticed a recurring practice: parching seeds before storage or as part of their preparation. Believe me, it wasn't a rare occurrence. For example, most seed and grain treatments by native peoples in the American Southwest began with parching. This included thistle sage, wild oats, white sage, common sunflower (*Helianthus annuus*), fringed amaranth (*Amaranthus fimbriatus*), and countless others.

Parching was also a common practice worldwide. In Africa, millet and sorghum were parched to make porridge or before they were ground into flour for flatbreads. Similarly, in Asia, grains such as barley, sesame, and wheat were roasted for use in teas, snacks, and traditional dishes. In Europe, the ancient Greeks and Romans parched wheat and barley for use in bread and porridge, while in the Middle East, grains like wheat and barley were parched to preserve them for later use in stews and bread. And the list goes on . . .

Before we take a deeper dive into the various reasons for parching, let's take a closer look at the differences between parching, toasting, and roasting.

Parching is a simple method whereby seeds or grains are heated directly on a dry pan or hot stone, without oil or water, to remove moisture and enhance flavor through browning. However, the extent to which browning occurs can vary. Sometimes, parching is just about drying the seeds to make them easier to store, without significant flavor changes.

Toasting involves heating seeds, grains, or other foods—usually without oil—to develop deeper flavors and color, as with toasted sesame seeds or bread. This can be done on a dry pan or hot stone, or in an oven.

Roasting uses dry heat, usually in an oven or over an open flame, at higher temperatures. Like toasting, it enhances flavor, but the higher heat often caramelizes sugars and browns the surface, creating rich, complex flavors. Roasting is used for nuts, seeds (like pumpkin or sunflower seeds), coffee beans, vegetables, and meats. Coffee beans are probably the best-known example, with their varying roast levels.

If you research historical methods of preparing seeds or grains, you might get confused between the terms "parching" and "toasting." Even dictionaries sometimes blur the line. To keep it simple, "parching" and "toasting" are often used interchangeably. For example, Merriam-Webster defines parching as "to toast under dry heat." These days, both terms generally refer to drying food by applying heat, usually resulting in some browning and a crispy surface.

From a Native American perspective, a great explanation I found comes from the Pechanga Band of Indians website:

> Seeds and nuts that are stored for long periods are usually parched first. Parching is a process where foods are dried quickly by heating them. Our people still parch seeds and other foods: the traditional method was to toss them repeatedly in a shallow basket with hot pebbles, but modern cooks usually parch seeds in a frying pan. This pulls the moisture out of the food and keeps it from spoiling, sort of like freeze-dried foods today.*

* "Traditional Foods," Pechanga Band of Indians, pechnaga-nsn.gov/index.php /culture/customs-and-traditions/traditional-foods.

While researching, I found that parching techniques vary slightly between cultures, and even from one individual or tribe to another.

There is much more to parching than I initially thought. From my uneducated perspective, I assumed it was all about flavor, but it turns out heating or toasting grains and seeds offers many advantages over dealing with raw seeds and grains.

For instance, if you forage seeds or grains, let them dry at room temperature, and store them in sealed containers, you may find insects or pests getting into your harvest. One October, I foraged a bunch of nettle seeds, dried them for a week, and stored them in a jar. When I opened it a couple of months later, I found tiny spider webs and discovered that about 20 percent of my harvest had been eaten.

A simple heating step would have killed any critters inside, which would have been crucial in the old days when food storage was less secure and losing your harvest could be disastrous.

But toasting—I'll use that term for simplicity—has even more benefits.

Preservation: Heating or lightly toasting removes moisture, preventing mold and spoilage and making seeds and grains easier to store.

Ease of processing: Toasting seeds and grains prior to extracting them makes them easier to hull, winnow, or grind into flour.

Versatility: Toasted seeds and grains can be ground into flour, eaten whole, or added to cakes, porridges, and stews.

Portability: Dry, roasted seeds are lightweight and easy to transport in large quantities, perfect for a nomadic lifestyle.

Antinutrient reduction: Toasting can reduce antinutrients like phytic acid and tannins, which interfere with mineral absorption.

One standout example of parching is parched corn, a traditional preparation method used by Native Americans and early settlers in North America. Corn kernels were heated on a dry surface, often until lightly browned, resulting in a nutty, roasted flavor. Not only did this process enhance the taste, but it also made the kernels lighter and easier to carry, turning them into a practical and shelf-stable food source. Parched corn is still enjoyed today as a snack, showing how parching serves the dual purposes of flavor enhancement and preservation.

However, it's important to note that not all parching involves browning or developing flavor. In some traditional practices, the goal was solely to dry seeds or grains to extend their shelf life or prepare them for further processing without altering the flavor significantly. This is especially true for seeds that don't benefit much from browning and for which gentle heating is more appropriate.

Experiment with your foraged seeds and grains. If you're using parching as a food preservation technique, browning might not be necessary. Try gently heating or toasting, too, and see what works best for you.

Basic Procedure for Toasting Grains and Seeds

1. Place a dry frying pan over medium heat. No oil or butter is needed—the seeds' natural oils are enough. Let the pan heat up for about a minute to ensure even toasting.

Heat the pan, then add your seeds or grains, spreading them out in a single layer. This helps ensure they toast evenly. Avoid overcrowding the pan, as this can make it harder to achieve a consistent result.

Stir frequently with a spoon or gently shake the pan to keep the seeds or grains moving as they toast. They are ready when they give off a nutty, fragrant aroma. Be cautious not to over-toast, as they can go from perfect to burnt in seconds.

Immediately transfer the seeds or grains to a bowl or plate to cool. Leaving them in the hot pan will cause them to continue cooking. In this case, I toasted thistle sage seeds, which can be used similarly to toasted sesame seeds.

2. Spread the seeds or grains in the pan in a single layer, avoiding overcrowding. Stir frequently or gently shake the pan to prevent burning.
3. Toast until fragrant and lightly golden. Be careful not to over-toast—seeds can go from perfect to burnt in seconds. Immediately transfer them to a plate to cool.

In the past, many cultures used flat stones or clay bowls heated over a fire for toasting. Seeds or grains were spread over the hot surface and stirred with sticks or spoons for even toasting. Similarly, as described by the Pechanga Band of Indians, seeds and nuts were traditionally tossed repeatedly in a shallow basket with hot pebbles to parch or toast them.

Fermenting Grains

Fermenting grains is an ancient practice. For thousands of years, cultures worldwide have fermented grains to create foods like sourdough bread, fermented porridges, and beverages such as beer and kvass.

This process relies on natural microbes—wild yeasts and lactic acid bacteria—to break down the starches, proteins, and fibers in grains, transforming them into more digestible and nutrient-rich foods.

But my main reason for fermenting grains is that it significantly boosts their flavor. Fermentation enhances the natural taste of grains, creating deeper, more complex, and often unexpected flavors. The process brings out subtle sweetness, tanginess, and umami qualities that are impossible to achieve through regular cooking or baking methods.

Fermentation enlivens grains with character. A simple grain porridge, for example, transforms into something creamy and slightly tangy with a richer flavor profile when the grains are fermented. Fermented bread like sourdough develops a distinctive depth—both nutty and slightly sour—that makes every bite unique.

This flavor transformation is what excites me the most. It's not just about making grains more digestible or nutrient rich—though those are great benefits. For me, it's about the taste experience:

Tips for Success

Temperature: Fermentation slows down in cooler conditions. If it's cold, give it extra time.

Grain type: Harder grains like wheat might take longer to ferment than softer grains like oats.

Clean water: Chlorine inhibits natural fermentation. Use filtered or spring water.

elevating humble grains into something extraordinary with layers of complexity that are deeply rewarding. That's the magic of fermentation.

Basic Procedure for Fermenting Grains

Materials

Whole grains: Wild grains such as wild barley, wild oats, wild rice, and the like. You can also use cultivated varieties of wheat, rye, barley, rice, oats, etc. There is a lot of experimentation possible.
Water: Clean, nonchlorinated water.
Salt: This helps suppress unwanted microbes and encourage beneficial lactic acid bacteria. You want around 1 to 2 teaspoons (5–10 g) per quart (1 L) of water.
Container: Glass jar, ceramic bowl, or food-grade plastic container.
Starter (optional): Whey or brine from a previous ferment can help speed up things.

Method

1. Rinse the grains under cold water to clean them. If the grains are large and whole—like barley or wheat—you can crack or coarsely grind them to speed up fermentation. This helps the wild yeast and bacteria access the starches more easily.
2. Place the grains in your container and cover with water—use enough to fully submerge the grains (at least double the grain volume).
3. Add salt to help create a stable environment. If desired, introduce a small amount of whey or fermented brine as a starter culture to jump-start the process. (I always do.)
4. Close the container and fasten the lid tightly. Let the grains ferment at room temperature (68°–75°F / 20°–24°C). Twice a day, burp the container to release excess pressure and shake it to ensure even fermentation. Watch for bubbles, a tangy smell, or a slight cloudiness in the water—these are signs of successful fermentation.
5. Taste the grains after 1 to 3 days. They should have a mild tangy flavor. If the water becomes slimy or smells unpleasant, discard and start fresh.
6. Once fermented, rinse the grains thoroughly with clean water. Use immediately for cooking, grinding, or baking, or refrigerate for up to a week. You can also dehydrate the fermented grains to make flour later on.

California buckwheat
Wild rye
Cheatgrass
Rocky Mountain beeplant
Roasted thistle sage
Curly dock
Sprouted proso millet
Wild oat

Wilder Flours

Researching and experimenting with wild flours for this book has been an eye opener for me as a wildcrafter. Making wild flours wasn't entirely new to me; I'd already made flour with acorns, curly dock seeds, burdock, cattail roots, and even pine and cattail pollen. But diving deeper into making flours with foraged wild grains and seeds really opened my eyes to the incredible diversity around us.

Before exploring all the possibilities, let's take a look at the equipment needed to process wild grains and seeds into flours. I'll be honest, I don't have a lot of money to spend on expensive equipment, so I stick with the simple, reliable tools I've used for years. The only pricey pieces are my Vitamix and a large stone grinder that was a gift. Some of these tools are old-school, but they all get the job done, and each serves a purpose, depending on the quantity and texture I need. You'll recognize some of them from the chapter on grain and seed extraction—it is a bonus that they have multiple uses.

Stone grinder: A classic tool that grinds grains slowly. As a forager, this is a must-have tool due to its versatility.

Metate/quern: A big flat stone with a smaller one on top that you can use to crush grains by hand. Perfect for small batches.

Hand-crank coffee grinder: These tools work well for grains, too. In fact, it is one of my favorite tools. Great for small amounts.

Rotary quern or hand mill: Widely used in ancient and medieval times for hand-grinding grains. Mine was

The stone grinder, also called a *molcajete,* is classic tool that grinds grains slowly. A must-have tool due to its versatility.

A metate is a big flat stone with a smaller one on top to crush or grind grains by hand. Perfect for small batches.

The hand-crank coffee grinder is one of my favorite methods for small batches.

Rotary querns or hand mills were widely used in ancient and medieval times for hand-grinding grains and are precursors to modern milling technology.

a gift and is mostly a teaching tool, but I've used it a couple of times with wild oat grains.

Electric coffee grinder: Fast for small amounts, though not always great for producing fine flour.

Vitamix: Strong enough to grind flour. It's best if you don't grind large quantities often, as it can overheat. I use a classic Vitamix 5200.

If you already own a high-end flour mill, feel free to use it. If you're considering buying one, prices range from $300 to $700.

WonderMill Electric Grain Grinder: Fast and handles dry grains well.

Country Living Grain Mill: Durable manual mill with adjustable settings.

Mockmill 100 Stone Grain Mill: Ideal for fine-textured flour and compact design.

KoMo Classic Grain Mill: Combines efficiency with an attractive design. Seriously, I love the "look."

NutriMill Classic High-Speed Grain Mill: Offers variable texture control.

Electric coffee grinders are fast for small amounts, but they're not great for producing very fine flour.

At high speed, the Vitamix efficiently makes fine flour. It's another one of my favorite methods.

On Making Flours

Creating my own flours has been a lesson in diversity, both in nutrition and flavor. Most North American supermarkets sell wheat-based flours, like all-purpose, bread, whole wheat, cake, and pastry. Other options include rye, almond, rice, and coconut flours. Some flours, like self-rising, have baking powder and salt mixed in. In general, there are about eight to ten types of flours readily available.

Well, as a wildcrafter, you can add a lot more to these store-bought options. So far, I've made flour from the following foraged grains and seeds:

- Wild barley
- Wild oats
- Indian ricegrass
- Wild rice
- Cheatgrass
- Proso millet
- Wild rye
- Bulrush
- Curly dock
- Thistle sage
- Rocky Mountain beeplant
- Smilo grass
- Einkorn
- Thistle sage
- California buckwheat
- Sunflower seeds
- Jungle rice

Keep in mind that some wild seeds, like chia and thistle sage, may "gunk up" these machines.

Even as a full-time wildcrafter and teacher, I can't justify the cost of a high-end flour mill. My seeds and grains are special and time intensive to forage and extract, so I'm happy with my basic equipment. My Vitamix does a wonderful job making flours from the wild seeds and grains I collect.

Quick and Simple Method with a Vitamix 5200

This method is fast and efficient, and prevents the machine from overheating.

1. Ensure the container is clean and dry.
2. Pour ½ to 1 cup (125–250 ml) of grains into the container. Avoid overfilling for even grinding.
3. Secure the lid. Start on the lowest speed, then gradually increase to the highest.
4. Blend for 30 seconds to 1 minute, or until the grains reach the desired texture. Stop sooner for coarse flour or blend longer for fine flour.
5. If the flour feels warm, let it cool before storing to prevent clumping or moisture buildup.
6. Transfer to an airtight container and store in a cool, dry place.

Antinutrients and Wild Flours

Antinutrients are not usually an issue with commercial flours. All-purpose flour and bread flour are made by removing the bran and germ from wheat, which eliminates most antinutrients. This process results in smoother, more shelf-stable flour but also removes a significant portion of nutrients, including fiber and minerals. These flours are not treated to reduce antinutrients further because the milling process already achieves this. While versatile for baking, they are less nutritious than whole wheat flour.

That said, whole wheat flours are generally not treated to reduce antinutrients either. Since they include the entire wheat kernel—bran, germ, and endosperm—they retain higher levels of nutrients, including fiber, vitamins, and minerals, but they also contain more antinutrients, like phytic acid, which can interfere with mineral absorption.

Is this antinutrient thing really important? Yes and no. From my perspective, if you eat a balanced diet with varied foods, the impact of antinutrients is minimal. Also, you probably won't eat breads or flatbreads made with wild flours daily.

However, if you were to eat a diet that was heavily reliant on wild flours due to inconvenient circumstances—like the end of the world or being on a survival TV show like *Naked and Afraid*—then you need to take antinutrients into consideration.

I'm joking a little, but seriously, if you want to cultivate your own grains, use wild flours, and rely on them as an important part of your diet, reducing antinutrients becomes more important.

The simplest method for removing antinutrients is soaking. Here is how I do it:

1. Rinse the grains or seeds to remove dirt.
2. Soak them in water for 8 to 12 hours at room temperature. Add a splash of vinegar or lemon juice to the water for better results.
3. Dry the grains completely before grinding them into flour.

I know it's a pain to add this step, but if you're really into making your own flours, it's worth it.

There's a whole art to preparing grains to make flours. The following additional methods not only reduce antinutrients but can also boost nutrition and add flavor to your final product. This is where things get exciting.

Fermentation: Soak grains with a natural starter for 24 to 48 hours, stirring occasionally. Drain, dry completely, and grind into flour.

This process breaks down phytic acid and other antinutrients while developing complex, tangy flavors.

Sprouting: Soak grains for 8 to 12 hours, drain, and let them germinate, rinsing twice daily, until small sprouts appear. Dry completely and grind into flour. This activates enzymes, reduces antinutrients, and imparts subtle sweetness to the final product. See chapter 6 for more information on sprouting.

Roasting/toasting: Spread grains on a dry pan or baking tray. Roast them lightly over medium heat or in the oven at 200 to 250°F (90–120°C) until aromatic and slightly golden. Cool before grinding into flour.

Boiling: Boil grains for 10 to 20 minutes, then drain and dry completely before grinding. This works well for harder grains like millet or amaranth.

These methods vary in complexity and effectiveness, so choose one based on your time and needs.

Cleaning and Soaking Seeds for Flour

Cleaning and soaking seeds is an essential step when making flour, especially with seeds whose husks or dried flower heads are included in the processing because separating the seeds is impractical. These include curly dock, California buckwheat (*Eriogonum fasciculatum*), canaigre (*Rumex hymenosepalus*), water dock (*Rumex aquaticus*), and patience dock (*Rumex patientia*), among others.

Many of these seeds can be quite dirty, especially if they've been exposed to wind. This is particularly true for the California buckwheat flowers I forage in the desert, where fine sand particles are carried by the wind. Additionally, as explained earlier, some seeds and husks have a natural bitterness that can be reduced by soaking.

Method

1. When collecting seeds or flowers, choose areas free of pollution or contaminants. For example, when I lived in Los Angeles, I avoided public parks due to vehicle emissions and other pollutants.
2. Sort through your harvest to remove leaves, stems, and any unwanted debris. This step makes the cleaning process easier and more effective.
3. Place the seeds or flower heads in a large bowl and cover them with cold water, ensuring they are fully submerged. Gently stir

with your hand to loosen dirt and dust. Pour out the dirty water, refill the bowl with clean water, and stir again to complete the cleaning process.

4. Soak the seeds or flower heads in fresh water for 8 hours, or overnight. This helps reduce any inherent bitterness in seeds like dock or California buckwheat. If you soak during the day, changing the water periodically can help, too.
5. Spread the cleaned seeds or flowers in a single layer to dry. You can dry them in the sun or use a dehydrator set at 115°F (46°C). The relatively low temperature will allow the seeds to retain their nutrients.
6. Once dried, the seeds or flower heads are ready to be ground into flour. For small batches, I use a high-speed blender like a Vitamix.

This method ensures your flour is clean, free of sand, less bitter, and ready for use in recipes. If you're working with particularly sandy or dirty foraged materials, an extra rinse might be helpful.

Tips on Bitter Seeds and Flours

During the COVID-19 pandemic, I visited my daughter in Longmont, Colorado. I was traveling across North America, learning about plants and collecting wild clay for pottery. Most of my time was spent outdoors, exploring, identifying plants, and snapping photos. I was already deep into writing this book and the grasses in Colorado absolutely fascinated me—so different from the types in Southern California.

On my walks, I kept noticing this strange plant. I ignored it at first since I was focused on grasses and grains. But the plant wouldn't let me ignore it, practically begging me to take notice. Foragers will get this; sometimes it feels like plants are yelling, "Hey, check me out!"

Finally, I gave in, took a photo, and identified it. Turns out, it was Rocky Mountain beeplant (*Cleomella serrulata*). A little research revealed it was an important food source for Native Americans that was also used for making dye. The seeds were traditionally cooked into a mush, like porridge.

Here's the issue: the seeds were bitter. Too bitter for my taste. I tried working with them but gave up. Then, one day, as I was looking into ways to prepare local edible seeds, I stumbled upon a small but important detail. Traditionally, beeplant seeds were boiled first, then dried, and finally made into mush.

How had I not thought of this? It's the same concept as boiling dandelion greens or leaching acorns to remove tannins. So, if you've got bitter seeds or grains that you know were once staple foods, try boiling the seeds to reduce bitterness. Dehydrate them. Grind them into flour or make mush. It's simple but effective.

Curious about other options, I tried removing bitterness from flour instead of whole seeds. For this experiment, I chose curly dock seeds because of their natural bitterness. I ground them (chaff and all) into fine flour using my Vitamix, then tested two methods:

1. **Coffee filter method.** I treated the flour like coffee, placing it in a filter and pouring boiling water over it. The bitterness did reduce (by around 50 percent), but the process was slow. Straining took hours, so I eventually removed the wet flour and dried it in my dehydrator.
2. **Cold leaching method.** This method was the clear winner. I mixed the dock flour with cold water in a jar (about 25 percent flour to water by volume) and let it sit overnight. The flour settled at the bottom, making it easy to pour off the water. I removed the flour with a spoon, dried it, and was pleasantly surprised—no noticeable bitterness, and the flour had a mild, nutty flavor.

Until I find a better method, I'm convinced cold leaching is the way to go when dealing with bitter curly dock flour.

Let's summarize a little. If you're working with bitter seeds or flour, you have a few options to try:

Seed Soaking

- Soak seeds overnight (or longer), then dehydrate and grind into flour.
- For stubborn bitterness, change the water periodically until the seeds taste less bitter.

Seed Boiling

- Boil the seeds until they're no longer bitter, then dehydrate and grind into flour.

Flour Bitterness Removal—Coffee Filter Method

- Place the flour in a coffee filter, pour hot water over it, and let it strain.
- Dry the leached flour afterward.

Seed soaking: Soak seeds overnight (or longer), then dehydrate and grind into flour.

Seed boiling: Boil the seeds until they're no longer bitter, then dehydrate and grind into flour.

Coffee filter method: Place the flour in a coffee filter, pour hot water over it, and let it strain. Dry the leached flour afterward.

Cold leaching method: Mix one part flour with four parts water, let sit overnight, pour off the water, and dry the leached flour.

Flour Bitterness Removal—Cold Leaching Method

- Mix flour with water in a jar or bucket.
- Let it sit overnight, then pour off the water.
- For extra bitterness removal, repeat the process once or twice daily until the flour tastes neutral and then dry the leached flour afterward.

Each method has its pros and cons, but the cold leaching method stands out for its ease and effectiveness—especially with curly dock flour. Try these techniques and see what works best for your foraging adventures!

Putting It All Together

It's important to step back and decide what works for your needs when it comes to the various methods for processing wild grains and seeds. If foraging is just a side project, you can skip many of the detailed methods for removing antinutrients. If what you harvest is a small addition to your meals, the antinutrient content won't significantly impact your overall nutrition, especially if you eat a balanced diet. In these cases, you can focus on cleaning to remove debris, grinding if you're baking, and cooking them as is for porridge and other simple recipes.

On the other hand, if wild (or commercial) grains and seeds are a regular part of your diet or if you're aiming for the best flavor and texture, extra processing is worth the effort. Parching, for instance, can bring out rich, nutty flavors and make grinding easier. Soaking softens tougher grains, improving their texture and making them easier to work with. Fermenting takes things a step further, unlocking complex flavors and adding a unique twist to bread, wild crackers, or other baked goods.

Even if you're not concerned about antinutrients, these methods offer creative ways to explore the full potential of wild seeds and grains. Think of them as fun tools to enhance your foraging experience and culinary possibilities.

CHAPTER 4

Common Wild Varieties

Let's get started! You should be able to find the seeds and grains featured in this chapter on almost every continent—except maybe Antarctica, of course. If you're in the desert, some might be harder to come by, although even there you'll find some surprises.

In Southern California, where I spend much of my time foraging, these seeds and grains are abundant. I've also seen many of the same varieties while teaching in Vermont and during visits to Europe. Their adaptability is impressive—they seem to pop up everywhere people have settled. In fact, many of these plants are considered non-native and invasive. So, by foraging and eating them, you're not only filling your pantry but also helping the environment.

This chapter covers the grains and seeds you're most likely to encounter, whether you're wandering through meadows, walking near the woods, or ambling along roadsides. Some, like wild mustard, thrive in disturbed areas, while others, such as plantain and lamb's-quarter, are known to follow human activity closely. If you've ever thought, "There's nothing edible growing around here," I guarantee these plants will change your mind. Once you learn to identify them, you'll start to see them everywhere.

Not only are these seeds and grains easy to find, but they're also rich in nutrients. Some, like amaranth, have high protein content, while others, such as black mustard seeds, pack bold flavors that can transform simple meals. Many also store well for long periods, which is why ancient cultures relied on them for food security. Today, they're perfect for anyone wanting to reconnect with nature, eat seasonally, or reduce their reliance on commercial food sources.

What's fascinating about many of these seeds and grains is their long history of use. They were key foods for many of our ancestors. These plants were spread across continents, whether intentionally or accidentally, and some, such as wild barley and oats, are wild relatives of crops now grown in large-scale agriculture. They offer a glimpse into what people relied on

long before modern farming practices took over.

As you read through this chapter, I encourage you to approach these plants with curiosity and a sense of adventure. While they may not always look like the grains and seeds you find at the store, they offer a unique connection to the land. Keep an open mind, experiment with recipes, and enjoy the process of learning from the natural world.

Amaranth

AMARANTHUS SPP.

Amaranth is a diverse genus with about seventy recognized species. We have ten native species in North America, and the remaining species can be found pretty much anywhere in the world. According to Calflora (a nonprofit database providing information on wild California plants), we have over twenty different types in California alone. Three of them showed up in my garden last year. Amaranth plants can grow in a variety of conditions and are often found in disturbed soils, gardens, fields, and roadside areas. They are known for their resilience and can thrive in both dry and moist conditions.

Amaranths vary widely in appearance and usage, from grains to leaf vegetables to ornamental plants. For this book, our main interest is the seeds, but so far all the wild amaranths I have encountered boast edible sprouts, microgreens, and leaves, too.

Some amaranths are considered "ancient grains," having been cultivated and consumed for thousands of years in various parts of the world, including Africa, Asia, and the Americas. They are a rich source of protein, fiber, and micronutrients.

Here are some of the most common (wild) amaranths:

Redroot amaranth (*Amaranthus retroflexus*): Widespread in North America, Europe, and Asia. It thrives in disturbed habitats such as agricultural land and urban areas.

Spiny amaranth (*Amaranthus spinosus*): Native to tropical America, it has spread across many tropical and subtropical regions worldwide, including Asia, Africa, and the southern United States. It's known for its spiny stems.

Palmer amaranth (*Amaranthus palmeri*): Originally from the southwestern United States and northern Mexico, it has spread extensively across North America. It prefers agricultural fields and disturbed areas.

Slender amaranth (***Amaranthus viridis***)**:** Found in tropical and subtropical regions around the world, including Africa, Asia, and the Americas. Common in open, disturbed areas.

Tumbleweed amaranth (***Amaranthus albus***)**:** Native to the western United States but now found in many parts of North America, as well as Europe and Asia. Known for its seed dispersal method, resembling a tumbleweed.

Waterhemp (***Amaranthus tuberculatus***)**:** Predominant in North America, especially in the central and eastern parts. It grows along waterways and in agricultural fields.

Spleen amaranth (***Amaranthus dubius***)**:** A species found in the tropical Americas but has spread to parts of Asia and Africa. It is often found in disturbed sites and is used as a leaf vegetable in some regions.

Red amaranth (***Amaranthus cruentus***)**:** Originating from Central and South America, it has been introduced to regions in Africa and Asia. Cultivated for its grains and leaves, it also thrives as a wild species in various climates.

Joseph's coat (***Amaranthus tricolor***)**:** Native to Southeast Asia, it is used as an ornamental plant and a leaf vegetable. It has been introduced to other tropical and subtropical regions.

Livestock amaranth (***Amaranthus blitum***)**:** Common in Mediterranean regions but has spread to many parts of Europe, Asia, and the Americas. It grows in disturbed soils and is also consumed as a leafy vegetable in some areas.

Redroot pigweed (*Amaranthus retroflexus*).

There are several key features to look out for when identifying wild amaranth (also known as pigweed, among other names). Across species, you're likely to be looking at a plant with the following characteristics:

Alternating leaves that are often notched at the tips and can sometimes appear reddish at the center, especially in the red amaranth varieties. The young leaves of redroot pigweed are often purple.

The stem of the amaranth plant can be green or red/purple, depending on the species. It is usually upright, can grow quite tall (up to several feet in some cases), and may have a somewhat rough or hairy texture.

Flowers are nondescript and densely packed in spike-like clusters. They can range in color from green to red to gold, depending on the species.

The seeds of the (wild) amaranth plants I've encountered are very small, round, and typically black or brown. They are found within the flowers once they have matured.

With so many different species, you will encounter variations, so use as many tools as you need to identify wild amaranth until you have a 100 percent positive identification. For example, you can compare the plant to high-quality images or descriptions in a field guide or online search engine, share the photo with plant identification groups on social media, use a plant identification app, and so on.

Collection and Extraction

The average number of seeds produced by a wild amaranth plant can vary greatly based on factors like species, environmental conditions, and the plant's health. Generally, it's reported that a single wild amaranth plant can produce anywhere from about 10,000 to over 100,000 seeds or even greater under typical conditions—great news for foragers! For example, Palmer amaranth plants can produce up to 250,000 seeds. The seeds remain viable for 3 to 5 years.

Wait until the amaranth plants have matured and their seed heads are dry and starting to drop seeds. This usually occurs in the late summer or early fall. Bring along some paper bags or envelopes to collect the seeds. It's better to use something breathable to avoid moisture trapping, which can lead to mold.

You can use a few different collection methods:

Method 1: Use a plastic or paper bag to cover the plant's top. Carefully tilt the plant sideways and give it a shake. This will dislodge the seeds.

Method 2: If the plants are densely seeded, you might find it easier to cut the entire seed head off and place it into your bag. Once you have collected several heads, you can shake and rub them together inside the bag to separate the seeds from the plant material.

Once you've collected your seeds, place them in a shallow bowl or pan, then gently blow on them. The lighter chaff will blow away, leaving the heavier seeds behind. You can also set the bowl outside on a breezy day, using the wind's natural flow to assist in the separation process.

Spread the seeds out on a clean, dry surface in a well-ventilated area away from direct sunlight. Allow them to dry thoroughly to prevent mold. This can take 1 to 2 weeks depending on humidity levels. Store the dry seeds in a cool, dry place (see Drying and Storage, page 18).

Preparation

Wild amaranth seeds are extremely hard, resembling tiny black pebbles. This hardness makes it necessary to soften them through boiling before they are suitable for consumption. If you try eating them raw, you may find

A ferment of lamb's-quarter leaves, daikon roots, and wild seeds and grains (including amaranth) in progress.

them too tough to chew properly. Boiling helps unlock their nutritional value and makes them easier to digest.

To prepare a small amount for personal use, I typically use 2 tablespoons (26 g) of seeds combined with 1 cup (250 ml) of water. The ratio of water may seem a bit excessive, but it ensures the seeds have enough moisture to soften completely.

1. Combine the seeds and water in a pot.
2. Heat the water over medium-high heat until it begins to boil.
3. Once the water reaches a boil, reduce the heat to a simmer. Cover the pot partially, letting it cook for about 25 minutes.
4. After 25 minutes, taste a few seeds to make sure they are tender. If they're still firm, continue simmering for a few more minutes, checking intermittently until they reach the right texture.
5. The seeds should double in volume by the time they finish cooking. This means for every tablespoon of seeds, you will end up with around 2 tablespoons of cooked seeds.

Culinary Uses

Amaranth seeds are an excellent addition to your wild pantry, and you'll find them featured in many of my recipes. Their mild, nutty flavor and small size make them a great way to boost the nutritional content of meals. Once properly cooked, wild amaranth seeds are versatile and can be incorporated into a variety of dishes, such as:

Tabbouleh: Mix them with parsley, tomatoes, and lemon juice as an addition to wild rice, bulgur, or couscous.

Rice dishes: Combine them with cooked rice for added texture and nutrition.

Porridge: Stir them into porridge for a nutritious breakfast boost.

Crackers: Mix them (after cooking) into cracker dough to create crispy, nutrient-dense crackers.

Lacto-ferments: Add cooked seeds to lacto-fermented foods like sauerkraut or kimchi. The seeds absorb the brine, softening over time while adding a subtle crunchy texture.

Pickling: Add them to pickled seed blends for extra variety and texture (see Pickled Wild Seeds, page 262).

Broadleaf Plantain

PLANTAGO MAJOR

Broadleaf plantain, also known as white man's footprint or common plantain, originally comes from Eurasia but is now found across most continents, including North America, South America, and Europe.

To identify broadleaf plantain, look for its broad, oval-shaped leaves that grow close to the ground in a rosette pattern. The leaves are smooth with 5 to 7 noticeable veins running parallel from the base to the tip. This plant also has unique flower stalks that emerge from the center, standing upright and bearing cylinder-shaped spikes of tiny greenish flowers. The stalks are usually longer than the leaves. Broadleaf plantain is often found in lawns, parks, and paths where the soil is compacted.

Collection and Extraction

To harvest the seeds, wait until the flower spikes turn brown in late summer or early fall. Cut the spikes off with scissors or a knife, put them in a paper bag, and place them in a warm, dry location for a few days to ensure they are moisture-free. Once dry, rub the spikes over a bowl to shake the tiny seeds out of the husks. To separate the seeds from the husks, pour them back and forth between two bowls in a light breeze; the lighter husks will blow away, leaving the heavier seeds. Store the dry seeds in a cool, dry place (see Drying and Storage, page 18).

Culinary Uses

Young broadleaf plantain leaves are good to eat, either raw or cooked. I like to boil the leaves for 3½ minutes and then add a soy sauce marinade, as described on page 116 of my book, *The New Wildcrafted Cuisine*.

I use the seeds in the following ways:

Smoothies and drinks: When mixed with liquids, the seeds become thick and gel-like, similar to chia, making them a great fiber-rich addition to smoothies and other beverages.

In baking: The seeds can bind ingredients together in baking. When ground into a powder, they help give structure and moisture to breads and pancakes.

Soups and sauces: The seeds can thicken soups and sauces. They can also be added to oatmeal or homemade granola for extra fiber and a bit of texture. I like using these seeds in my Pickled Wild Seeds recipe (page 262).

Brome

BROMUS SPP.

If you've ever walked through a field of dried grasses in the late summer in Southern California, only to end up with a bunch of painful, spiky burrs stuck in your socks, congratulations! You've found my favorite grain. The grains of great brome are designed to disperse by attaching to the fur of animals or the clothes of humans. Their long awns (bristle-like structures) with barbed tips allow the grains to easily catch onto fabric but make them difficult to remove.

Great brome—also known as foxtail—originally comes from Europe, and the hills of Southern California are covered with it. Another name for it is "ripgut brome," because its sharp leaves and grains can cause cuts, or "rips," in the mouths and stomach linings of herbivores. This can be especially problematic for livestock like cows and sheep. So, people started calling it ripgut brome to warn others about this potential danger.

I became fascinated with great brome because it is invasive, but the grains inside are quite large. They're not impressive at first glance—they're rather flat and super hard—but the secret is to boil them. You end up with the most beautiful red, rice-like grains. Evidence of brome grain consumption in prehistory and history is typically indirect, inferred from archaeological finds of seeds or residues on ancient tools and pottery, but I found some references to this grain being found mixed with other edible seeds and grains in Neolithic Europe.* Further research confirmed these grains as a food source for some native tribes (e.g., Luiseño, Karuk, Miwok) once great brome was introduced in North America.†

I find it amazing that one of the most invasive plants in my area was actually a food source for some of my European ancestors, but I'm not surprised. Quite a few so-called invasive plants in Southern California are commonly eaten in other countries.

Bromus is a large genus of around 200 different grasses that have their own special group called Bromeae. They're known as the bromes, brome grasses, cheatgrasses, or chess grasses. While some bromes, such as great brome, have large grains, others, such as red brome (*Bromus madritensis* ssp. *rubens*), have small grains with little nutritional value. Not all *Bromus* grains are worth the effort of foraging and processing.

* Sue Colledge and James Conolly, eds., *The Origins and Spread of Domestic Plants in Southwest Asia and Europe* (Walnut Creek, CA: Left Coast Press, 2007).

† Daniel E. Moerman, *Native American Ethnobotany* (Portland, OR: Timber Press, 1998).

Bromus grasses are widespread and native to many parts of the world. For example, California brome (*Bromus carinatus*) grows in the Rocky Mountain and Pacific Coast regions of North America. These grains were parched, ground into flour, and used to make bread, pinole, or mush by native tribes such as the Nisenan, Karuk, Luiseño, Miwok, and Mendocino.*

When I did some research about the use of edible *Bromus* grains in Europe, I found an interesting article titled "Should *Bromus secalinus* (Rye Brome) Be Considered a Crop?" The study explains how Iron Age rye brome seeds have been found in large quantities in living areas and among other farmed plants. Researchers looked at findings from 338 locations and found hints that people might have eaten brome grass during the Iron Age—cake fragments made with brome were discovered in two rural settlements. The study suggests that people might have been too quick to label rye brome a "weed," and that for people in the past, the thin line between a useful plant and a weed wasn't always clear.†

Today, rye brome is considered invasive in several parts of the world. It originates from parts of Europe and Asia but has become invasive in North America and Australia. In these regions, rye brome invades agricultural lands, disturbed soils, roadsides, and natural habitats. Its invasive nature is due to its ability to produce a large number of grains, its tolerance to different soil types, and its capacity to compete with native plants and crops.

So, as a forager, you might stumble upon this ancient crop in your locale. In fact, it's pretty much guaranteed that you have some sort of brome grass growing in your environment. In Southern California, I'm mostly interested in great brome and cheatgrass.

---

* Daniel E. Moerman, *Native American Ethnobotany* (Portland, OR: Timber Press, 1998).

† Véronique Zech-Matterne et al., "Should *Bromus secalinus* (Rye Brome) Be Considered a Crop?: Analysis of Bromus Rich Assemblages from Protohistoric and Historic Sites in Northern France and Textual References," *Vegetation History and Archaeobotany* 30 (2021): 773–87, https://doi.org/10.1007/s00334-021-00830-5.

Cheatgrass

BROMUS TECTORUM

Cheatgrass is probably the most invasive grass where I live in the mountains. It's pretty much everywhere. Although it's not obvious when you look at the plant, cheatgrass grains are extremely abundant. It completely fooled me in the beginning—the awns obscured the grains inside.

Extraction

It was a challenge to figure out how to extract cheatgrass grains efficiently. After experimenting with various techniques, I ultimately adopted the Flame Winnowing method (page 42), which proved quite effective. I placed a bunch of cheatgrass awns in a large bowl and lit everything on fire. The goal isn't to fully carbonize the contents but to agitate the bowl slightly, ensuring a swift combustion that doesn't excessively harm the grains. You can also use a stick to stir the burning awns. It takes a bit of practice, but the flames typically die down rapidly on their own. Blow on the remaining grains to get rid of the ashes, and voila! You end up with tons of "parched" grains. (Make sure to read about Vitamix Threshing on page 47, too, which works extremely well and can save you a lot of time.)

Great brome.

Cheatgrass. Notice the obvious awns that look like dried-up flowers.

Preparation

Boil the grains for around 45 minutes, and they're ready to use. Don't get overexcited about them; on their own, they are barely palatable, but mixed into a gruel, porridge, tabbouleh, or wild salsa, they're quite acceptable. Actually, I change my mind; you can get excited about their culinary potential! I've barely scratched the surface in terms of their possible uses.

You can also make an interesting tea using parched cheatgrass grains. The taste is similar to barley tea, known as *mugicha* in Japan and *bori-cha* in Korea. It has a toasty, slightly bitter flavor and can be enjoyed hot or cold as a caffeine-free alternative to tea. See Wild Grains Tea, page 227, for instructions.

Great brome grains.

Cheatgrass grains after flame winnowing.

Great Brome

BROMUS DIANDRUS

Great brome grains are quite chewy due to their thick bran (outer layer), but gosh, they are beautiful. If you press one between your fingers after cooking it, you'll notice how starch-rich they are too.

These grains are incredibly versatile in my cooking. I don't use them on their own, but I love adding them to various recipes alongside other grains and seeds. For example, I mix them into ferments, toss them in my wild guacamole and salsa, and even use them as part of artistic dish presentations. However, I've found they don't work well in crackers or bread since the outer skin becomes too tough and chewy when dried.

Great brome grains, roasted thistle sage seeds, and seaweed served with a touch of soy sauce.

Collection and Extraction

Harvest great brome when the grains are ripe and dry, typically in the late summer or early fall, depending on your region. Make sure to wear gloves for protection and check for mold on the grain clusters or panicles (page 21). It takes me about 15 minutes to gather enough great brome grains for most of the year. Here's my method:

1. With your gloves on, grab a bunch of stems just below the grain clusters. Use a knife to cut beneath the clusters with your other hand.
2. Quickly stuff the clusters into a plastic or paper bag, moving from plant to plant until you have enough grains. It should not take long, maybe 10 to 15 minutes.
3. Secure the top of the bag to keep the grains from escaping. They will try . . .
4. If you aren't using your grains right away, spread the clusters in a thin layer on a clean surface or mesh screen to dry. Stir occasionally for even drying, which takes about a week. Alternatively, you can put them in an oven at a low setting (below 200°F / 93°C) or a food dehydrator for several hours. Honestly, leaving the bag

open in a shaded spot for a couple of weeks works too—my favorite lazy method!

5. Once dry, transfer the grain clusters to airtight containers. Glass jars, metal containers, or heavy-duty plastic containers work well. Store them in a cool, dry place out of direct sunlight.

I've successfully separated the dried grains from their husks and awns using a stone grinder. The method is simple: I gently grind the content, applying just enough pressure to strip away the husk and awns. While this method works to some extent, it can also damage the grains, making them look less appealing later on.

My favorite method of extraction for harvesting beautiful grains is straightforward: just boil the grains and use your fingers (see Hand Extraction, page 26). Place a large bunch of grain clusters in a pot and cover them with water, using a ratio of about 25 percent clusters to 75 percent water. Bring the water to a boil, then reduce the heat and let it simmer for 60 minutes. Turn off the heat, cover the pot, and allow the grains to sit in the hot water for an additional hour to soak. After they've soaked, strain the cooked grains. Once you've boiled the grains, it's very easy to remove the outer layers, and you end up with a lot of stunning grains in no time. This is the method I use if I want the grains to be a visible feature in a dish. You can also freeze portions of the cooked grains for later use, completing the hand extraction when you thaw them.

And, finally, the *best* method of extraction is using a Vitamix (see Vitamix Threshing, page 47). Place 2 cups (480 ml) of loose, unprocessed grains, including husks and awns, into the Vitamix. Set the speed to low (dial on 2), turn on the machine, and use the tamper to press the grains down until they rotate smoothly. Let the blender run for 20 minutes to fully separate the husks from the grains. Once done, transfer the contents to a bowl and winnow them in the wind to remove any remaining debris.

While the grains may not look as perfect as those from hand extraction, they're still excellent for use in any dish with a more rustic presentation.

Preparation

If you use the Vitamix method to extract your grains, you'll need to boil them after extraction. Simply add the desired amount to a pot with water, using a ratio of 1 part grains to 4 parts water. Bring to a boil, then reduce the heat to simmer for about 60 minutes.

Taste and check the texture of the grains. If needed, continue simmering or leave the grains soaking in hot water for another hour. Strain them and use immediately or store them in a jar with water in the fridge for up to 2 days.

Grab a bunch of stems just below the grain clusters. Use a knife to cut beneath the clusters.

Stuff the clusters into a plastic or paper bag, moving from plant to plant until you have enough grains.

Put the clusters in a pot of water, bring to a boil, then simmer for 60 minutes. Turn off the heat, cover the pot, and let the grains soak in the water for an additional hour.

If using the grains right away, use your fingers to remove the husk and awns. You can also freeze them—husks, awns, and all—for later extraction and use.

Your grains are now ready to eat. You can also store them in water in the fridge for a couple of days.

Add the grains to ferments, toss them in salsa, or use them to garnish your dishes.

Chickweed

STELLARIA MEDIA

Chickweed is native to Eurasia and presently naturalized throughout the world. We have so much chickweed in the Los Angeles area! But when I traveled in an RV exploring North America in 2020 and 2021, I found it in pretty much every state I visited. It thrives in cool, damp environments and is often found in gardens, fields, and shady areas. This plant is easily recognizable by its tiny, white, star-shaped flowers, which typically have five deeply divided petals, making them appear as if they have ten. The leaves of chickweed are small and oval, and grow in pairs opposite each other on the stem. The plant's stems are thin and delicate, with a distinctive line of fine hairs running along one side, which is a key identifying feature.

Chickweed is usually low growing, forming dense mats that can cover the ground. Its ability to spread quickly makes it a common weed in many areas, but it is also valued for its edibility. Chickweed can be used in salads, soups, and other dishes, offering a mild, slightly sweet flavor. Additionally, it is sometimes grown as food for poultry. It's one of those edible wild greens that are liked by chefs because of its strong earthy flavors.

Collection and Extraction

Collecting chickweed seeds is easy, but timing is crucial. Technically, you can pick the seedpods individually, but it's so tedious it will drive you insane. The most efficient method is to gather the dense mats of plant material as they dry and release their seeds. I typically fill a grocery bag in 5 to 10 minutes since the mats are easy to collect. This method, similar to the Natural Seed Release method described on page 28, involves transferring the gathered plants to a large container at home. Allow them to dry slowly in a shaded, dry area, stirring daily to ensure even drying and seed separation. Once dry, shake, sieve, and winnow to extract the seeds for use. Store the seeds in a cool, dry place (see Drying and Storage, page 18). I mostly use the seeds to grow delicious microgreens.

Cleavers

GALIUM APARINE

I thought I should include cleavers in this book, as their seeds may help you survive the apocalypse. One of my biggest phobias, if the end of the world comes, is definitely coming face to face with Starbucks zombies. Heck, the company even named a Frappuccino for them. Yes, one of the biggest dangers you might face is coffee-addicted zombies, never able to fully wake up, wandering the streets in search of their favorite drink. I assume they could be dangerous if you can't provide them with a cup of joe, but fear not, the solution is here!

But first, let's talk about the plant. I think cleavers can be found pretty much everywhere in the world, either as a native or introduced plant. Its status in North America is somewhat controversial, but it seems it's actually native.

Cleavers can be identified by their unique leaf and stem characteristics. The leaves are small and narrow, and grow in whorls (circles) of 6 to 8 around the stem. Both the stems and leaves are covered in tiny, hooked hairs, giving them a rough or sticky feel. This feature allows the plant to cling to clothing or fur, hence the name "cleavers."

Additionally, cleavers have a weak stem and often sprawl or climb over other plants, forming tangled mats. They produce tiny, white, star-shaped flowers in clusters at the tips of the stems. These flowers eventually turn into small, round, green to brownish seeds, also covered in hooked hairs. Our main interest lies in these seeds. Cleavers are part of the coffee family, known as Rubiaceae, so yes, you can make a coffee substitute using cleaver seeds.

I wouldn't say the drink is fantastic, but the flavors are quite interesting—kind of a cross between coffee and tea, like a mild coffee with some earthy flavors.

Collection

First, you'll need to collect the mature seeds. Each plant can produce hundreds of seeds, but collecting them is easier said than done. It's quite a tedious process of collecting them by hand. I've tried other methods, such as grabbing the dried plants full of seeds and stuffing them into a bag for future extraction, but it was even messier trying to extract the seeds. So, you'll need patience, but it's kind of a fun project.

You don't want to collect the seeds when they're still green; you want them dried up and grayish-brownish. The seeds are often quite dusty or dirty, mixed with dried pieces of old stems and leaves. You can rub them

between your hands or use a sieve, then blow gently to remove any excessive debris, but there's no need to go crazy trying to remove all unwanted particles or even to wash them in water.

Preparation

Just as coffee beans are roasted, you'll need to roast the cleaver seeds. One option is to spread the "cleaned" seeds on a baking sheet and roast them in the oven at a low temperature (around 320°F or 160°C) until they turn dark brown. This usually takes about 10 to 15 minutes, but keep an eye on them to avoid burning.

My preferred method is to roast them in a skillet; it takes me around 5 minutes at medium-high heat. You can go by the smell and the color of the seeds; they should turn dark brown.

Once roasted, grind the seeds using a coffee grinder or a mortar and pestle until they reach a fine, coffee-like consistency.

Prepare your beverage as you would coffee. I tend to use 1 to 1½ tablespoons (3.5 to 5 g) of ground seeds per cup (250 ml) of water. You can brew it using a French press or a drip coffee maker, or simply by steeping it in hot water and then straining the grounds. That's it! Now you'll survive the apocalypse and the Starbucks zombies.

Cleavers and Caffeine

The fact that cleavers belong to the Rubiaceae family, the same family as the coffee plant (*Coffea* spp.), has led to the assumption that they might share some chemical properties, including the presence of caffeine. Quite a few foraging and herbalism resources mention that cleaver seeds contain caffeine and can be used to make a coffee-like beverage, but these claims are not typically backed by rigorous scientific analysis. The reality is that cleaver probably doesn't contain caffeine, but it still does a damn good job fooling those Starbucks zombies.

Dock

RUMEX SPP.

There are over 200 species within the *Rumex* genus worldwide, and they can be found in various habitats across the globe, including temperate regions, grasslands, and disturbed areas. The one I've encountered the most in North America and Europe is curly dock.

Based on my experience, the vast majority of docks have edible seeds, but it's essential to identify each plant accurately and research their seed edibility. Keep in mind, "edible" doesn't always mean "tasty." For example, the seeds of bitter dock (*Rumex obtusifolius*) live up to their name—they're far too bitter for my liking.

Curly dock seeds and many other dock seeds are easy to identify: the egg-shaped seeds are enveloped in three wing-like papery sections. The surface texture can vary, ranging from smooth to slightly ridged or wrinkled. The seeds are produced in late spring to early summer and remain on the plant until they are mature and ready for dispersal in the late summer or early fall. Initially green, the seeds gradually transition to a dark brown or black coloration as they mature.

These are some of the most common dock plant species with edible seeds that can be found in each region:

North America and Europe

Curly dock (*Rumex crispus*)
Broad-leaved dock (*Rumex obtusifolius*)
Common sorrel (*Rumex acetosa*)
Patience dock (*Rumex patientia*)

Asia

Japanese dock (*Rumex japonicus*)
Nepalese dock (*Rumex nepalensis*)

Middle East

Bladder dock (*Rumex vesicarius*)
Toothed dock (*Rumex dentatus*)
French sorrel (*Rumex scutatus*)

I wouldn't classify dock seeds as "gourmet" food. The flavors vary depending on the species and how they are prepared. Generally, the seeds have a nutty and slightly sour taste. When collected past their prime, they tend to be rather insipid. Toasting the seeds in an oven for a few minutes at 350°F (175°C) can enhance their nutty flavor and aroma. My main method is to grind them into flour and use them as a gluten-free addition to bread, pasta, or crackers. You can also grow fancy lemony sprouts (see page 210), which are a great addition to salads and other dishes.

Culinary Uses

Curly dock flour has several interesting culinary uses:

Breads and flatbreads: Mix curly dock flour with other flours like wheat or rye to create rustic breads or flatbreads. I usually keep the ratio of 20 to 25 percent dock flour and 75 to 80 percent other flour. Curly dock flour adds an earthy flavor with a touch of bitterness, as well as a denser texture. Bitterness is not a bad flavor profile if it's not excessive; sourdough breads can be quite bitter.

Pancakes and crepes: Use curly dock flour in pancake or crepe batters to add color and an interesting flavor twist. For people who enjoy foraging, it's a fun way to turn this often-unwanted weed into healthy food.

Pasta or noodles: You can blend dock flour with regular flour to make homemade pasta or noodles. The addition of dock flour gives the dough a firmer texture.

Crackers and biscuits: Incorporate curly dock flour into crackers or biscuits for a nutty, crispy snack. Again, I tend to stick with 20 percent dock flour, but by all means feel free to experiment. There are online recipes for crackers using mostly curly dock flour.

Breading for meat and vegetables: I've used curly dock flour as part of a coating mixture for fried octopus—the brown color made the dish quite unusual-looking in a good way.

Simple Curly Dock Pancake Flour

INGREDIENTS

¼ cup (30 g) dock flour
¾ cup (90 g) all-purpose flour
1 tablespoon (12 g) sugar (optional)
1 teaspoon (4 g) baking powder
¼ teaspoon (1.5 g) salt
1 egg
¾ cup (180 ml) milk (or plant-based milk)
1 tablespoon (15 ml) olive oil

I'm sure there are many other culinary uses to explore. For example, I plan to experiment with incorporating curly dock and acorn flour into my turkey stuffing recipe.

MAKING FLOUR WITH CURLY DOCK SEEDS

The following procedure can also be applied to other dock seeds. When making the flour, there's no need to separate the seeds from the fibrous papery husk surrounding them. Everything is utilized, and the resulting flour consists mostly of husk fibers. But, hey . . . fiber is supposed to be beneficial for your health!

1. Curly dock seeds are quick to harvest. Simply grasp the stems with one hand and use the other to strip the seeds from the stems into a bag. Within minutes, you can amass several cups of this wild food.
2. Remove any debris, dried stems, or old leaves from the seeds. Typically, you can simply use your fingers to separate the seeds from the unwanted material.
3. Rinse the seeds briefly, as they often accumulate dirt. Transfer the seeds to a bowl of cold water, give them a brief stir with your hands, and then remove them using a strainer. I usually soak the seeds overnight to remove some of the bitterness.
4. Because I live in warm, sunny climate, I place the clean seeds on a tray in the sun to dehydrate them. You can also spread the clean seeds in a single layer on a baking sheet and dehydrate at 150°F (65°C) until fully dried, around 6 hours. If you don't have a dehydrator, use your oven at the lowest setting.
5. Transfer the dried seeds to a grinder or food processor and grind to the consistency you like. I've made coarse dock flour using my stone grinder, but you'll get better results using an electric coffee grinder, high-speed blender, or Vitamix. You may need to do this in batches, depending on the size of your grinder or food processor.
6. Transfer the curly dock flour to an airtight container such as a glass jar or a plastic container with a tight-fitting lid. Store the flour in a cool, dry place away from the sun for up to a year.

Lamb's-quarter

CHENOPODIUM SPP.

Chenopodium is a genus of over 132 recognized species, commonly known as lamb's-quarter or goosefoot. There are both perennial and annual varieties, and you can find them almost anywhere in the world.

The *Chenopodium* genus includes plants like white goosefoot (*Chenopodium album*), kañiwa (*Chenopodium pallidicaule*), and quinoa (*Chenopodium quinoa*), which are used as food in various ways. They can be eaten as leafy greens, similar to spinach, or used as pseudocereals (they are grain-like but not true grains). These plants have been part of human diets for a very long time. For example, the pitseed goosefoot (*Chenopodium berlandieri*) was a key food for Native Americans over 6,000 years ago, and white goosefoot was consumed in Europe around the same time.

Generally speaking, all lamb's-quarter leaves are safe to eat, but they taste better when they're young. As they get older, the leaves develop a stronger flavor because they contain more oxalic acid, which can make it harder for your body to absorb minerals. This is especially important for people with kidney issues or rheumatism to consider. (See Managing Oxalic Acid, page 55, for more information.)

That said, obviously I've not collected or cooked the leaves and grains of all 132 species, so you'll still need to do your homework, identify the plant properly, and research its edibility.

To get you started, here are some of the most common edible varieties around the world:

Common lamb's-quarter or white goosefoot (*Chenopodium album*): This is the most widely known and consumed species. Both its leaves and seeds are edible and highly nutritious, and they can be used in a variety of dishes. *Chenopodium album* can be found nearly worldwide. It is native to Europe, but its adaptability has allowed it to become naturalized in many parts of North America, Asia, Africa, and Australia.

Good-King-Henry (*Chenopodium bonus-henricus*): Also known as poor-man's asparagus, Good-King-Henry is native to much of Europe and parts of West Asia and has been introduced to some areas of North America.

Nettleleaf goosefoot (*Chenopodium murale*): This one is found across many parts of the world. Originally native to Europe, Asia, and North Africa, it has become naturalized in many other regions, including North and South America, Australia, and New Zealand.

Pitseed goosefoot (*Chenopodium berlandieri*): Pitseed goosefoot is common across North America. In Mexico, the flower buds are prepared similarly to broccoli and used in traditional dishes.

Kañiwa (*Chenopodium pallidicaule*): Also called cañihua or cañahua, kañiwa is grown in the Andes mountains of South America.

Seaberry saltbush (*Chenopodium candolleanum*): Native to Australia, seaberry saltbush has edible leaves that can be eaten either raw or cooked, similar to spinach, offering a salty flavor that adds a unique taste to dishes. The seeds are also edible, providing a source of vitamins and minerals.

Golden goosefoot (*Chenopodium auricomum*): This plant thrives in various habitats, including Australia, where it adapts well to disturbed soils and agricultural lands. The young leaves can be eaten raw or cooked, offering a spinach-like option rich in nutrients. The seeds are edible too.

Lamb's-quarter thrives in places where the soil has been disturbed, like gardens and fields. It's a tough plant that pops up all over the place. These plants, particularly common lamb's-quarter and nettleleaf goosefoot, are easy to spot once you know what to look for. Expect some variations across the many different species, but the following applies to the most common varieties:

Leaves: The leaves are a giveaway. They're light green, maybe with a bit of blue, and shaped like a diamond or the foot of a goose, which is how it gets one of its names. They often have a whitish, powdery coating that you can rub off. On some species, the young top leaves may have a reddish hue.

Stem: Lamb's-quarter has a green or reddish stem that can grow pretty tall, up to about 6 feet (2 m). The stem usually has red lines running up and down it.

Flowers and seeds: Look for tiny green flowers that grow in clusters. Later, these flowers turn into small, edible black or brown seeds.

Feel: If you touch the leaves, they might feel a bit gritty because of the powdery coating. The plant is generally pretty sturdy.

Collection and Extraction

Locally, most of the seeds I collect are from white goosefoot. There are other *Chenopodium* varieties around, but this one is really common and has lots of seeds. It's also considered somewhat invasive where I live, so I can do my part in helping the environment by eating them.

There is more than one method to collect lamb's-quarter seeds. One of my favorite methods is Hand Rubbing (see page 38). Other effective methods include Stone Grinder (page 46) and Vitamix Threshing (page 47).

Method

1. Wait until the lamb's-quarter seeds on the stalk have dried out a bit. Grasp a stalk that has seed clusters, and with your other hand, carefully slide your fingers from the base of the seed cluster toward the tip, allowing the seeds to fall off. Use a container or bag to catch the seeds as you detach them from the stalks.
2. Spread the seeds on a flat, clean surface in a thin layer. Paper towel or cloth beneath the seeds will help absorb excess moisture. Place them in a warm, airy spot out of direct sunlight so they don't overheat and are protected from moisture. They should dry within 1 to 2 weeks.
3. After the seeds are dry, pour them through a sieve or mesh strainer over a bowl. Choose a sieve with holes small enough to catch any dried leaves and debris but large enough to let the seeds pass through.

To harvest, grasp a stalk that has seed clusters and, with your other hand, slide your fingers from the base of the cluster to the tip, allowing the seeds to fall off into your bag or container.

Place the dried seeds in a stone grinder and use back-and-forth motions with the pestle to break the seeds free from the chaff.

Pour the seeds and chaff from one bowl into another below. The lighter chaff will blow away with the breeze, while the heavier seeds will fall into the second bowl.

Your seeds are now ready to be used or stored.

4. Take a handful of the sieved seeds and rub them between your palms over the bowl. This action helps separate the seeds from their outer covering, also known as chaff.
5. Pour the seeds and chaff from one bowl into another below. The light chaff will blow away with the breeze, while the heavy seeds will fall into the second bowl. If there's no breeze, gently blow over the seeds as you pour to achieve the same effect. You might need to repeat the rubbing and winnowing process several times to fully remove the chaff.

   A friend of mine uses a thin screen for separating the seeds from the chaff. Using his hands, he rubs the seeds against the screen, letting the finer chaff fall through its mesh while the seeds remain on top. Any remaining chaff is then winnowed away by the wind.
6. Store the seeds in a cool, dry place. Use paper bags or jars with tight-fitting lids. Label them with the date and type of seed for future reference (see Drying and Storage, page 18).

Preparation

Don't expect these seeds to turn out exactly like the quinoa you buy from the store. Lamb's-quarter seeds are smaller and retain a bit of a crunch. However, this cooking method eliminates any bitterness, making them quite tasty.

Once you've cooked your lamb's quarter, check out the Lamb's-Quarter "Quinoa" and Wild Rice on page 264.

1. Place ½ cup of dry seeds in a large jar. Fill the jar with hot water and let it sit for 15 minutes, stirring occasionally.
2. Drain the water from the jar and move the seeds to a bowl. Pour in new warm water. You'll notice a lot of bubbles start to form. Continue to replace the water until no more bubbles appear on the water's surface.
3. Transfer the seeds to a pot and fill it with enough water to cover them. Forget about the usual quinoa-cooking ratio of 2 parts water to 1 part seeds. Instead, just make sure there's enough water to boil the lamb's-quarter seeds thoroughly for about 20 to 25 minutes. For ½ cup of seeds, I use around 6 to 7 cups of water.
4. Once boiled, drain off the remaining water and put the seeds into a clean jar with a tight lid. Store this jar in the refrigerator, where the cooked seeds will stay fresh for 4 to 5 days.

Milk Thistle

SILYBUM MARIANUM

Milk thistle is a species of thistle native to Southern Europe and Asia but now found worldwide. I frequently spot it in Southern California and the Los Angeles area. In some parts of North America, the plant is considered invasive.

The plant is somewhat easy to identify with its white-veined spiky leaves and purple flower heads, which typically bloom from late spring to early fall.

Many herbalists and health enthusiasts are familiar with the benefits of milk thistle. It has been used for millennia as an herbal remedy for liver dysfunction. The seeds contain silymarin, a compound that helps heal and protect liver cells from toxins. You can find these seeds at health food stores or online, though they can be quite pricey. They are commonly used to assist with conditions such as fatty liver disease, hepatitis, and cirrhosis, and have even been used to treat mushroom poisoning and alcohol abuse.

Aside from their medicinal benefits, milk thistle seeds are simply tasty to eat. The seeds I forage vary in color from darkish brown to tan, a variation I've also observed in seeds sold online. One of my favorite ways to prepare them is to roast them in a pan or oven, which gives them a nutty flavor similar to sesame seeds. There is a slight touch of bitterness, but it's not excessive. Toasted milk thistle seeds are an excellent addition to various dishes, including ferments, acorn hummus, wild tabouleh, and wild food salads.

If you plan to use these seeds daily as a supplement, it's wise to do some research or consult your doctor. My research indicates

that milk thistle seeds can interact with certain medications and are not suitable for those allergic to plants in the daisy or ragweed families. However, allergies aside, it seems that enjoying roasted or parched seeds occasionally is generally safe and trouble-free.

Collection and Extraction

To forage milk thistle seeds, come prepared with gloves to protect your hands from the sharp thorns. Use a knife or scissors to cut the flower heads once they have dried and turned fluffy white. Collect these heads in a bag or container.

At home, separate the seeds by breaking apart the flower heads over a bowl or paper towel. I often cut the flowers in two using scissors. It's very easy to separate the seeds from the fluffy parts, but keep your gloves on while doing so.

Once they are dry, store the seeds in a cool, dry place. Use paper bags or jars with tight-fitting lids. Label them with the date and type of seed for future reference (see Drying and Storage, page 18).

Miner's Lettuce

CLAYTONIA PERFOLIATA

Miner's lettuce is a very common edible plant that can be found in North America and parts of Europe, Asia, and Australia. It is popular among foragers worldwide for its mild grassy flavors.

The leaves of miner's lettuce are its most noticeable feature. The younger (and lower) leaves are oval and have long stems, while the upper leaves are round and appear as if the stem goes through the middle. These leaves are smooth and a bit fleshy. The plant's stems are thin and usually green, but they can sometimes be reddish. The stems can grow up to 12 inches (30 cm) long, and the plants form dense mats or clusters.

Miner's lettuce has small white or pink flowers that grow in clusters at the center of the upper round leaves. These flowers usually appear in early spring but can bloom throughout cooler months if conditions are right. The flowers help in identifying the plant.

Miner's lettuce prefers cool, moist locations such as forests, hiking trails, grasslands, stream edges, and gardens. It thrives in rich, moist, well-drained soil with plenty of shade.

I collect seeds from miner's lettuce every year for several reasons. It's a native plant where I live, and I even like to grow it in my vicinity when appropriate. The seeds (as well as the plant) are edible, although they're pretty tiny and super hard. Their flavor profile is quite bitter, so I mainly use the seeds for sprouting or growing microgreens during the winter.

Collection and Extraction

Collect the mature plants when their seeds are ready and place them in a box. Let them dry slowly in a dry but shaded area. Stir the plants daily to ensure even drying and seed separation. Once dry, shake, sieve, and winnow to extract the seeds for use (see Natural Seed Release, page 23).

Mustard

BRASSICACEAE FAMILY

I don't even know where to start with this one—there are so many wild mustards and related plants in this world that it would take several pages just to name them all. The mustard family, Brassicaceae, comprises around 338 groups and more than 3,700 types of flowering plants found all over the world.

There are many mustard-family plants that you can find at your local supermarket, such as: bok choy (*Brassica rapa* var. *chinensis*), broccoli (*Brassica oleracea* var. *italica*), cabbage (*Brassica oleracea* var. *capitata*), cauliflower (*Brassica oleracea* var. *botrytis*), collards (*Brassica oleracea* var. *acephala*), and countless others.

As a forager, when I speak to my students about wild mustards, I often refer to plants that follow the usual identification characteristics and are closely related to some of the common cultivated mustards, such as brow mustard (*Brassica juncea*), black mustard (*Brassica nigra*), white mustard (*Sinapsis alba*), and a few others.

This helps new foragers, allowing them to learn and safely explore the various wild mustards that can be found in their particular environment. For example, in the Los Angeles area, I've found over 16 different varieties with the following features:

Flowers: Mustard flowers have four petals arranged in the shape of a cross, giving them a characteristic cruciform appearance. The petals

Three different mustard leaves. From left to right: shortpod mustard (*Hirschfeldia incana*), black mustard (*Brassica nigra*), and tumble mustard (*Sisymbrium altissimum*).

are typically bright yellow, although in some species, such as wild radish and arugula, they can be white, light pink, or even purple. Mustard flowers grow in clusters at the tops of tall, branching stems, forming noticeable groups of blooms.

Leaves: Most mustard plants, such as black mustard, wild mustard (*Sinapis arvensis*), hoary mustard (*Hirschfeldia incana*), and the like, have leaves that are identifiable by their shape and texture. The leaves at the bottom of the plant are usually large and deeply divided, forming a rosette close to the ground. These lower leaves can be quite broad and have a jagged, toothed edge. As you move up the stem, the leaves become smaller and less divided, and may clasp the stem. Here is a good tip for you: A typical mustard leaf is composed of a main stem with smaller leaflets along the sides and a larger leaflet at the end.

The overall texture of the leaves will vary with each mustard. For example, black mustard leaves are somewhat prickly, while hedge mustard (*Sisymbrium officinale*) leaves are quite fuzzy.

Of course, you will have some variations. For example, garlic mustard (*Alliaria petiolata*) has kidney-shaped leaves with rounded teeth the first year, while second-year plants have more triangular leaves. *Descurainia sophia*, also

Black mustard (*Brassica nigra*).

Young shortpod mustard (*Hirschfeldia incana*).

known as fine-leaved tansy-mustard or flixweed, has fern-like leaves.

Overall, if you find a plant that has yellow flowers with four petals each growing in clusters at the top of the stems and leaves composed of a main stem with smaller leaflets along the sides and a larger leaflet at the end, you probably have a mustard plant. Mustards are often found in open, sunny areas, such as fields, roadsides, and disturbed soils.

As I write this book, I don't know of any mustard that is poisonous, though some may not be edible due to flavors or texture.

The most common wild mustards you'll find worldwide are:

Black mustard (*Brassica nigra*): Black mustard is found in various regions around the world, including North America, Europe, Asia, North Africa, and Australia. It thrives in temperate climates with plenty of sunlight and well-drained soils, often growing in disturbed areas such as fields, roadsides, and coastal regions. Native to Europe and parts of Asia, it has spread widely due to its adaptability to a variety of habitats. Black mustard can reach up to 10 feet (3 m) tall, with bright yellow flowers and long, slender seedpods. Its seeds taste very much like wasabi and make a great Dijon-Style Mustard condiment (see page 259).

Wild mustard (*Sinapis arvensis*): Wild mustard is prevalent in North America, where it grows in fields, roadsides, and disturbed areas throughout the United States and Canada. In Europe, wild mustard is native and commonly found in agricultural lands, wastelands, and along roadsides. It is also widespread in Asia and

Australia. It is a robust plant with yellow flowers and round seed pods, known for its resilience and widespread distribution. Its seeds are spicy and have a characteristic mustard taste.

Hedge mustard (*Sisymbrium officinale*): Found in Europe, North America, and Asia, hedge mustard grows in disturbed areas and along roadsides. It has small yellow flowers and its seeds are mild in flavor.

Garlic mustard (*Alliaria petiolata*): Garlic mustard is common in North America and Europe and invasive in many regions. It has white flowers, a garlicky aroma, and edible leaves and seeds. The seeds are spicy and garlicky, but not as strong as black mustard and wild mustard.

Charlock (*Sinapis arvensis*): Also known as field mustard, charlock often grows in agricultural fields across Europe and North America. It has bright yellow flowers.

Hoary mustard / shortpod mustard (*Hirschfeldia incana*): Common in the Mediterranean and parts of North America (and super invasive in Southern California), hoary mustard has yellow flowers, hairy leaves, and thrives in dry, disturbed areas. The seeds are somewhat tasteless, but they are great for sprouting. The sprouts taste like broccoli.

London rocket (*Sisymbrium irio*): Found in North Africa, Europe, and North America, London rocket grows rapidly in disturbed soils. It has yellow flowers, medicinal properties, and tiny, spicy seeds with hints of wasabi and . . . gasoline (in my opinion).

Tumble mustard (*Sisymbrium altissimum*): Also known as tall hedge mustard, tumble mustard is widespread in North America, Europe, and Asia, and known for its ability to spread rapidly. It has small yellow flowers, and its seeds are one of my favorites—they taste like hazelnuts and beets put together.

Field mustard (*Brassica rapa*): Widespread in Europe, Asia, and North America, field mustard is typically found in fields

Mustard seeds vary greatly in size and color.

and disturbed areas. The seeds are somewhat flavorless but great for sprouting and microgreens.

Western tansymustard (*Descurainia pinnata*): Found in dry, disturbed areas in North America, western tansymustard has yellow flowers, finely divided leaves, and seeds with a delicious nutty flavor.

Wild mustards are often invasive. Here in Southern California, black mustard and field mustard have taken over the local hills. Across North America and Canada, garlic mustard is particularly problematic, invading forest understories, outcompeting native plants, and disrupting local ecosystems. It spreads rapidly in shaded areas, such as forests, woodlands, and riverbanks.

Speaking from experience, foraging wild invasive mustards is beneficial for the environment primarily because it helps control the spread of these aggressive species that threaten biodiversity.

Seedpods

Of course, everyone has heard of edible mustard seeds and their culinary uses, but what you can purchase at the local supermarket is nothing compared to the sheer quantity, variety, and flavors that can be found in the wild.

But before we talk about seeds, let's talk about mustard seedpods, which are known as *siliques*. These pods vary in size, shape, and color depending on the species. Common characteristics include a long, slender pod with a beak-like tip, though some may be shorter and more rounded. The pods usually grow in clusters along the stems of the plant, and as they mature, they transition from green to shades of yellow or brown.

To identify mustard seedpods accurately, look for these distinctive features, and note the plant's growth habit, leaf structure, and location, which can help distinguish between different mustard species.

Collection and Extraction

Extracting mustard seeds is often quite straightforward. I primarily use two methods: Bag Threshing (page 41) and Twist and Gather (page 31).

The Bag Threshing method is simple and works very well with black mustard, shortpod mustard, and other mustard plants with relatively short seedpods.

1. Start by filling a sturdy bag with dry seedpods, packing in as many as possible. It's advisable to wear gloves to protect your hands, as the seedpods can sometimes be quite sharp. Once the bag is

Black mustard
(*Brassica nigra*)
Shortpod mustard
(*Hirschfeldia incana*)
Arugula
(*Eruca sativa*)
Tansymustard
(*Descurainia pinnata*)
Tumblemustard
(*Sisymbrium altissimum*)

about three-quarters full, seal it securely, place it on the ground, and stomp on it with your feet. Adding a little dance at this stage makes the process more enjoyable.

2. After stomping for a minute or so, tip the bag at an angle and shake it. Using scissors, cut a hole in the bottom corner where the seeds have accumulated. Position a strainer below the opening and above a bowl so the seeds can fall through while the chaff is retained in the strainer.
3. Gently shake the bag to let the seeds and chaff fall into the strainer. Collect the seeds that pass through into the bowl. This method is incredibly easy and efficient.

The Twist and Gather method is even more straightforward and works very well with mustard plants that have long siliques, such as tumble mustard and western tansymustard.

1. Collect the dry plants in a bundle, then move your hand slowly down the bundle, toward the seedpods. Using your hands, gently crush and squeeze the seedpods, letting the seeds fall into a large bowl below.
2. Transfer the contents of the bowl to a strainer over a smaller bowl. Any chaff or debris will stay in the strainer, while the seeds will fall into the small bowl.

For both methods, if you still have a bit of chaff or debris, you can remove it by gently blowing on the seeds or winnowing the contents in the wind. Store the dry seeds in a cool, dry place. Use paper bags or jars with tight-fitting lids. Label them with the date and type of seed for future reference (see Drying and Storage, page 18).

Culinary Uses

The various culinary uses of mustard seeds are determined by their distinct flavors. For example, black mustard seeds are the most pungent of the mustard seed varieties. They possess a strong, spicy flavor that can be quite intense, making them a staple in many Indian and Middle Eastern dishes. The seeds release a sharp, hot taste when they're chewed, and like brown mustard seeds, their flavor is enhanced when they're heated in oil. These are the seeds I use to make my wild Dijon-Style Mustard condiment (page 259).

The mildly bland seeds of plants like field mustard and shortpod mustard are excellent for sprouting into microgreens. These microgreens will carry the same flavor as the mature mustard plant.

Sedges

CYPERUS SPP.

Sedges, or *Cyperus*, are grass-like plants that grow in many parts of the world. You can find them in wetlands; along rivers, lakes, and marshes; and in grasslands and forests. They are common in North America, Europe, Africa, Asia, and Australia. Sedges usually thrive in places with plenty of water but can also grow in drier regions. They are adaptable and grow in both temperate and tropical climates.

There are more than 700 species of *Cyperus*, and they often have triangular stems, which is one of the characteristics that makes them different from regular grasses.

One of my first wild food teachers, Christopher Nyerges, used to tell me that "Sedges have edges, rushes are round, and grasses have nodes all the way to the ground." It's a simple rhyme that can help you remember the key differences between these three grass-like plants, which often grow in the same areas.

Quite a few sedges have culinary uses. One well-known species, *Cyperus esculentus* (also called chufa or tiger nut), has edible tubers that have been used as food for thousands of years. Another species, *Cyperus papyrus*, was important in ancient Egypt, where it was used to make paper. Some references suggest that parts of the plant, particularly the roots and shoots, were also occasionally consumed by people in ancient Egypt and other regions in times of scarcity.

Another sedge with edible tubers is *Cyperus rotundus*, also called purple nutsedge. It is one of the most aggressive weeds in the world, spreading across tropical and temperate areas. It has been called the world's worst weed, because it is a problem in more than 90 countries and affects over 50 crops globally.

In North America, many other sedges were recorded for the edible use of their tubers by native tribes. This includes: *Cyperus fendlerianus* (Fendler's nutgrass), *Cyperus odoratus* (fragrant flatsedge), and *Cyperus squarrosus* (bearded flatsedge).

Tall flatsedge (*Cyperus eragrostis*).

But for the purpose of this book, the main question is: are sedge seeds edible?

There are experienced foragers who claim all sedge seeds are edible, as I discovered during my research on the topic. I tend to be a tad more conservative on the issue and say: "Maybe, possibly, probably." While it is true that many sedge species produce edible seeds, the claim that all sedge seeds are edible isn't entirely accurate because not every species has been widely studied for edibility or safety. There is very little documentation of their use as a primary food source, and they are overshadowed by the more commonly eaten tubers. I also think that sedge seeds have not always been recorded as edible because many of them are just too small and insignificant in terms of nutritional value to have been used on a large scale. So, in essence, we simply don't know, but overall, their edibility seems to be a safe assumption. As usual, I think it's best to research individual species before consuming them.

That said, there are examples of sedge seeds being used as food historically. *Carex pendula* (pendulous sedge) is native to most parts of Europe and is also found in northwest Africa and parts of the Middle East. The seeds can be harvested, ground into flour, and made into bread. You'll find numerous recipes online.

The book *Native American Ethnobotany* lists the seeds of *Cyperus erythrorhizos* (redroot flatsedge) and *Cyperus odoratus* (fragrant flatsedge) as being eaten by some native tribes, including the Kamia, Cocopa, and Mohave.* *Cyperus eragrostis* (golden nutsedge) seeds were also eaten by the Yokuts in California.†

For more than twenty years, I have used the seeds of *Cyperus esculentus* (yellow nutsedge), *Cyperus eragrostis* (tall flatsedge), *Cyperus virens* (green flatsedge), *Cyperus surinamensis* (tropical flatsedge), and *Cyperus squarrosus* (bearded flatsedge). These are pretty much all the sedges I could find in my area. The seeds are really tiny, but I love to mix them with other edible seeds and grains when I make wild crackers. I use a ratio of around 5 percent sedge seeds and 95 percent other edible seeds and grains (e.g., chia, wild oats, sages, and so on).

Collection and Extraction

To gather sedge seeds, I simply crumble the seed heads or flowers by hand. Another method is to shake them into a paper bag. I usually do this on-site while foraging. Dry the seeds and store them in a cool, dry place. Use paper bags or jars with tight-fitting lids. Label them with the date and type of seed for future reference (see Drying and Storage, page 18).

* Daniel E. Moerman, *Native American Ethnobotany* (Portland, OR: Timber Press, 1998).

† Stephen Powers, "1877 Tribes of California, Contributions to North American Ethnology," vol. 3, in *California Indians and USA*, 2016, https://digitalcommons.csumb.edu/hornbeck_usa_2_c/1.

Stinging Nettle

URTICA SPP.

Ouch! This is an easy plant to identify. The genus *Urtica*, to which stinging nettles belong, comprises about 30 to 45 species. One of their most noteworthy characteristics is the painful sting you get if you touch them.

Aside from the sting, nettle leaves are one of their most distinguishing features; they're dark green and shaped like hearts or long ovals with saw-like edges. These leaves grow in matching pairs on opposite sides of the stem.

The stems are somewhat slender, squarish, and can grow anywhere from 2 to 6 feet (0.5–2 m) tall at maturity. Both the stems and the undersides of the leaves are covered with tiny needles that are responsible for the plant's sting.

Imagine the needles are tiny syringes. If you touch the plants, the needle's tip breaks off under your skin and releases irritating substances like histamine and formic acid. This usually leads to a sharp, burning feeling along with redness and swelling, lasting a few minutes to hours depending on the kind of nettle. While it's unpleasant, the sting from a stinging nettle has been used in old healing practices for its possible benefits against inflammation. In Belgium, I recall my neighbor hitting his own hands with it to ease his arthritis pain. But I'm not suggesting you try it.

These plants also have small green or white flowers that hang in bunches. You'll usually find them in shady spots like woods or streams. Despite their painful reputation, stinging nettles are generally edible, especially the common stinging nettle (*Urtica dioica*) and the small nettle (*Urtica urens*). However, they must be cooked or otherwise processed to remove the stinging chemicals from the hairs on the leaves and stems.

Nettles are highly nutritious. They are loaded with protein and are a great source of vitamins A, C, and K, along with many minerals. They are used in a variety of dishes, including soups, teas, and pesto. Their seeds, too, are edible and quite versatile. My favorite seeds come from small nettle, originally native to Eurasia and now found as an introduced species in North America, Australia,

and South Africa. They are rich in essential fatty acids, especially omega-3s, and contain vitamins A and C, iron, and magnesium. They also offer adaptogenic qualities, which can help regulate energy and manage fatigue.

Collection and Extraction

Collecting nettle seeds is somewhat easy. The best time to harvest is late summer to early autumn, when the seeds are ripe but before they have fully dried and fallen from the plant.

Wear gloves to protect your hands from the stinging hairs. Find a nettle patch where the plants are healthy and robust. Look for the hanging strands of seeds beneath the upper leaves. Using scissors or your fingers, snip off these strands into a paper bag or container.

Spread the seeds out in a dry, airy space on a paper towel or cloth. Let them dry completely, which will take a few days. Store the dried seeds in a paper bag or an airtight container in a cool, dry place until you're ready to use them.

The seeds of small nettles are a bit harder to collect, because these plants don't have hanging strands. The seeds are held in small clusters close to the stem, beneath the leaf nodes, similar to the common nettle but on a smaller scale.

My solution to this is cut the entire plant when it is going to seed, then spread the plants on a table to dry. Once the nettles have thoroughly dried, I shake them to release the seeds, then sweep the seeds into a paper bag or an airtight container. They should be stored in a cool, dry area.

Culinary Uses

Nettle seeds have an herbaceous, slightly nutty flavor. The consensus seems to be that you can consume 1 to 2 teaspoons (0.5–1 g) of seeds per day—any more can be overstimulating. I like to use nettle seeds in the following ways:

Salad and grain topper: These seeds can be lightly sprinkled on salads, soups, or cooked grains (like rice or quinoa) to add nutrition and a touch of "green" flavors. They pair well with leafy greens, roasted vegetables, and soft cheeses.

Toasting the seeds enhances their nutty flavors. Start by heating a dry pan over medium heat. Once the pan is warm, add a thin layer of seeds, spreading them evenly. Stir or shake the pan frequently to prevent burning and ensure the seeds toast evenly. After about 2 to 5 minutes, the seeds will darken slightly and release a warm, nutty aroma, signaling they are ready.

Immediately remove them from the pan to prevent overcooking and spread them on a plate or paper towel to cool. Once cooled, the seeds can be used right away or stored in an airtight container to keep their flavor fresh.

Energy-boosting smoothies: Small nettle seeds have healthy fats and are used by herbalists to help the body handle stress, making them great for smoothies or protein shakes. Add them to fruit smoothies or green blends for a gentle energy boost.

Breads, crackers, and granola: Incorporate the seeds into baked goods like crackers, granola bars, or bread dough. You can also sprinkle them over granola mixes before roasting.

Fermented foods: I like to incorporate the seeds into my wilder fermented foods, adding extra texture and nutrition. Just stir them in with the other ingredients prior to the fermentation process.

Tea and tonic infusions: Nettle seeds can be steeped to make a mild herbal tea, often blended with leaves for an earthy infusion. When mixed with honey or lemon, the tea becomes a soothing, restorative drink. For added nutty flavors, toast the seeds first.

Trail mix and energy snacks: Add the seeds to trail mix with nuts and dried fruits for a portable energy snack. You can also use them in homemade energy bites or protein bars.

Topper for yogurt or porridge: Nettle seeds are excellent sprinkled over yogurt, oatmeal, or porridge, adding a nutty note and subtle crunch. This makes a healthy breakfast option, boosting the nutritional profile with extra vitamins and minerals.

Sprouts: As you'll read about in chapter 6, you can cultivate attractive and tasty sprouts from nettles. During the sprouting phase, the tiny, hair-like needles are negligible.

Seed strands (*Urtica dioica* ssp. *gracilis*).

Sunflowers

HELIANTHUS SPP.

Let's talk about sunflowers!

Sunflowers are a group of plants known for their big, bright yellow flowers. They belong to a plant group called *Helianthus* and are predominantly native to North America, with a few species extending into Central America. The most famous sunflower is the common sunflower.

Sunflowers are easily identifiable by their large, bright yellow petals that surround a dark central disk; sturdy and hairy stems; and large, rough-textured leaves often shaped like hearts. You'll typically find them in sunny, open areas like fields and gardens.

Outside of North and Central America, wild sunflowers can also be found in some regions of South America, particularly in Argentina. They have been introduced in various parts of Europe, Asia, and Australia via their seeds as a result of agricultural practices and human activities.

In the Los Angeles area, the main species I find in abundance are called California sunflowers (*Helianthus californicus*). While the seeds are technically edible, they are generally not considered a significant source of food compared to the seeds of the common sunflower.

I kept looking for the common one locally, but I had no luck until I started writing this book—they magically showed up in my yard in the summertime! Yay! I am super thankful for this gift.

Common sunflower (*Helianthus annuus*).

Here is a list of sunflower species that can be found across North America:

Helianthus angustifolius (swamp sunflower)
Helianthus annuus (common sunflower)
Helianthus argophyllus (silverleaf sunflower)
Helianthus californicus (California sunflower)
Helianthus debilis (beach sunflower)
Helianthus divaricatus (woodland sunflower)
Helianthus giganteus (giant sunflower)
Helianthus grosseserratus (sawtooth sunflower)
Helianthus hirsutus (hairy sunflower)
Helianthus laetiflorus (showy sunflower)
Helianthus maximiliani (Maximilian sunflower)
Helianthus mollis (ashy sunflower)
Helianthus occidentalis (western sunflower)
Helianthus petiolaris (prairie sunflower)
Helianthus salicifolius (willow-leaved sunflower)

Helianthus schweinitzii (Schweinitz's sunflower)
Helianthus silphioides (rosinweed sunflower)
Helianthus smithii (Smith's sunflower)
Helianthus strumosus (pale-leaved sunflower)
Helianthus tuberosus (Jerusalem artichoke or sunchoke)

As with the California sunflower, not all of these species have seeds worth collecting. The primary sunflower species in North America with edible seeds commonly used by humans are:

Common sunflower (*Helianthus annuus*): The seeds are widely cultivated and consumed as a snack, used in cooking, and pressed for oil.
Jerusalem artichoke or sunchoke (*Helianthus tuberosus*): While sunchokes are primarily known for their edible tubers, the seeds are also edible, though they are not as commonly harvested for this purpose.
Maximilian sunflower (*Helianthus maximiliani*): The seeds are edible, though they are not as widely harvested as those of *H. annuus*.

You'll find common sunflowers with flowers of various sizes. Some can be quite large. The size varies because there are different types bred for farming. Some types, like Mammoth and Russian Giant, grow very tall—between 10 and 12 feet (3–3.7 m)—and produce large seeds.

The typical size of the wild common sunflower ranges from 3 to 10 feet (1–3 m) in height. The flower heads typically range from 3 to 6 inches (7.5–15 cm) in diameter. The size of the flower heads can vary based on environmental conditions.

History and Uses

The common sunflower is an important plant for many Native American tribes, who utilize the seeds for various culinary purposes. Different tribes developed unique methods of processing and consuming sunflower seeds, often tied to the availability of other resources and cultural preferences. Here is a quick look at some of the culinary uses of sunflower seeds by various Native American tribes:

Apache: Ground and sifted seeds, made into dough, and baked on hot stones.
Cahuilla: Dried and ground seeds and mixed with flour from other seeds.

Cherokee: Roasted seeds for snacks or made seed balls with honey or maple syrup.

Chumash: Mixed seeds with other nuts and seeds to create a nutritious trail mix.

Hopi: Combined sunflower seed meal with blue cornmeal to make thin, crispy piki bread.

Iroquois (Haudenosaunee): Ground seeds into flour for bread and porridge.

Lakota (Sioux): Ground seeds into meal to make sun-dried or lightly cooked cakes.

Navajo: Ground seeds and made into bread and dumplings.

Paiute: Made a coarse meal porridge by boiling ground seeds with water, often sweetened with berries or honey.

Collection and Extraction

My method is a variation of the Natural Seed Release method on page 28, with the main difference being that we'll rub the dry flower heads to remove the seeds instead of stirring or shaking them.

1. Locate mature sunflower heads. Most of the petals will have fallen off, and the back of the head will be brown and dry. Cut the sunflower head off the stem, leaving a few inches of stem attached for handling.
2. Hang the harvested sunflower heads upside down in a dry, well-ventilated area. This helps further dry out the seeds and makes them easier to extract.
3. Once the heads are thoroughly dry, rub them with your hands or use a stiff brush to dislodge the seeds. You can also place the head in a bag and shake it vigorously to release the seeds.
4. Separate the seeds from the plant debris. This can be done by winnowing, which involves tossing the seeds in the air and allowing the wind to blow away the lighter debris. Alternatively, use a sieve or colander to help sift out unwanted material.
5. Once dry, store the seeds in a cool, dry place. Use paper bags or jars with tight-fitting lids. Label them with the date and type of seed for future reference (see Drying and Storage, page 18).

Watercress

NASTURTIUM OFFICINALE

Watercress is a fast-growing, aquatic or semi-aquatic perennial plant native to Europe and Asia. It is one of the oldest leaf vegetables eaten by humans. Watercress belongs to the Brassicaceae (formerly Cruciferae) family, making it a mustard. Like its relatives—garden cress, radish, arugula, and, of course, mustard—it is well known for its spicy flavors. This nutritious leafy green is highly valued for its peppery flavor and is used in salads, soups, and garnishes.

Watercress thrives in clean, slow-moving streams, springs, and ponds, and is often found in cool, slightly alkaline waters. In the wild, it is common across Europe, Asia, and North America, having naturalized in many regions due to its widespread cultivation and adaptability.

To identify watercress, look for the following characteristics:

Leaves: The leaves are compound, meaning they have multiple leaflets. They are usually around 2 to 6 inches (2–15 cm) long and have two to eight oval-shaped leaflets in opposite pairs, with a larger leaflet at the end.

Flowers: The flowers are small and white with four petals and yellow stamens. They grow in long clusters along the stem, similar to other mustard plants.

Seeds: After flowering, usually in early fall, watercress produces long, narrow, green seedpods, known as siliques, similar to other cresses and mustards.

Look for watercress plants in clean, unpolluted water sources. Avoid areas with potential contamination from agriculture or urban runoff.

Collection and Extraction

Foraging for watercress seeds is not too difficult, but timing is important. The best time to find and collect watercress seeds is summer to early fall, when the flowers have bloomed and started to form seedpods. The seedpods will mature and turn brown as they dry. The brownish color is an indication that it is the right time to forage them.

1. Gently pinch or snip the seedpods from the plant. Place them in a paper bag or container to finish drying. I usually put them in a bowl and churn the content once daily for a few days. Although churning helps, the seedpods have a tendency to open on their own, and the seeds will accumulate at the bottom of the bowl.
2. Allow the seedpods to dry completely in a cool, dry place for a week or so. Once dried, the pods usually split open, releasing the seeds.
3. Store the seeds in a cool, dry place. Use paper bags or jars with tight-fitting lids. Label them with the date and type of seed for future reference (see Drying and Storage, page 18).

Culinary Uses

You might think the seeds are very tasty since watercress leaves are packed with flavor, but this is not the case; they are rather bland. The best use for them is to grow microgreens. Watercress microgreens are versatile and nutritious, offering a peppery flavor that can enhance a variety of dishes. They can be added to mixed green salads; used as a fresh, crunchy layer in sandwiches and wraps; blended into smoothies for added nutrients; or used as a garnish for soups.

You can also mix the microgreens into omelets and scrambled eggs or add them to tacos and burritos for extra flavor and texture. They work well sprinkled over pasta dishes, as a topping for homemade pizzas after baking, or included in fresh spring rolls. See chapter 6 for more information and instructions on how to grow wild microgreens at home.

Wild Barley

HORDEUM SPP.

Chances are you'll find this plant in your yard or nearby, as many wild barley species are common "weeds." The genus *Hordeum* includes about 30 species found worldwide, especially in temperate areas of Europe, Asia, and North America. The most common wild barley types include:

Wall barley (*Hordeum murinum*): Found in Europe, Asia, and North America, this species typically grows in disturbed areas such as roadsides and fields. In Southern California, it's considered an invasive weed. The goat farm where I'm currently staying is full of it.

Archaeobotanical evidence shows that it was likely part of the diet in various regions of prehistoric Europe, although it was not a primary crop like domesticated barley (*Hordeum vulgare*). Wall barley seeds have been found in archaeological sites, indicating that it may have been gathered and used as a wild food resource by ancient populations.

This wild barley was likely collected along with other wild grains during the Mesolithic and Neolithic periods, before grains were widely domesticated. From my research into prehistoric grains and seeds, as well as discussions with archaeologists, it was probably used as a supplemental food, ground into flour, or used as an addition to porridge—similar to other wild cereals of the time.

Foxtail barley (*Hordeum jubatum*): Native to North America, this species thrives in meadows and grasslands, and along roadsides. Its bristly seed heads make it easily recognizable. Indigenous tribes such as the Kawaiisu and Paiute of the Great Basin region harvested its seeds, grinding them into flour for porridge or bread. However, its awns made processing difficult, so it was not a primary food source.

Wild barley (*Hordeum vulgare* ssp. *spontaneum*): This species is considered the wild ancestor of cultivated barley. It is native to the Fertile Crescent, found in countries like Israel, Jordan, Syria, Lebanon, Turkey, Iraq, and Iran. It also grows in parts of the Caucasus, Southwest Asia, North Africa, and Southern Europe.

Several other wild barley species have been harvested around the world for human consumption. *Hordeum marinum*, also known as sea barley, was collected by coastal communities in Europe, North Africa, and parts of

Asia, and even in North America after its introduction. In the Mediterranean region, *Hordeum bulbosum* (bulbous barley) was sometimes collected for its underground bulb, but its grains were also consumed.

Wild barley is a tall grass that grows between 1 and 3 feet (30–90 cm) tall, with long, narrow leaves similar to blades of grass. The plant has a distinctive seed head at the top, which looks like a long, dense spike or brush with small seeds lined up in a row. One of the main features of wild barley is the long, bristle-like hairs that stick out from the seed head, giving it a spiky appearance.

From my perspective as a non-botanist, some types of wild rye resemble wild barley, particularly when it comes to the leaves and seed heads. These plants grow in similar environments, making them easy to confuse at first glance. Not to worry—both have edible grains!

Detached spikelets.

Collection

While barley seeds remain in the plant's grain-bearing tips—known as *ears*—those tips are referred to as seed heads or spikelets. These terms describe the part of the plant where the seeds, along with their protective chaff, remain intact. However, once the seeds are removed from the plant and separated from the chaff, they are called grains. The distinction is important: seed heads refer to the entire structure before harvest, while grains refer to the clean, edible seeds used after processing.

The best time to collect wild barley is usually in late spring to mid-summer, depending on the climate and growing conditions. The ears of wild barley change color as they mature, transitioning from bright green to golden brown. Wild barley is typically harvested when the seed heads have matured but before they fully dry out and start to fall apart. It's important to monitor the heads regularly, because wild barley will shed its seeds if left too long. My personal method is to monitor a wild barley field until some of the ears start shedding spikelets. That's when I know it's the perfect time to collect them.

To collect wild barley, I grasp the seed heads and place them into a basket or bag. After harvesting, leave the bags wide open or spread the ears or spikelets in a dry, shaded area to air-dry fully. Most of the time, the spikelets will detach as the ears dry out. Once dried, store the spikelets in a cool, dry place for future use. I usually leave the seed heads in the same bag I collected them in, closing it after they've air-dried for a couple of weeks.

Extraction

Here are two effective methods for extracting wild barley grains.

FLAME WINNOWING

For this method, use spikelets that haven't been stored for too long—it's best to process them within a week or two of foraging, while the grains still contain some moisture. Place the spikelets in a large, heat-safe bowl. Use a kitchen torch, lighter, or another flame source to ignite the plant material. As it burns, shake and stir the contents to ensure an even burn. Avoid letting the fire become too intense or burn too long, as it could damage the grains.

Once the chaff burns away and the fire dies down, you should be left with mostly grains. Use a sieve to remove any remaining charred bits. For cleaner grains, you might need to rub the burned material between your hands.

VITAMIX THRESHING

Place 2 to 3 cups (480–720 ml) of loose spikelets into the Vitamix and set the speed to low (between 1 and 2). With wild barley, you'll need to use the tamper to keep the spikelets from escaping—they'll try! Turn on the blender and use the tamper to press the spikelets down until they rotate smoothly. Once they're turning consistently, let the machine run for 15 minutes. When finished, transfer the contents to a bowl and winnow them in the wind to separate the chaff from the grains. This is the best method I've found so far for extracting wild barley grains.

Once dry, store the grains in a cool, dry place. Use paper bags or jars with tight-fitting lids. Label them with the date and type of seed for future reference (see Drying and Storage, page 18).

Culinary Uses

I like to use these grains in my ferments, sauces, salads, and soups. I first soak them overnight in water, then rinse them and add them to my preparation. If you're short on time, you can simmer the grains for around 30 minutes, until tender, instead of soaking them overnight, but some of the grains may break open in the process.

Crushed grains can also be boiled into a porridge or gruel. Once you have a large batch, you can grind the grains into flour to make crackers, flatbreads, or regular bread. Roasted barley grains also make a delicious and nutritious tea (see Wild Grains Tea, page 227).

Wild Oats

AVENA SPP.

Wild oat is another plant that covers the hills of Southern California. They're quite easy to identify. Wild oats are a tall, thin grass that typically grows between 3 and 4 feet (90–120 cm) tall. Its leaves are flat and a bit rough, and sharpen to a point. The most noticeable feature is the drooping cluster of grains at the top of the stem, known as a panicle. Each cluster includes many florets, each holding a single grain encased in a somewhat tough, hairy hull. This gives wild oats a distinctive, shaggy look. These plants are usually green to pale yellow and are commonly found in fields or disturbed areas from late spring through summer.

There are several types of wild oats. Locally, I've found:

Common wild oat (*Avena fatua*): One of the most widespread and well-known species, *Avena fatua* is often found in agricultural fields and disturbed soils. It is native to Eurasia but now found across temperate zones globally. It is often considered invasive and noxious, especially in agricultural areas, due to its competitive nature.

Slender wild oat (*Avena barbata*): This species is similar to common wild oat but tends to be a bit finer in texture. It is native to the Mediterranean region and parts of Asia and has also become invasive in similar climates worldwide, like California and Australia. In the Mojave Desert area where I currently live, slender wild oats are abundant.

Animated oat (*Avena sterilis*): Larger and more robust than the common wild oat, this species grows on all continents except Antarctica.

I don't bother much with the slender wild oat; the grains are smaller and tougher to extract, so I tend to focus my foraging on common wild oat. That said, if slender wild oat is all you have, go for it.

Collection and Extraction

Wild oat grains are a pain to extract with traditional equipment and methods such as stone grinders, the fire method, and so on. Vitamix Threshing, which I detail on page 47, was truly a game-changer for these grains.

Wild oats have a history of use as food grains, and perhaps someone will discover a traditional extraction method that proves effective. After it was

introduced to the North America, common wild oat became a food source for various tribes, including the Pomo, Miwok, and Yuki.

The book *Kashaya Pomo Plants* by Jennie Goodrich, Claudia Lawson, and Vana Parrish Lawson eloquently details how Pomo women collected and prepared wild oats for pinole:

> The grain [*Avena fatua*] was integral to pinole, a very fine dry meal. The women gathered the seeds in June or July, timed with the onset of the first warm inland winds that dried the grasses and prompted them to release their seeds. Anticipating these winds, the women knew they had a narrow window to harvest the seeds before they dropped to the ground. They removed the seeds from the grass tops using a basketry seed beater, catching them in a closely woven burden basket. Prior to storage, the seeds underwent winnowing in a work tray; they were rubbed to

> loosen the chaff, then tossed into the air so that the heavier grains fell back into the basket while the lighter chaff was carried off by the wind. To parch the grain, small amounts were placed in a circular coiled tray basket with tanoak coals and agitated back and forth. The grain was ground into a fine powder in a hopper mortar as needed. Various mixes of wildflower seeds and grains were combined to create different flavors.*

I wish I could have been there to witness the actual process. Rubbing to remove the chaff is a time-consuming task on my end, but perhaps there's a critical aspect of the technique I'm overlooking.

Hand Extraction (see page 26) is another method that yields beautiful grains, though it's difficult to extract a large quantity with this method. It took me and my friend a couple of hours to collect just ⅕ of a cup (around 20 g).

As a note, some people (me included) experience irritation or itching from the hairs on the chaff of wild oats. These fine hairs are designed to protect the plant but can cause discomfort when they come into contact with human skin.

If you extract the grains by hand and experience irritation, washing the area with soap and water and using a soothing lotion can help alleviate the discomfort.

Culinary Uses

There are many possibilities for integrating wild oats in your diet. Here are some of my favorites.

Porridge and oatmeal: Wild oats need to be crushed or lightly rolled to break the outer hull for easier cooking. Once prepared, they

* Jennie Goodrich, Claudia Lawson, and Vana Parrish Lawson, *Kashaya Pomo Plants* (American Indian Studies Center, 1996), 85–86.

can be simmered with water or milk to create a hearty porridge. Add honey, wild fruits, berries, or nuts for a satisfying breakfast.

To crush wild oat grains, I use a stone grinder. The process involves placing small batches of the grains between the grinding surfaces and rotating the top stone to apply even pressure. This breaks the outer hull and crushes the grains into coarse pieces, perfect for cooking porridge, adding to baked goods, or toasting for enhanced flavor. The stone grinder allows me to control the coarseness, ensuring the grains are processed just right for different uses.

Baked goods: Grind the grains into flour (see page 65) and use it in bread or crackers. Mixing wild oat flour with other flours adds a nutty flavor and texture to baked goods.

Wilder granola: Toast crushed oats and mix them with store-bought oats, wild seeds, dried berries and fruit, and honey or maple syrup to create a wilder granola. This works well as a snack or a topping for yogurt or desserts.

To toast crushed wild oat grains, heat a dry pan over medium heat. Once the pan is warm, add the crushed oats in a thin layer. Stir or shake the pan frequently to ensure even toasting and prevent burning. Toast for 3 to 5 minutes, or until the grains become golden-brown and release a nutty aroma. Immediately transfer them to a plate to cool, as they can continue to cook in the hot pan.

Wild ferments: Wild oat grains can be included in kimchi- or sauerkraut-style wild ferments (see Wilder Kimchi, page 253). The grains add texture and nutrition and enrich the flavors of the ferment.

Soup and stew thickener: Ground wild oats can thicken soups, stews, or gravies, adding body while enhancing nutritional content.

Tasty pilaf or grain bowl: Cook wild oats as a base for grain bowls or pilafs. Toss them with roasted vegetables, herbs, or sauces for a satisfying dish.

Energy snacks: Combine oats with dates, nuts, and seeds to make energy bars or protein balls. These snacks are perfect for a quick energy boost.

Sprouts for salads and sandwiches: Sprouting wild oats increases their nutritional value (see chapter 6). Add the sprouts to salads, sandwiches, or wraps for extra crunch and freshness.

Wild Rye

ELYMUS SPP., *LEYMUS* SPP., *PSATHYROSTACHYS* SPP.

This one is interesting. Before I started researching for this book, I thought that when wild rye plants were mentioned in foraging circles, we were talking about very few plants—maybe four or five—and that all of them had edible seeds or grains. But as I delved deeper into the subject, I realized that this wasn't the case at all—it's much more complicated.

"Wild rye" is really a common name used for many grasses. Wild ryes belong to one of three groups:

1. *Elymus* (wheatgrasses)
2. *Leymus*
3. *Psathyrostachys*

And within these three groups, we're not just talking about a few plants—we're actually looking at around 200 different species.

Not all "wild rye" species are worth foraging for their seeds or grains—in fact, most of them aren't. While the term "rye" often brings to mind the cultivated cereal grain (*Secale cereale*), it's important to note that many plants referred to as "wild rye" actually belong to the *Elymus* group, not the *Secale* one. The name "wild rye" is used because these *Elymus* species share some similarities with cultivated rye, such as their grass-like appearance and growth habits. However, they are distinct in both botanical classification and use. Cultivated rye is primarily grown as a grain crop, while wild rye species are often valued more for landscaping or ecological benefits than for their edible grains.

Here's some more detailed information about the various groups to which wild ryes belong, if you are interested in exploring the differences further.

Elymus

Elymus is a genus of perennial plants in the grass family with approximately 150 species, related to rye, wheat, and other widely grown cereal grains.

Not all species in the *Elymus* group are edible or suitable for grain production. While some, like Canada wild rye and slender wheatgrass (*Elymus trachycaulus*), have been used for food in the past, most *Elymus* species are not consumed by people. They're often valued more for their ecological roles, such as soil stabilization, and as forage for livestock.

Leymus

The *Leymus* group, closely related to *Elymus*, comprises around 50 species commonly found in temperate regions of the Northern Hemisphere, including North America and Eurasia. Most *Leymus* species are also valued more for ecological purposes and livestock forage, although some species have historically been used by foragers and Indigenous peoples for their edible grains.

For example, mammoth wild rye (*Leymus racemosus*), native to Europe and Asia, has occasionally been used for food due to its larger seeds compared to other wild ryes. Similarly, sheepgrass (*Leymus chinensis*), widespread in Eurasia, has been consumed by local populations in times of scarcity.

In North America, species like creeping wild rye (*Leymus triticoides*) and basin wild rye (*Leymus cinereus*) have edible grains, but the yield is quite negligible in my experience.

Psathyrostachys

I'm not even going to try pronouncing that word! *Psathyrostachys* is a small group of plants in the grass family, with about 10 species, depending on how they are classified. These plants mostly grow in Central Asia and Siberia.

I have absolutely no experience with these plants, so this information is solely based on research. Unlike *Elymus* or *Leymus*, plants in the *Psathyrostachys* group are not usually eaten or used for their seeds. Instead, they are studied for their ability to survive in harsh conditions, which could be helpful for breeding stronger crop plants.

Collecting wild rye grains has been one of my most frustrating challenges. Local species such as giant wild rye (*Elymus condensatus*), creeping wild rye, and, further north, basin wild rye, along with a few others, offered truly minimal yields, and I'm not usually very picky. The seeds were either negligible in size (if I could even find them) or simply not worth the effort to gather.

In terms of getting a decent yield, foragers in North America usually stick to Canada wild rye. Your best bet in Europe is probably mammoth wild rye. While edible uses of other wild rye species are relatively rare, there is still potential for exploring these species as food sources.

Feral Rye

Don't forget feral rye (*Secale cereale*)! Over time, some cultivated rye plants spread beyond agricultural fields and became wild again. Feral rye grows well in tough conditions, especially in dry areas, and is common along roadsides or abandoned fields. It's found in North America, Europe, and parts of Asia. It looks like cultivated rye, but it's usually smaller and tougher. While it can still produce edible seeds, its grains are generally smaller.

Canada Wild Rye

ELYMUS CANADENSIS

Canada wild rye is a tall perennial grass native to North America. It grows widely throughout Canada, the United States, and parts of Mexico. Occasionally, it is cultivated or used as an ornamental grass in Europe. This grass is most common in the central regions of North America. Although the USDA map lists it as present along parts of the West Coast, I've never personally seen it here, even when I went looking for it!

You'll find Canada wild rye in a variety of environments, including prairies, riverbanks, and woodlands. It's hardy and adaptable, thriving in various soil types, including sandy, loamy, and clay soils. While it prefers full sun, it can also handle partial shade, making it suitable for many different habitats.

Canada wild rye grows in dense bunches and can reach up to 5 feet (1.5 m) in height. The leaves are long, narrow, and slightly rough to the touch. When young, the foliage is bluish-green, but it turns golden or brown as the plant matures. Its flowers appear on drooping, curved spikes, which are 6 to 10 inches (15–25 cm) long. These spikes have fine bristles called awns that stick out. Canada wild rye flowers in summer, and its seeds are ready to harvest by late summer or early fall.

Collection and Extraction

Harvest the seed heads once they turn brown or golden, cutting them off the plant with scissors and placing them in a basket or paper bag to keep them dry. Spread them on a tarp

or screen in a warm, dry place for 1 to 2 weeks to ensure they are fully dried, making the grains easier to extract.

I find Canada wild rye seeds quite tricky to process using traditional methods like stone grinding. However, the Vitamix Threshing method (described on page 47) works perfectly and requires minimal effort. I grind the seeds for 20 minutes at low speed, then pour the contents into a bowl and winnow in the wind to remove excess chaff and debris.

Culinary Uses

Though Canada wild rye grains look small and unremarkable, they swell nicely when boiled for about 50 minutes. I've used them in some of my classes, adding them to a wilder version of tabbouleh and in my kimchi-like ferments.

The grains can also be ground into flour for baking rustic bread, flatbreads, or crackers. Whole grains can be boiled or steamed to make a hearty side dish, similar to farro or barley, and are great in soups, stews, or wild food salads. Some foragers and homebrewers use wild rye grains to enhance the flavor of beer or other fermented drinks.

Are All Grass Seeds Edible?

I've been wondering about this for a while. If you dig around online, you'll come across all kinds of opinions about whether grass seeds—or even grass itself—are edible. Some survivalist sites confidently claim that all grass seeds are safe to eat, while others flat-out say they're not without really explaining why.

The truth is, it's tricky to get a clear answer. There are over 11,000 recognized species in the grass family (Poaceae), and not all of them are worth foraging. Many grass seeds are so tiny that they aren't worth the effort to collect.

There are many factors to consider when it comes to grass seed edibility, including:

Palatability: Many grass seeds are unpalatable due to their flavor or texture. Furthermore, even if some grass seeds are technically edible, they might not provide significant nutritional value.

Small size and hard hulls: Many grass seeds are too small to be practically harvested and processed for food. Take Bermuda grass (*Cynodon dactylon*)—those seeds are so tiny, it's just not worth the effort. I'd rather look for more exciting and abundant forage nearby. And red brome? Honestly, I'm not even sure that stuff has seeds. I'm half-joking, but I've never managed to find any! When it comes to foraging, size really does matter.

Additionally, some grass seeds have hard, inedible hulls that are difficult to remove. Heck—some seeds are so hard, I'm pretty sure they would simply go through your digestive system fully intact. Sprouting grass seeds could be a solution.

Processing requirements: Some seeds require extensive processing, including husk removal, lengthy soaking, fermentation, sprouting, cooking, and so on to improve digestibility and taste and eliminate potential toxins.

Potential toxicity: Some grass seeds may contain substances that are toxic to humans and can cause health issues if consumed.

Let's talk more about the big one: toxicity. Are some grasses toxic? And are some of their seeds unsafe to eat? Honestly, that's a tough question to answer.

There are organizations in North America and Europe that research the edibility of grains and seeds, both for people and animals. Some of the key players include the United States Department of Agriculture (USDA), European Food Safety Authority (EFSA), Agriculture and Agri-Food Canada (AAFC), and the French National Institute for Agricultural Research (INRAE).

The catch? The main focus of these organizations is crops with high economic value—such as wheat, corn, and rice—that already have well-developed markets, production systems, and distribution networks. Wild grains just don't offer the same economic incentives. Low yields, niche demand, and the challenges of domestication make them less appealing for large-scale research. As usual, it all comes down to money. It feels like these organizations aren't really concerned with helping people forage food for free.

To be blunt, there isn't much research into whether wild seeds and grains are safe for human consumption. Even when a wild grain is edible—like great brome—you won't find USDA recommendations about eating it. Instead, you'll see advice on how to get rid of it because it's invasive in some areas. Maybe if someone invents a machine that makes processing wild grains super easy and profitable, that perspective will shift. But for now, you're pretty much on your own.

Now, back to the main question: are some grasses actually toxic? Surprisingly, the answer is *yes*. I really hoped all grass seeds would be edible, but that dream got squashed. But here's the silver lining: toxic grass seeds are extremely rare. I also haven't found any reports of people dying from munching on wild grass seeds specifically.

In short: some grass seeds are perfectly safe. A few aren't. But with a little care, there's still a lot to explore.

The main guilty party I found is darnel (*Lolium temulentum*). Also known as poison ryegrass, this grass produces seeds that contain temuline, a narcotic alkaloid. Consumption can lead to symptoms similar to drunkenness, and severe cases can be dangerous.

You might say, "Wait a minute, drunkenness sounds interesting." Well, historically, darnel is famous for causing trouble in the grain world. It often sneaked into wheat fields, pretending to be a cultivated grain—kind of like the wild cousin who shows up without an invite—mixing its slightly poisonous seeds into the wheat. People in the past might have accidentally baked darnel into their bread and ended up feeling dizzy and wobbly, almost as if they were drunk, but without any of the fun of drinking actual ale.

Seriously, though, this is a book about edible grains and seeds and I'm not going to get into the psychotropic properties of some of them. From what I've read, it looks like darnel could be really bad news if eaten in large enough quantities. Let's skip that one: we're not eating it.

Certain grasses, like sorghum varieties—think Sudan or Johnson grass—contain cyanogenic glycosides, which release hydrogen cyanide when the plant gets damaged. This makes them a concern when used as animal fodder. The good news? Based on my research, these compounds are mostly in the leaves and stems, not the seeds.

When sorghum plants are grown and harvested for their seeds, the cyanide risk drops significantly since the seeds don't contain much of these compounds. That's why eating sorghum seeds or grains is considered safe and doesn't carry the same risks as munching on the other parts of the plant. And here's a bonus: cooking or processing parts of plants that do contain cyanide can reduce their toxicity.

Boiling works well because hydrogen cyanide evaporates at high temperatures. It's the same process people use to make cassava roots safe to eat—they boil them to remove the toxic compounds.

Personally, I always cook Johnson grass or sorghum seeds before eating them or mixing them into dishes.

So, yes, many grass seeds are edible and full of good stuff like carbs, protein, and fats. But not every grass seed is easy to eat straight off the plant. Some need processing to make them safe or tasty, some are too hard and tough, and a few, like darnel, can even be toxic.

The bottom line: it's important to know which grasses you're dealing with and how to prepare them properly. A little knowledge goes a long way toward staying safe and enjoying what you forage, and, as usual, doing your own research and properly identifying plants is key to avoiding harmful or toxic plants.

And finally, don't forget to check grass seeds for signs of contamination like mold or fungal infections. Ergot, for example, can grow on certain wild grasses, especially rye, and can be harmful if consumed (see Fungal Infections: Ergot and Smut, page 19). Make sure seeds are stored properly to prevent molds like those that produce aflatoxins. Keeping seeds dry and well ventilated helps maintain their quality and safety.

What are the most common edible grass seeds found on most continents?

Barnyard grass (*Echinochloa crus-galli*): Native to many parts of the world, including Asia, North America, Europe, and Australia. It is commonly found in fields and disturbed areas. This grass is a significant agricultural weed, but its seeds are edible and have been used as a food source in various cultures.

Canary grass (*Phalaris canariensis*): Originally native to the Mediterranean region, it has spread to North America, Europe, and other regions as both a cultivated plant and a wild grass often found in wet environments. The seeds are used in bird feed but are also edible for humans.

Cheatgrass (*Bromus tectorum*): Originally from Eurasia, it is now found extensively across North America, particularly in the Western United States, and has also spread to parts of South America and Australia. As explained earlier in this book, I use the grains.

Crabgrass (*Digitaria sanguinalis*): This grass is found worldwide, particularly in temperate zones, including North America, Europe, Asia, and Australia. Often considered a weed, the seeds of crabgrass are edible and have been used traditionally as a grain in some cultures.

Foxtail millet (*Setaria italica*): Although cultivated in many areas, wild forms of this grass are found across Asia, Europe, North America, and Australia. It has been used for thousands of years for its nutritious seeds, which are still a staple in many regions.

Quackgrass (*Elytrigia repens*): Native to Europe and Asia, this grass has become widespread in North America and can also be found in parts of Australia. It is a persistent weed with edible seeds that have been used historically in times of scarcity.

Wild oats (*Avena fatua*): Found across many regions, including North America, Europe, parts of Asia, and Australia, typically in agricultural lands and disturbed soils. A relative of common oats, these seeds can be harvested and eaten.

Wild rye (*Elymus* spp.): Various species of *Elymus* are native to temperate regions of North America, Europe, and Asia and have adapted to a variety of climates and conditions. The seeds are used by Indigenous peoples in various parts of the world. Many species of wild rye have seeds that are not easy to extract using traditional methods.

Witchgrass (*Panicum capillare*): Native to North America but found in parts of Europe, Asia, and Australia as well, often in disturbed soils. It is sometimes used as a grain substitute, though it is commonly considered a weed.

From there, you venture into the vast landscape of edible grass seeds, potentially numbering in the hundreds. Below are some that I've personally tried or that are listed as edible from various online sources.

June grass (***Koeleria macrantha***): Native to North America, it grows across the United States and Canada in prairies and open woodlands. It is known for its small but edible seeds.

Brome grass (***Bromus*** **spp.**): These species are widely distributed across Europe, North America, and Asia, with some species also found in Australia. Many of them have edible seeds.

Little barley (***Hordeum pusillum***): Predominantly found in North America, especially in the United States, where it was historically an important food grain for Indigenous peoples.

Wild sorghum (***Sorghum*** **spp.**): These species are mainly found in Africa, with some species also in Asia and the Mediterranean region. The seeds of wild sorghum varieties are edible.

Hair grass (***Deschampsia*** **spp.**): Found in cool climates across Europe, North America, and Asia. The seeds of various *Deschampsia* species are used in traditional diets in cooler regions.

Common reed (***Phragmites australis***): This grass is ubiquitous along water bodies across Europe, Asia, North America, and Australia. The seeds are edible, and in some cultures, other parts of the plant are used for their nutritional and medicinal properties.

Ryegrass (***Lolium perenne***): Widely distributed across temperate climates, including Europe, Asia, and North America. It is primarily used for pasture and fodder, but in historical contexts, its seeds were also used for making flour.

Buffalo grass (***Bouteloua dactyloides***): Native to the Great Plains of North America, it has small seeds that were traditionally used as food by Indigenous peoples. It is adapted to arid environments and is drought-resistant.

Manna grass (***Glyceria*** **spp.**): Found in temperate regions of North America, Europe, and Asia, typically in wet, marshy areas. The seeds are sweet and were historically gathered and used by various Indigenous peoples.

Sweet vernal grass (***Anthoxanthum odoratum***): This grass is found in Europe, Asia, and North America, primarily in pastures. While known for its sweet scent when cut, the seeds are also edible and have been used traditionally. Some caution is advised due to the presence of coumarin.

Wood millet (***Milium effusum***): Found in the forests of Europe and Asia, with sporadic populations in North America. The seeds of this grass are edible and have been used in traditional European diets, especially in porridges.

Spike trisetum (***Trisetum spicatum***): Common in the mountainous regions of Europe, Asia, and North America, this grass thrives in alpine and subalpine zones. Its seeds are edible and were used by mountain-dwelling peoples.

Common Wild Seeds as Spices

Nowadays it's easy to go to the store and buy your spices, but I think that in the process, we are missing so much! The use of wild seeds as spices allows you to explore your true local flavors and create a deeper connection to the land.

In every region, you can find seeds that reflect the environment. Arid Southern California is a land of wonderful aromatic sages and sagebrush. Sprinkling toasted thistle sage seeds on a humble side dish like boiled watercress leaves with a touch of soy sauce can truly elevate it to a new dimension.

So, which wild seeds-as-spices are the most common?

Well, obviously we have wild mustard seeds, which can be found all around the world and offer a huge range of flavors. Mustard seeds apart, here are some of the most common wild seeds I've encountered during my travels in North America and Europe.

Alexanders

SMYRNIUM OLUSATRUM

This one is mostly for European foragers. I haven't found Alexanders in the North American wilderness . . . yet. So—disclaimer—I ended up purchasing some seeds online to experiment with them.

Native to the Mediterranean region, Alexanders now grows abundantly in temperate parts of Europe and the British Isles. It thrives in coastal areas and prefers well-drained soils. It is often found along cliffs, hedgerows, meadows, and roadsides.

Though less common in North America, you might encounter Alexanders in gardens or wild spaces with Mediterranean-like conditions. Its ability to spread easily has led to it being labeled as invasive in some regions.

To identify Alexanders, start by looking at the leaves. They are large, glossy, and divided into three lobed segments, resembling celery leaves in their bright green color. The plant's stems can grow up to 5 feet (150 cm) tall, are hollow and ridged, and often exhibit a reddish-purple tinge. During the flowering season, from April to June, Alexanders produces small yellow-green flowers arranged in umbrella-like clusters called umbels. The seeds of the plant are oval and ridged, transitioning from green to black as they mature.

Culinary Uses

Alexanders was used in ancient Roman cuisine and medicine. Known for its versatility, Alexanders can be used in a wide range of dishes, from salads to soups to stews, making it a valuable plant for foragers and cooks alike.

By using Alexanders, modern foragers can reconnect with a piece of ancient culinary history and rediscover the plant's unique flavors and uses.

The seeds, with their peppery and slightly bitter flavor, are a wonderful spice for both sweet and savory dishes. Their taste is reminiscent of black pepper, but with a unique earthy undertone. Here are some creative ways to use Alexanders seeds:

Seasoning vegetables: Sprinkle ground seeds on roasted root vegetables, or use them whole in stir-fries for a warm, peppery kick.

Soups and stews: Add whole seeds to broths, soups, or stews. They work well in hearty dishes like vegetable soups or lentil stews.

Pickling spice: Include Alexanders seeds in your pickling spice blends for a more complex, aromatic layer of flavor.

Homemade spice blends: Combine ground Alexanders seeds with salt, black pepper, and other herbs for a custom seasoning mix.

Breadseed Poppy

PAPAVER SOMNIFERUM

I almost skipped this one, but I decided to include it because I found it growing wild in California and Colorado. Per the USDA, the plant has been introduced in most of the United States. It can also be found on other continents. *Papaver somniferum*, known as the opium poppy or breadseed poppy, is a flowering plant in the poppy family (Papaveraceae). It is famous for its use in medicine, cooking, and baking. Originally from the Mediterranean region, it is now grown worldwide for its seeds, which are popular in many dishes, and for the latex sap used to make opium and its derivatives. The wild ones I find locally are likely spread by birds.

The poppy family includes over 700 species. Many look similar, but most do not have edible seeds, and some are even poisonous. In my research, I have found several mentions of corn poppy (*Papaver rhoeas*) and Oriental poppy (*Papaver orientale*) seeds used similarly to opium poppy seeds. Although some websites list California poppy (*Eschscholzia california*) seeds as edible, I could not find any reliable sources to confirm this. So, if you're exploring edible poppy seeds, research very carefully. Personally, I'll stick to the opium poppy and corn poppy for now. I have to research the Oriental poppy much more before attempting consumption.

Breadseed poppy grows 12 to 60 inches (30–150 cm) tall with smooth, bluish-green stems and gray-green, lobed leaves. The large flowers, which bloom in late spring to early summer, are 4 to 6 inches (10–15 cm) wide and come in white, pink, red, and purple, often with darker spots. The round seed capsules, about the size of a golf ball, have star-shaped tops and turn from green to brown as they mature. They contain a large number of tiny black or blue-black seeds.

Collection and Extraction

To collect seeds from breadseed poppy, wait until the seed capsules turn from green to brown and dry out, usually a few weeks after the flowers bloom. Once dry, cut the capsules off the plant and place them in a paper bag. Gently shake the bag to release the seeds, or open the capsules by hand and pour the seeds out. Allow the seeds to dry thoroughly to prevent mold. This can take 1 to 2 weeks depending on humidity levels. Once dry, store the seeds in a cool, dry place (see Drying and Storage, page 18).

Culinary Uses

Poppy seeds are widely used in cooking and baking for their nutty flavor and crunchy texture. They are commonly sprinkled on bread, rolls, and bagels, and used in pastries, muffins, and cakes. Ground poppy seeds are used as fillings in pastries, cakes, and desserts, especially in Eastern European and Middle Eastern baking. Examples include *hamantaschen*, poppy seed rolls (*makowiec*), and strudel.

Poppy seeds are also used as spices and seasonings. They can be sprinkled on salads, yogurt, or fruit dishes to add texture and flavor. Sometimes, they are mixed into spice blends or used to flavor sauces and dressings. A paste made from ground poppy seeds, sugar, and milk or water is used in sweets and desserts. In some cuisines, this paste is also used to thicken and enrich savory dishes like curries or stews. In Indian cooking, poppy seeds, known as *khus khus*, are used to thicken sauces and add texture to dishes, and as a main ingredient in spice blends.

When I use ground poppy seeds in spice blends or to make a savory paste as part of a dessert, I usually roast the seeds in a skillet first. The following method allows you to control the roasting process, ensuring the seeds don't burn and their flavor is maximized.

1. Place a dry skillet on the stove over medium heat. Allow the pan to heat up for a couple of minutes.
2. Pour the desired amount of poppy seeds into the pan. Ensure they are spread out in an even layer for consistent roasting.
3. Roast for 3 to 5 minutes, or until the seeds become fragrant and slightly darker. Be attentive, as poppy seeds can burn quickly. Stir the seeds continuously using a wooden spoon or spatula to prevent them from burning.
5. Once roasted, remove the pan from the heat and transfer the seeds to a plate to cool.

(WILDER) SAVORY PASTE WITH ROASTED SEEDS

To make a rich and flavorful poppy seed paste for desserts like galettes, *hamantaschen*, poppy seed rolls, and strudel, start by combining ¼ cup roasted poppy seeds, ¾ cup of your favorite wild jam, and 2 tablespoons cocoa or cacao powder in a food processor.

For a smoother paste, you can also grind the roasted seeds prior to putting them in the food processor using a spice grinder, coffee grinder, or mortar and pestle until they form a fine paste.

What is my favorite wild jam? Elderberry jam! But any jam, wild or not, will do. You can skip the cacao powder if you don't have any on hand.

Process the mixture until it becomes smooth and has the consistency of a thick jam. This delightful paste can be used immediately as a filling for your favorite desserts.

Galette made with acorn flour, wild currant jam, and roasted poppy seed paste.

White Sweet Clover

MELILOTUS ALBA

Not many people use the seeds of white sweet clover as a spice, but I've done so for many years, mostly in stews and similar dishes.

White sweet clover originally comes from Europe and Asia. Now, it grows all over North America. This plant prefers open fields, roadsides, and disturbed grounds. It is often found close to rivers and streams. In Canada and some parts of North America, the plant is considered invasive.

You can recognize white sweet clover by its three-part leaves and clusters of small white flowers that bloom from late spring to early fall. The plant has a sweet smell and taste, making it popular among foragers. The plant belongs to the Fabaceae or Leguminosae family, commonly known as the legume, pea, or bean family. The seeds resemble tiny lentils.

The culinary use of white sweet clover can be slightly controversial because it contains a natural compound called coumarin—responsible for the plant's characteristic sweet odor—that can act as a blood thinner in large amounts. However, humans typically do not consume it in large quantities, so eating it in moderation is generally not a problem. That said, I would not advise anyone taking blood-thinning medication to eat white sweet clover.

Coumarin isn't really toxic in its original state, but when it ferments (as happens when plants mold or aren't dried properly) it can convert into dicoumarol, a compound that disrupts blood clotting.

I've noticed that some white sweet clover plants, especially those near water and at a later stage of growth, develop a white mold on their leaves that can lead to dicoumarol formation. I avoid those plants and focus on healthy green ones.

Coumarin is naturally present in many wild plants, including sweetgrass (*Hierochloe odorata*), woodruff (*Galium odoratum*), and bison grass (*Hierochloe odorata*). Coumarin is also naturally present, albeit in small amounts, in various cultivated plants and fruits, including parsley, celery, licorice, apricots, cherries, strawberries, black currants, and many others.

Collection

Begin by harvesting the seed heads when they are fully mature and dry, usually indicated by the seedpods turning brown. Collect them in paper bags.

Once home, remove the seedpods from the bag and dry them completely by spreading them out in a well-ventilated area for a few days. Many seeds will fall out on their own, but for the remaining seeds, gently crush the dried seed heads to release them.

Removing the seeds from their outer husks is relatively easy. You can crush them vigorously between your fingers or use a stone grinder, applying firm pressure with the pestle to separate the seeds from their outer layers.

Transfer the contents to a bowl, then winnow them by gently blowing to remove the loose chaff and debris.

Culinary Uses

If you work with white sweet clover seeds, you'll find that they are as hard as rocks. A good solution is to soak the seeds in water overnight, which softens them considerably by the next day. Their flavor is quite potent, so a little goes a long way. I often sprinkle them on shellfish or various side dishes to add a tasty touch.

Another way to use the dry seeds is to powder them using a hand-crank spice or coffee grinder. I often mix the powder with salt and garlic, then sprinkle a dash on seafood; it's quite awesome on cooked clams, mussels, and sea snails.

You can also use the seeds in small amounts in stews.

Remember to use this spice sparingly. I use it mostly on special occasions, such as a small dish that is part of a tasting menu.

Wild Carrot

DAUCUS CAROTA

Wild carrot, also known as Queen Anne's lace, is native to Europe and southwestern Asia. It has spread widely and now thrives in temperate regions worldwide, including North America, where it is naturalized and often considered invasive. Wild carrot prefers open, sunny spaces like fields, meadows, roadsides, and disturbed areas, making it a familiar plant in many parts of the world. The seeds of wild carrot are a flavorful spice with great culinary potential.

Wild carrot plants are easily identifiable by their fern-like leaves and distinctive umbel flower clusters, which are typically white but can sometimes feature a central purple floret. The seeds are small, ridged, and covered with tiny bristles that help them disperse by attaching to animal fur.

The best time to harvest wild carrot seeds is in late summer to early autumn, when the flower heads have dried and turned brown. Carefully cut the dried umbels and place them in a paper bag to finish drying. Once fully dried, the seeds can be easily separated by gently rubbing the flower heads.

When foraging for wild carrot seeds, it is crucial to avoid confusing them with the seeds of poison hemlock or water hemlock, which are highly toxic. Ensure proper identification by checking multiple plant characteristics, and if in doubt, consult an expert.

Culinary Uses

Wild carrot seeds carry an intense, earthy aroma with peppery undertones and hints of cilantro. Their flavor lies somewhere between coriander, fennel, and cultivated carrots, offering a complex taste that works well in many dishes. Wild carrot seeds shine in both savory and sweet recipes.

Roasted vegetables: Sprinkle whole or ground seeds on roasted carrots, potatoes, or root vegetables.

Soups and stews: Add ground seeds to soups or stews for a warm, aromatic note.

Breads and crackers: Mix ground seeds into doughs to enhance flavor.

Desserts: Try sprinkling the seeds on ice cream or sorbet for an unexpected twist.

Spice blends: Incorporate them into spice mixes for a unique, earthy addition.

These versatile seeds bring depth and warmth to any dish, making them a valuable ingredient for creative cooking.

Wild Celery

APIUM GRAVEOLENS

Wild celery originally comes from the Mediterranean region. It has been used since ancient Greek and Roman times. Today, wild celery can be found in many parts of the world, including North America and Australia. It grows best in wet areas like marshes, riverbanks, and wetlands, where the soil is rich and damp.

Wild celery (*Apium graveolens* var. *graveolens*) and the celery you buy at the store (*Apium graveolens* var. *dulce*) are different in several ways. Wild celery has thinner, more fibrous stalks and smaller leaves. It tastes stronger and a bit bitter. Store-bought celery, on the other hand, has thick, crisp stalks and broader leaves. It tastes milder and more watery.

Here in Southern California, I've occasionally found wild celery near streams or in shaded forests close to rivers. However, it's not too common here, likely due to the harsh climate and the plant's need for a substantial amount of water.

Wild celery usually grows to about 1 to 3 feet (30–90 cm) tall and has hollow, grooved stems. The leaves are divided into smaller, jagged-edged leaflets that smell strongly of celery when crushed. In the summer, wild celery produces small white or greenish-white flowers in umbrella-shaped clusters. By late summer, it forms small, dark brown seeds.

Culinary Uses

Similar to domesticated celery seeds, wild celery seeds are a flavorful spice that can be used to flavor soups, stews, and pickles. You can also sprinkle them on bread before baking or add them to marinades and rubs for meats and fish. The seeds are always a welcome flavorful addition to my ferments.

Wild Dill

ANETHUM GRAVEOLENS

Wild dill is originally from the Mediterranean region and western Asia. It has spread and can now be found in various parts of the world, including North America. I can't tell the difference between cultivated dill and the wild dill I've encountered while foraging in Colorado; they're probably the same plant species with similar characteristics and uses.

There is another plant in North America that goes by the common name "wild dill." The Latin name is *Perideridia americana*. It's also called the American wild carrot or yampah, but this plant has nothing to do with dill. While both are members of the Apiaceae family, they are different plants.

Identifying wild dill involves observing several specific characteristics. The plant is known for its delicate, feathery leaves that are finely divided and thread-like and typically bright green in color. These leaves give wild dill a soft, airy appearance. The plant produces small yellow flowers that grow in flat-topped clusters called umbels, which can be 4 to 6 inches (10–15 cm) across. These clusters are a distinguishing feature during the blooming season, which usually occurs from midsummer to early fall. Wild dill commonly reaches a height of 2 to 3 feet (60–90 cm), making it easy to spot in the environments it thrives in.

Like wild carrots and fennel, wild dill is most often found in fields, meadows, and along roadsides, preferring well-drained soil and full sunlight. The plant has a distinct, strong, aromatic scent similar to that of cultivated dill, which becomes especially noticeable when the leaves or stems are crushed. This characteristic scent is a key identifying feature and can help distinguish wild dill from other similar-looking plants. Dill seeds are another important feature; they are flat, oval, and brown with light brown lines.

When identifying wild dill, it's essential to be aware of poisonous lookalike plants such as poison hemlock. Poison hemlock, which is highly toxic, has similar feathery leaves but can be identified by the purple blotches on its stems. Due to the risk of confusing wild dill with poisonous plants, proper identification is crucial. Always use a reliable field guide or plant identification app, and consider taking a foraging workshop or joining a local foraging group for practical, hands-on experience. There are numerous identification groups on social media that can be helpful as well.

A harmless, edible lookalike is fennel (*Foeniculum vulgare*), which also has feathery leaves but can be distinguished by its licorice or anise scent.

Culinary Uses

Dill seeds are used extensively in various cuisines around the world. They taste slightly sweet and remind some people of caraway or anise. They also have a mild citrus flavor. If you pay close attention, you might also notice a mild sweetness like carrots, but this isn't its main flavor. Dill seeds contribute a strong, tangy taste that works well in pickles, stews, breads, and vegetable dishes. They have a strong smell, making them a popular spice in many recipes.

Seasoning: Dill seeds can add a bright, citrusy flavor to vegetables, meat, or fish dishes. They can be used whole or crushed, either at the beginning of cooking for a mellower flavor or toward the end to preserve their pungency. Dill seeds pair well with cream dishes and root vegetables. I often toast dill seeds prior to using them.

Pickling: Dill seeds really shine with pickling. They are a key ingredient in pickling spice and can be added to brines for cucumbers, beets, carrots, and other pickled vegetables.

Soups, stews, and sauces: Dill seeds can be used to flavor soups, stews, braised dishes, and sauces, especially in the winter.

Other dishes: I sometimes add dill seeds to my sourdough or curly dock breads.

LEMON DILL WEED SEASONING

I use this seasoning on vegetables, roots like carrots, and my wild food salads. It can also be used in dips or on fish and chicken.

Ingredients

2 tablespoons minced lemon zest (about 2 large lemons)
1 tablespoon dried dill weed
1 teaspoon dill seeds (preferably toasted)
½ teaspoon wild fennel seeds
½ teaspoon onion powder
½ teaspoon ginger powder
½ teaspoon garlic powder
½ teaspoon salt

Method

1. Spread the lemon zest on parchment or wax paper. Cover loosely with a paper towel and let sit at room temperature until completely dry, about 1 day.
2. Once the lemon zest is dry, add it to a stone mortar along with the remaining ingredients. Grind the mixture with a pestle until well combined. Alternatively, you can use a coffee grinder, but be careful not to overdo it—keep the ingredients somewhat coarse.
3. Transfer the seasoning to a spice jar. This seasoning can be stored at room temperature for several months.

Wild Fennel

FOENICULUM VULGARE

Wild fennel grows naturally in many places, including North America. Known for its feathery leaves and licorice-like scent, this plant is versatile. You can eat different parts of it, such as the leaves, stems, flowers, and seeds.

Wild fennel can spread quickly and take over local plants, so it is considered invasive in some areas, including where I live in Southern California. Using fennel seeds can help control the plant population.

Wild fennel leaves have a feathery, delicate appearance similar to cultivated fennel (or dill), but they are usually a bit coarser. The leaves are bright green and emit a strong, sweet aroma reminiscent of anise or licorice when crushed. Wild fennel grows from thin, hollow stems that are green and sometimes have a slight purple tinge. Unlike cultivated fennel, wild fennel does not typically form a large bulb at the base. These features, along with its strong fragrance, make wild fennel leaves easy to recognize in their natural habitat. Wild fennel likes sunny, dry spots like roadsides and fields. It can grow up to 6 feet (2 m) tall and has bright yellow flowers that bloom in clusters during summer.

Collection

To collect fennel seeds, wait until late summer or early fall when the flowers turn into seed heads. The seeds change from green to brown when they are ready. Cut the seed heads and place them in a paper bag to dry. Once dry, shake the bag or rub the seed heads to separate the seeds.

Culinary Uses

Fennel seeds are known for their sweet, anise-like flavor. They are

used in many dishes, especially in Indian, Mediterranean, and Middle Eastern cooking. They're also a common addition to pickling spices. Wild fennel also makes for some tasty sprouts and microgreens (see chapter 6).

Meat: Rub generously on chicken, pork, beef, or lamb before grilling, roasting, or smoking.
Vegetables: Sprinkle on roasted or grilled vegetables for added flavor.
Fish: Use as a seasoning for fish fillets before baking or grilling.
Fennel seed tea: Crush fennel seeds and steep in hot water for a soothing tea.
Spice mixes: Fennel seeds are often used in spice blends like herbes de Provence. I use them in my spice mixes with other local native plant seeds.
Baking: Add fennel seeds to bread, cookies, and cakes for a unique flavor.
Digestive help: Chew fennel seeds after meals to aid digestion and freshen breath.
Cough syrup: Boil fennel seeds with honey and ginger to make a simple cough syrup.

FENNEL SEED SPICE RUB

Ingredients

2 tablespoons fennel seeds
1 tablespoon coriander seeds
1 bay leaf (I use ½ California bay leaf)
2 teaspoons paprika
1 teaspoon black peppercorns, ground
1 teaspoon dried thyme
1 teaspoon garlic powder
1 teaspoon onion powder
1 teaspoon salt

Instructions

1. In a dry skillet over medium heat, toast the fennel and coriander seeds until fragrant, about 2 to 3 minutes. Stir frequently to avoid burning.
2. Allow the toasted seeds to cool slightly, then transfer them to a spice grinder or mortar and pestle, along with the bay leaf. Grind them into a fine powder.
3. In a small bowl, combine the ground seeds with the remaining ingredients and mix well.
4. Transfer to an airtight container. This spice rub can be used immediately or stored in a cool, dark place for up to 6 months.

Wild Onion and Garlic

ALLIUM SPP.

After foraging wild onion seeds in the Mojave Desert and finding them pretty much tasteless, I received some samples of various wild onion seeds from fellow foragers and learned that the flavor and intensity and can vary widely depending on the species. In general, the seeds will carry the characteristic onion taste, but as I learned, that's not always the case, so you'll need to experiment with your local wild onions.

There are some poisonous plants that look like wild onions that can be dangerous for foragers. In North America, those toxic lookalikes include death camas, star-of-Bethlehem, autumn crocus, and lily of the valley. One forager's rule is to always check for the onion smell to help identify real wild onions.

Wild Garlic Versus Wild Onions

When we talk about wild garlic, we usually mean *Allium ursinum*, also called ramsons or bear's garlic. This plant is common in Europe and has a strong garlic smell and taste. It has broad, flat leaves and white, star-shaped flowers. The plant usually grows in moist, shady woods and is commonly used by foragers for its tasty leaves, flowers, and bulbs.

In North America, a similar plant that is often called wild garlic is ramps, or *Allium tricoccum*, also known as wild leeks. Ramps are popular with foragers and chefs for their combined garlic and onion flavors.

One of our local wild onions in Southern California: fringed onion (*Allium fimbriatum*).

To make it simple—and I know some may disagree—people are usually referring to a few specific plants when they talk about "wild garlic":

Ramsons (***Allium ursinum***) is the plant most commonly referred to as wild garlic in Europe. It has broad, flat leaves and white star-shaped flowers and is found in woodlands across much of Europe, particularly in damp, shaded areas. Although not native to North America, it can occasionally be found in certain areas where it has been introduced.

Field garlic (***Allium vineale***) is often called wild garlic in North America and Australia. It has slender, hollow leaves and clusters of small, bulbous flowers and is commonly found in fields and meadows, and along roadsides.

Three-cornered leek (***Allium triquetrum***) is also known as wild garlic, especially in the Mediterranean region. It has triangular stems and white flowers with green stripes and grows in coastal regions and along riverbanks. It is not native to North America but can sometimes be found in areas where it has been introduced, particularly in coastal regions.

Ramps (***Allium tricoccum***) are commonly called wild garlic in North America, particularly on the East Coast. They have broad leaves and a strong garlic-onion flavor and are often found in rich, moist deciduous forests from the southern Appalachian Mountains up to Canada. Ramps are native to North America.

Wild garlic (***Allium canadense***) is native to North America and is also known as wild onion or meadow garlic. It has slender, grass-like leaves and clusters of small white-to-pink flowers. This species is common in open fields and meadows, and along roadsides, particularly in the eastern and central United States.

Culinary Uses

I've not been able to play a lot with wild onion or wild garlic seeds, and on top of that, my local onion seeds are rather tasteless, so you'll need to experiment with what you have locally.

That said, onion and garlic seeds have the following traditional uses:

Seasoning: Wild onion and garlic seeds can be dried and ground into a powder and used as a seasoning in dishes like soups, stews, and marinades. They add a pungent, garlicky flavor similar to commercial garlic powder.

Pickling: The seeds can be used in pickling brines to add a distinctive flavor to pickles, vegetables, and other preserved foods. Their strong taste infuses well into the pickling liquid, enhancing the overall flavor profile.

If the seedpods are immature and tender but large enough, you can ferment them or make "capers" with them. Here's a simple method for making ramps capers:

Ingredients (for a quart jar)

1¼ cup ramp buds (unopened flower buds)
1¼ cup water
1¼ cup apple cider vinegar
1 tablespoon salt
1 teaspoon sugar or maple syrup (optional)
Spices such as peppercorns, mustard seeds, or bay leaves (optional)

Method

1. Harvest the unopened ramp buds. Rinse them thoroughly to remove any dirt or debris.
2. Bring a pot of water to a boil. Prepare a bowl of ice water. Blanch the ramp buds by boiling them for 30 seconds, then immediately transfer them to the ice water to cool. Drain and set aside.
3. In a small saucepan, combine the water, vinegar, salt, and sugar (if using). Bring the mixture to a boil, stirring to dissolve the salt and sugar. Remove from heat.
4. Sterilize a glass jar and its lid by boiling them in water for 10 minutes. Let them air-dry on a clean towel.
5. Place the blanched ramp buds in the sterilized jar. If desired, add any spices you like.
6. Pour the hot brine over the ramp buds, ensuring they are completely submerged. Leave a little headspace at the top of the jar.
7. Seal the jar with the lid and let it cool to room temperature. Once cooled, store the jar in the refrigerator.
8. Allow the ramps capers to sit in the refrigerator for at least a week before using to let the flavors develop. They can be stored for several months if kept refrigerated. Ramps capers can be used in any dish you would typically use capers.

Yampah

PERIDERIDIA SPP.

I visited my daughter and her partner in Idaho after they bought a new property, and of course, I had to check out what edible or medicinal plants were growing there. One plant really caught my attention. At first, I thought it was poison hemlock, but when I looked closer, the leaves were clearly different. I did some quick research using my plant ID app and an online search, and I realized I had found yampah. I was thrilled, because I had been searching for this plant for a long time, and now there it was, growing all around me!

Yampah is a native plant found in the western and central parts of North America. There are different types of yampah, like *Perideridia gairdneri*, *Perideridia bolanderi*, and *Perideridia pringlei* (which grows in Mexico). Native people use its seeds as a spice, and its roots are also a traditional food.

Yampah is a tall, slender plant that grows between 2 and 4 feet (60–120 cm) high. Its leaves are narrow and feathery, and look almost like fine threads. The flowers are small and white, and grow in umbrella-shaped clusters. The plant is found in open meadows and grasslands, and along streams.

As with wild fennel and carrots, be careful not to confuse yampah with poison hemlock or water hemlock, which are deadly. Yampah has smooth, green stems, while poison hemlock has purple spots and water hemlock has ribbed stems. The leaves of yampah are fine, feathery, and thread-like compared to the broader, coarser leaves of hemlocks.

Collection

Yampah seeds are ready to harvest when they turn dark brown. Gently shake the seed heads into a bag or bowl to collect them. You can also dig up yampah roots in late summer or fall, when the plant is fully grown. I use a regular garden spade with great success.

Culinary Uses

Yampah seeds have a mild, slightly spicy flavor, similar to caraway or fennel. They can be added to soups, stews, and breads for extra flavor. You can also sprinkle them on roasted vegetables, meats, or salads. The seeds can be used in spice mixes or brewed in tea for a refreshing, earthy taste.

Other Seeds as Spices

Many other wild seeds can be used as spices, adding unique local flavors and aromas to your dishes.

Nettle seeds (*Urtica urens*): These seeds have an interesting nutty flavor when lightly toasted. I use them in simple dishes such as boiled dandelion or watercress with a dash of soy sauce. They work as a nutty garnish, similar to roasted sesame seeds.

Virginia peppergrass seeds (*Lepidium virginicum*): Also called least pepperwort or Virginia pepperweed, this plant is part of the mustard family. It grows naturally in many parts of North America, including most of the United States, Mexico, and Southern Canada, as well as Central America. It has also been introduced elsewhere. The seeds are slightly peppery and spicy.

Feral arugula seeds (*Eruca sativa*): We have a lot of "wild" arugula in the Los Angeles area, probably escapees from the garden. This is strong stuff! Arugula seeds have a bold and distinctive flavor profile that mirrors that of arugula leaves but with greater intensity. They possess a strong mustard-like kick, a detectable nuttiness, and an earthy depth, accompanied by a slight bitterness. This combination of flavors makes arugula seeds a robust addition to ferments, fish seasoning, or hummus and yogurt dips, to give you a few ideas.

CHAPTER 5

Exploring Your Terroir . . . Past and Present

The more I've worked on this book, the more I've come to feel the history of farming needs a rewrite. The usual story about hunter-gatherers giving up their lifestyle to become farmers is way more complicated than it's often told. While agriculture is said to have started about 10,000 to 12,000 years ago in the Middle East's Fertile Crescent, reaching Northern Europe around 6,000 to 6,500 years ago, evidence shows that even thousands of years later, people were still foraging and eating wild seeds and grains alongside farmed foods.

It seems the decline in foraging and using wild foods is very recent. Heck, even my grandmother knew how to find and use wild foods in her area, and that wasn't so long ago. I think this knowledge has mostly disappeared with the rise of industrial farming and monoculture crops.

But don't despair! There's a lot of information out there—studies, papers, websites, and books—about what ancient people ate. No matter where you live, you can learn about the wild foods your ancestors relied on. It takes some time to dig into the research, but for a wildcrafter or anyone curious about their environment, it's worth the effort.

Archaeologists around the world have found evidence of wild seeds and grains in ancient diets, from Europe to the Middle East, Africa, and beyond: seeds stored in pottery, charred remains in caves, remnants of meals, and even fossilized human waste (coprolites). All of these discoveries highlight how much humans have always relied on wild foods.

When exploring this topic, it's important to remember the biases in early research, particularly in Europe. For instance, back in the 1950s, some researchers dismissed wild seeds or grains found with ancient remains as evidence of weeds contaminating crops—the classic narrative of "good" cultivated food versus "bad" weeds. It's only in more recent years, sometimes with input from foragers, that researchers have come to recognize how vital wild foods were for nutrition and dietary diversity. These weren't just accidental additions or fillers—they played a crucial role in our ancestors' diets.

For me as a forager, diving into this research has been inspiring and eye-opening. It's a reminder that wild food knowledge hasn't disappeared—it's just waiting to be rediscovered. Knowing that our ancestors were just as curious and resourceful as we are today is comforting. They experimented with flavors, preserved what they had, and created meals that reflected their environment.

If you're interested in wild foods and ancestral diets, there's so much to explore. Through archaeological studies as well as your own experiments in the kitchen, this journey is worth taking. It's not only about finding edible grains and seeds—it's about reconnecting with our past and learning what nature can provide for us now. For me, this journey has been about finding a sense of connection and carrying on traditions as old as humanity itself. We never really stopped foraging.

The Quest for My Own Ancestry

Ever since I started foraging, I've been fascinated by the question of what my ancestors would have eaten. I'm not sure why, but I think it's probably because foraging wild food drew out that desire—a sort of quest for a primal connection or an answer to the simple question, "Where do I come from?" I've never done a DNA analysis, but I get a hint from my extended family, which seems to be a blend of European descent (the Nordic countries, Germany, and central Europe) as well as a recent connection to the Mediterranean region (Spain and probably North Africa) through my maternal grandfather, whom I never knew aside from a couple of photos.

My brother definitely got the Spanish–North African genes—he looks like he was born there—but I seem to have inherited the European–Nordic genes. It's interesting that my cuisine has always been based mostly on traditional European food preservation techniques with a slight touch of Spanish-Maghreb influence. Sometimes I think our ancestors can speak through us and our artistic endeavors.

This quest for my ancestral culinary background received a strong kickstart while I was working on my book *The Wildcrafting Brewer*. I am from Belgium, so the connection to brewing was obvious, but I truly relished exploring the murky prehistoric period when my ancestors lived and imagining what their brewing concoctions might have looked like. I delved into old documents and archaeological studies of boozy remnants found in clay pots, sometimes discovered in tombs. Truly fascinating stuff!

Finding information about what my ancestors would have eaten became a borderline obsession when I started to research edible seeds and grains—and for good reason. I had a strong feeling that wild grains and seeds were an important part of their diet.

The problem, however, was that this information had been almost completely lost. What my European ancestors ate 2,000 or 3,000 years ago has essentially disappeared into the abyss of prehistory. One of the last major disruptions was the Roman invasion and colonization of Europe, which spread Mediterranean crops and techniques across the continent.

Trying to regain that lost knowledge felt hopeless, or so I thought.

One of my strengths is that I never give up once my mind is set on something. I began researching scientific and archaeological papers, focusing on charred remnants found in prehistoric pottery and caches, similar to the ancient brewing research I conducted for my previous work.

This research showed promise. Archaeological studies of Neolithic pottery revealed evidence of wild seeds in food residues, suggesting that people used wild plants alongside early domesticated crops. Analyses of these remnants uncovered traces of seeds from various wild plants, including goosefoot, brome grass, knotweed (*Polygonum* spp.), dock, and nutsedge. Goosefoot and knotweed seeds, rich in nutrients and starch, were likely added to stews or porridge, while brome grass and dock seeds provided bulk and calories.*

While I found plenty of fascinating information available online and in archaeological and scientific papers—and appreciated the work of those who conducted the research—the evidence of edible wild grains and seeds in ancient diets was still incomplete. I was missing stronger proof of an actual meal or recipe incorporating these ingredients. I had hit a culinary dead end. That changed when I stumbled across a documentary about bog bodies.

Bog Bodies: Dietary Time Capsules

Bog bodies are the naturally preserved remains of ancient people found in peat bogs, mainly in Northern Europe. These wetlands contain thick layers of peat, a type of soil formed from decayed plants. The cool, wet, acidic, and

* See Ceren Kabukcu, "The Real Paleo Diet: New Archaeological Evidence Changes What We Thought About How Ancient Humans Prepared Food," *The Conversation*, November 23, 2022, https://theconversation.com/the-real-paleo-diet-new-archaeological-evidence-changes-what-we-thought-about-how-ancient-humans-prepared-food-195127. This is a great article with numerous links and insights.

low-oxygen conditions in peat bogs prevent regular decay, allowing these bodies to stay preserved for thousands of years. Their skin, hair, and, sometimes, clothing remain intact, offering detailed insights into life in the distant past.

There's much speculation about why these people were buried in bogs. Some historians and archaeologists suggest that bog burials were ritualistic, perhaps to honor or connect with spiritual beliefs tied to nature. Bogs may have been seen as mysterious or otherworldly, making them significant for ceremonial practices. Others believe the burials were meant to symbolically preserve certain individuals, freezing them in time. The exact reasons remain unclear, but bog burials undoubtedly had cultural or spiritual importance.

Estimates suggest that hundreds of bog bodies have been found across Northern Europe, with more than one hundred well-documented cases. Notable examples include Tollund Man and Grauballe Man in Denmark and Lindow Man in England, all of whom have provided significant insights into ancient cultures.

Many bog bodies date back to the Iron Age, around 2,000 years ago. Because the bodies have been remarkably preserved, scientists can study what these individuals wore, how they looked, and—most importantly for this book—what they ate. Some bog bodies are so well preserved that their stomach contents reveal their last meals, reconstructed through detailed analysis.

This was the gold mine of information I had been searching for—actual recipes!

The last meals of many bog bodies, especially from the Iron Age, often consisted of porridge-like mixtures made from cultivated grains and wild seeds. Here are some specific examples based on gut content analysis.

Lindow Man (England, c. second century BCE): His stomach contents revealed a final meal of mostly cereals, and he likely ate slightly charred bread. Mistletoe pollen was also found.

Oldcroghan Man (Ireland, c. 362–175 BCE): His stomach contents revealed milk and cereals, though no wild seeds were documented.

Haraldskær Woman (Denmark, c. 490 BCE): Her last meal was a thick porridge made of unhusked millet and blackberries.

Huldremose Woman (Denmark, c. 160 BCE–220 CE): She ate coarsely ground rye with a large number of spurry seeds and other wild seeds.

Lots of other bog bodies have been studied, but the most detailed and recent work was done on Grauballe Man and Tollund Man. These discoveries gave me exactly what I was looking for—a solid connection between ancient diets and the use of wild grains and seeds!

Grauballe Man

Found in 1952 in a peat bog near the Danish village of Grauballe, Grauballe Man is one of the most famous bog bodies ever discovered. His body was so well preserved that even his hair, skin, and fingernails were intact, despite being over 2,000 years old. Scientists believe he lived during the Iron Age, around 290 BCE.

His last meal was a simple porridge made mainly using wild plants, some cultivated grains, and other simple ingredients. The findings show us that Iron Age people relied on both farmed and wild plants for food, reflecting a simple and resourceful diet.

Over 90 percent of the meal consisted of seeds from a wide variety of wild plants, with more than 60 different types identified. The two main wild seeds identified were corn spurry (*Spergula arvensis*) and pale persicaria (*Persicaria lapathifolia*), which made up a significant portion of the meal. Although traces of barley and other grains were initially noted, they appear to have been minimal, if present at all. This porridge also contained various grasses and herbs, typical of the local bog environment.

The bulk of the porridge consisted of approximately:

70 percent pale persicaria seeds (*Polygonum lapathifolium*) and persicaria seeds (*Persicaria maculosa*)
20 percent corn spurry seeds (*Spergula arvensis*)
8 percent grains—mostly emmer, but also oats, barley, and traces of rye (*Secale cereale*)
2 percent sheep sorrel seeds (*Rumex acetosella*) and other wild seeds

Although they constituted a very low percentage of the meal, the sheer diversity of the additional wild seeds and grains found is interesting and impressive:

Common wild oat (*Avena fatua*)
Lop grass (*Bromus hordeaceus*)
Flax (*Linum usitatissimum*)
Gold of pleasure (*Camelina sativa*)
Shepherd's purse (*Capsella bursa pastoris*)
Field pennycress (*Thlaspi arvense*)
Wild radish (*Raphanus raphanistrum*)
Curly dock (*Rumex crispus*)
Chickweed (*Stellaria media*)
Lamb's-quarter (*Chenopodium album*)

Goosefoot (*Chenopodium* spp.)
Orache (*Atriplex* spp.)
Meadow buttercup and creeping buttercup (*Ranunculus* spp.); see warning about cooking them on page 198.
Black bindweed (*Fallopia convolvulus*); note that there have been reports of members of this genus causing photosensitivity in susceptible people. The seeds are listed as edible at www.PFAF.org. Personally, I would advise caution and additional research before consuming.
Ribwort plantain (*Plantago lanceolata*)
Broadleaf plantain (*Plantago major*)
Black nightshade (*Solanium nigrum*); it was probably the berries, which are edible when ripe, that were added to the porridge, not the seeds. This plant is unrelated to deadly nightshade (*Atropa belladonna*).
Barnyard millet (*Echinochloa crus-galli*)
Yorkshire fog (*Holcus lanatus*)
Perennial ryegrass (*Lolium perenne*)
Mustard (Brassicaceae)
Oval sedge (*Carex ovalis*)

Note that some tiny quantity of seeds or seeds fragments found in the gut analysis might have been mistakenly gathered alongside the cultivated grains and might not be considered edible, including:

Hawk's beard (*Crepis tectorum*); considered somewhat edible, but there is no information on seed edibility.
Common fumitory (*Fumaria officinalis*); could not find information on seed edibility.
Field forget-me-not (*Myosotis arvensis*); could not find information on seed edibility.
Common hemp nettle (*Galeopsis tetrahit*); this plant is considered inedible, but it apparently has some medicinal uses. I could not find any mention of the seeds being edible, but, as you'll see, these seeds were also found in small quantities in Tollund Man.
Self-heal (*Prunella vulgaris*); a medicinal plant, but could not find information on seed edibility.

Tollund Man

Another well-known bog body that underwent extensive gut analysis is Tollund Man from early Iron Age Denmark (c. 405–380 BCE). His remarkably preserved body was discovered in 1950 in Bjældskovdal.

Scientists studied the contents of Tollund Man's large intestine, examining plant remains, pollen, and proteins. They discovered that his last meal was primarily made up of the following:

85 percent barley (*Hordeum vulgare*)
9 percent pale persicaria (*Persicaria lapathifolia*)
5 percent flax (*Linum usitatissimum*)
1 percent various other wild plant seeds

The presence of fish in Tollund Man's meal was confirmed through protein analysis, though no bones were found, likely due to digestion. The meal was probably cooked in a clay vessel, as suggested by charred food crusts. It's also possible that some of the seeds and grains were processed using fire.

What's so interesting about the gut analysis findings is how they resemble my approach to using wild seeds. When I cook cereals with wild seeds and grains, I typically use around 80 percent commercial grains, such as oats, and 20 percent wild ingredients such as berries, fruits, seeds, and grains. This balance makes sense for both nutrition and diversity. Eating oats alone doesn't provide adequate nutrition. Wild ingredients add not only essential vitamins and minerals, but also unique flavors, textures, and natural sweetness, making the meal more enjoyable and complex.

Tollund Man. *Photo by Liya Blumesser / Shutterstock*

The wild seeds found in Tollund Man's meal include:

Corn spurry (*Spergula arvensis*)
Lamb's-quarter (*Chenopodium album*)
Gold-of-pleasure (*Camelina sativa*)
Field pansy (*Viola arvensis*)
Hemp nettle (*Galeopsis* spp.)
Black bindweed (*Fallopia convolvulus*); note that there have been reports of members of this genus causing photosensitivity in susceptible people. The seeds are listed as edible at www.PFAF.org, but I would advise caution and additional research before consuming.
Marsh willow herb (*Epilobium palustre*)
Compact/soft rush (*Juncus conglomeratus/effusus*)
Dwarf marsh violet (*Viola palustris*)

The inclusion of these wild seeds suggests that Iron Age European meals were far from simple. Living in North America, I haven't been able to study or experiment with some of these seeds. But the lists of plants from these gut analyses reminded me of how the Pomo women of California processed wild oats, and other grains and seeds, into pinole.

Pinole is a finely ground powder made from roasted or parched grains, seeds, or a combination of both. Traditionally, seeds are gathered, winnowed to remove chaff, and lightly toasted to enhance flavor. The toasted grains are then pounded into a fine meal for use as needed. Different combinations of seeds and grains create unique flavors, making pinole both tasty and nutritious. Pinole is often prepared as a porridge to create a nourishing, energy-rich dish. Historically, it was a vital food for Indigenous peoples.

Today, pinole can still be found in some Hispanic stores in Los Angeles, though today's versions are usually made with roasted maize. This nutrient-dense powder is used in cereals, baked goods, tortillas, and drinks. A popular preparation is *pinolillo*, a beverage made by mixing pinole with cocoa, agave, cinnamon, chia seeds, vanilla, and other spices.

Returning to the Pomo women, *Kashaya Pomo Plants* by Jennie Goodrich, Claudia Lawson, and Vana Parrish Lawson describes how they processed wild oat into pinole:

> The grain (Wild oats) was parched by placing some in a circular coiled tray basket with some tanoak coals and shaking it back and forth. Small amounts were prepared as needed. The grain was pounded in a hopper mortar until it became a fine powder.

> Different combinations [of wildflower seeds and grains] could be mixed for different flavors.*

It's possible that a similar process was used in Europe, and that the small amounts of wild seeds found with Grauballe Man and Tollund Man were added for flavor. I often do this with my own local wild seeds, such as fennel and carrot, to enhance the taste of my dishes.

Caves, Caches, and Charred Materials

You can find more information about the ancient use of wild seeds and grains in archaeological studies and papers that focus on materials found in caves, storage caches (sometimes pottery), and charred food remains. This applies not only to Europe but also to regions like the Middle East, Asia, Africa, and beyond. Digging up this kind of information might take some research, but it's definitely possible to find useful details about local edible seeds and grains.

I came across some fascinating papers during my research, including one called "Food Storage in Two Late Bronze Age Caves of Southern France: Palaeoethnobotanical and Social Implications."† This paper shares insights from two Late Bronze Age cave sites in Southern France—Balme Gontran and Baume Layrou—that show how ancient people stored their crops.

Balme Gontran Cave

In the Balme Gontran cave, excavations uncovered a thick layer of charred seeds along with storage vessels. The site dates back to the Late Bronze Age (eleventh to tenth centuries BCE), confirmed through radiocarbon dating of the seeds and the ceramic styles.

The charred seeds showed a dense and well-preserved collection of grains, mostly spelt wheat (*Triticum spelta*) and proso millet (*Panicum miliaceum*), which were stored separately. There were also smaller amounts of barley, emmer wheat, einkorn wheat, and foxtail millet, in addition to a few bean and lentil species (*Lens culinaris*, horse beans [*Vicia faba*], and grass peas).

A small number of wild plant seeds were also found. Per the paper's authors, it seems possible that certain wild seeds, such as field mustard

* Jennie Goodrich, Claudia Lawson, and Vana Parrish Lawson, *Kashaya Pomo Plants* (American Indian Studies Center, 1996).

† Laurent Bouby, Gilbert Fages, and Jean Michel Treffort, "Food Storage in Two Late Bronze Age Caves of Southern France: Palaeoethnobotanical and Social Implications," *Vegetation History and Archaeobotany* 14 (2005): 313–28, https://doi.org/10.1007/s00334-005-0079-6.

(*Brassica rapa*), were stored alongside the cultivated grains, but it is difficult to say for certain. It's possible that some seeds, despite their edibility, were inadvertently mixed up with the cultivated grains.

The analysis of the charred seeds, grains, and organic materials from the site offers an incredible glimpse into ancient crop storage and food practices. Here is what was found:

Cultivated Seeds/Grains

Cereals (unspecified fragments): 402 fragments
Barley (*Hordeum vulgare*): 47 grains
Red or grass pea (*Lathyrus cicera* or *Lathyrus sativus*): 1 seed
Lentil (*Lens culinaris*): 462 seeds (pulses)
Broomcorn millet (*Panicum miliaceum*): 9,102 grains
Millet or foxtail millet (*Panicum* or *Setaria*): 8 grains
Foxtail millet (*Setaria italica*): 68 grains
Bread wheat or durum wheat (*Triticum aestivum* or *durum/turgidum*): 113 grains
Emmer wheat (*Triticum dicoccum*): 335 grains
Einkorn wheat (*Triticum monococcum*): 9 grains
Spelt wheat (*Triticum spelta*): 3,560 grains
Fava bean (*Vicia faba*): 87 beans

Wild Seeds/Grains

Black bindweed (*Bilderdykia convolvulus*): 14 seeds
Soft brome or rye brome (*Bromus hordeaceus* or *Bromus secalinus*): 109 grains
Cleavers (*Galium aparine*): 1 seed
Goosegrass (*Galium spurium*): 1 seed
Field mustard (*Brassica rapa*): 76 seeds
Lamb's-quarter (*Chenopodium album*): 4 seeds
Barnyard grass (*Echinochloa crus-galli*): 226 seeds
Wild oats (*Avena* spp.): 14 grains
Grass family (Gramineae): 1 grain
Knotweed family (Polygonaceae): 9 seeds
Dock (*Rumex* spp.): 18 seeds

Baume Layrou Cave

Baume Layrou is another late Bronze Age cave site in southern France, notable for its use as a storage location for agricultural products. Situated in a rocky limestone region, the cave provided a secure and stable environment for preserving grains and pulses.

As with the Balme Gontran cave, archaeologists found remains of charred seeds and grains, including barley, wheat, and some pulses. They also found fragments of storage vessels, which were likely used to hold and protect the stored grains and pulses.

An analysis of the charred plant remains from the site revealed the following:

Cultivated Seeds/Grains

Cereals (unspecified fragments): 12,305 grains
Barley (*Hordeum vulgare*): 23,174 grains
Germinated barley (*Hordeum vulgare*): 13 grains
Broomcorn millet (*Panicum miliaceum*): 25,349 grains
Aggregated broomcorn millet (*Panicum miliaceum*): 1,011 grains
Millet or foxtail millet (*Panicum* or *Setaria*): 1,754 grains
Aggregated millet or foxtail millet (*Panicum* or *Setaria*): 79 grains
Foxtail millet (*Setaria italica*): 645 grains
Aggregated foxtail millet (*Setaria italica*): 237 grains
Bread wheat or durum wheat (*Triticum aestivum/durum/turgidum*): 9,074 grains
Emmer wheat (*Triticum dicoccum*): 17,360 grains
Einkorn wheat (*Triticum monococcum*): 3,750 grains
Spelt wheat (*Triticum spelta*): 28,560 grains
Other wheat species (unspecified, *Triticum* spp.): 2,938 grains

Pulse (Legume) Seeds

Grass pea (*Lathyrus sativus*): 1,020 seeds
Lentil (*Lens culinaris*): 276 seeds (pulses)
Fava bean (*Vicia faba*): 146 beans
Other vetch (*Vicia ervilia*): 4 seeds

Nuts

Hazelnut (*Corylus avellana*): 216 fragments
Oak (*Quercus* spp.): 11 acorn bases

Wild Seeds/Grains

Wild oat (*Avena fatua/sterilis*): 4 grains
Black bindweed (*Bilderdykia convolvulus*): 13 seeds
Brome (*Bromus hordeaceus/secalinus*): 106 grains

Corncockle (*Agrostemma githago*): 88 seeds; note that corncockle (*Agrostemma githago*) is considered poisonous because its seeds and leaves contain high levels of saponin-like substances. However, saponins are poorly absorbed by the human body, meaning most pass through without causing harm. While saponins are present in many common foods like spinach, rhubarb, and certain beans, proper processing methods such as soaking, leaching, cooking, or fermentation can reduce their toxicity and improve edibility.
Cleavers (*Galium aparine*): 8 seeds
Wild mustard (cf. *Brassica rapa*): 5 seeds
Barnyard grass (*Echinochloa crus-galli*): 80 grains
Timothy grass (*Phleum pratense*): 11 seeds
Perennial ryegrass (*Lolium* cf. *perenne/rigidum*): 5 seeds
Clustered clover (cf. *Trifolium pratense*): 9 seeds
Wild oats (*Avena* spp.): 76 grains
Grass family (Gramineae): 21 grains
Sorrel (*Rumex* spp.): 4 fragments
Goosefoot (*Chenopodium* spp.): 1 fragment

An analysis of the uncharred materials (seeds, grains, beans, etc.) found in the cave revealed the following:

Cultivated Seeds/Grains

Broomcorn millet (*Panicum miliaceum*): 108 grains
Foxtail millet (*Setaria italica*): 39 grains

Nuts and Fruits

Wild strawberry (*Fragaria vesca*): 4 seeds
Oak (*Quercus* spp.): 3 acorn bases
Rose (*Rosa* spp.): 2 seeds, 9 fragments
Blackberry (*Rubus fruticosus*): 5 seeds, 12 fragments
Elderberry (*Sambucus nigra*): 2 seeds

Wild Seeds/Grains

Corncockle (*Agrostemma githago*): 22 seeds, 13 fragments (Caution: See prior note.)
Field gromwell (*Buglossoides arvensis*): 1 seed
Small bur-parsley type (*Caucalis platycarpos* type): 3 fragments
Self-heal (*Prunella vulgaris*): 5 seeds
Grass family (Gramineae): 1 seed

Exploring Your Unique Terroir

So, we've covered some of the most common wild edible seeds and grains (probably missing some) and taken inspiration from the diverse diets of our ancestors. Now, let's take things a step further and talk about foraging right in your own environment. Every place has a unique personality shaped by the land, the seasons, and the plants that call it home. In the world of foraging, we often use the word *terroir* to capture that sense of place. It's a fancy French word, sure, but it's just a way of saying that the land leaves its mark on the food that grows there. Just as wine tastes different depending on the vineyard in which it was grown, wild seeds and grains carry the flavor and spirit of the land that produces them.

When you forage close to home, you start to notice things you may have walked past a hundred times without a second thought. Maybe it's a patch of amaranth on the side of the road, some wild barley growing along a hiking trail, or even an abandoned field full of grasses ready to go to seed. There's so much interesting food waiting to be discovered when you tune in to what's growing naturally around you. The exciting part? You're not just gathering food—you're tapping into the landscape, learning what it offers in each season and how everything connects.

And, as we've seen, foraging also connects you to something even deeper—your ancestors. The activity of exploring and harvesting local seeds and grains isn't just about survival; it's part of your DNA. In a way, foraging is like stepping into our ancestors' footsteps, reconnecting with ancient traditions that kept people alive for thousands of years. That instinct to gather and use what the land offers is still within you—it just takes a bit of practice to awaken it.

You might be surprised how resilient wild plants are. They thrive in places where cultivated crops struggle—on rocky hillsides, in dry riverbeds, and even in the cracks of city sidewalks. These plants have been part of the landscape for millennia, often long before modern agriculture arrived. When you start exploring what grows wild in your area, it's like opening the door to a secret pantry stocked by nature. Once you develop a good eye for what's edible, even a short walk can turn into a treasure hunt.

There's a real joy in gathering seeds and grains that come from the land around you. It's satisfying to know that the food in your hand isn't the result of global shipping or big agriculture—it's local, natural, and often overlooked. Foraging also teaches you to be more in tune with the seasons. You'll notice that some plants go to seed right after the summer heat, while others wait for the first fall rain. With time, you'll know exactly when and where to look for specific seeds—whether it's chickweed popping up in winter or native ryegrass ripening in early summer.

A wonderful example of this connection to the landscape is found in Nordic cuisine. Around the early 2000s, chefs in Scandinavia began exploring their local environment in search of new flavors. Pioneers like René Redzepi of Noma in Denmark led the way in creating what's now called "New Nordic Cuisine." They focused on local, seasonal ingredients—berries, root vegetables, wild herbs, and fermented foods that captured the unique essence of the Nordic landscape. This new cuisine didn't just revive old ingredients; it emphasized the power of terroir, proving that the flavors of a region come from the land itself. When you forage locally, you're doing something similar—bringing the spirit of your environment directly into your kitchen.

To get started with your own exploration, begin by taking regular walks in natural areas or even your backyard, looking closely at the plants around you. Grasses, wildflowers, and shrubs all add to the landscape's character. Carrying a foraging guidebook or using a plant-identification app can help you get to know each plant safely and at your own pace. Social media groups focused on plant identification are also great resources. Many experienced foragers and botanists share their insights in these communities, allowing you to post photos of plants you're curious about and get guidance.

Proper identification is essential, as some edible plants have poisonous look-alikes. Always double-check each new plant with multiple sources to confirm it's safe to eat. This careful approach ensures safety while helping you become a more skilled forager, tuning into the land's seasonal rhythms and hidden offerings.

Foraging also brings a sense of connection—not just to the land, but to the animals and plants around you. Birds are natural seed carriers, spreading grains along trails and open spaces. Wind and water move seeds across the landscape, creating unexpected patches of bounty. The deeper you dive into your local landscape, the more these patterns become clear. You start seeing the land not as a random collection of plants but as a dynamic system with its own rhythm. This connection makes every outing an adventure, with new discoveries waiting just around the corner.

As you become familiar with local wild seeds and grains, you may start experimenting with new ways to use them. Perhaps you'll try grinding them into flour for baking or adding them to your next ferment. Some seeds are perfect for tossing into a salad, while others can be roasted to bring out a nutty flavor. The possibilities are endless, and part of the fun is figuring out what works for you.

And remember, foraging isn't just about gathering—it's also about respecting and caring for the environment. Responsible harvesting is a big part of working with the land. Sometimes, this means taking only what you need and leaving plenty for the plants to regrow or for wildlife to enjoy. In other cases, it's recognizing when a plant population might need time to recover and skipping a harvest to let it thrive. When I rely heavily on a particular native plant, I make a point of planting more of it to ensure it flourishes beyond what I take. Think of it as a partnership: you're nourishing yourself while helping the ecosystem thrive by staying mindful of what you take and how often you return.

Exploring your local area is about more than just food—it's about building a relationship with the land and becoming part of its story. It's a chance to slow down, pay attention, and appreciate the natural abundance that surrounds you. And in doing so, you're not just feeding yourself—you're reconnecting with the land in a way that goes back generations. No matter where you come from, your ancestors did this for thousands of years, relying on nature's gifts to survive. That same knowledge is still inside you, waiting to be rediscovered one seed, one grain, and one foraging walk at a time.

Your environment has its own hidden flavors and stories, and it's up to you to discover them. By exploring, you're diving into a culinary adventure much like the Nordic chefs did, uncovering flavors unique to your surroundings.

California: A Living Example

California is a place like no other. From 2020 to 2023, I traveled all over North America, but I never found the same diversity and abundance of wild foods as here. California reflects our modern world—a place where the land tells the story of migration, different cultures coming together, and history. Today, about 90 percent of what I forage here is made up of non-native—and often invasive—plants. This mix is shaped by California's mild climate and the incredible diversity of people who live here.

The landscape really started to change with colonization and settlement. As settlers arrived, they brought plants from Europe, the Middle East, Asia, and beyond. Crops were planted, and with them came extra seeds—some intentional, some accidental. Many of these non-native plants adapted well to California's ideal conditions, blending into the environment and, in some cases, even outcompeting native plants.

You see this especially in cities like Los Angeles and San Francisco, where people from all over the world have brought plants for farming, gardening, or simply by accident. Crop seeds like wheat often came with "unwanted" seeds, such as wild barley, great brome, and wild oats. With California's perfect climate—warmth and just the right amount of rain—these "weeds" grew quickly, spread widely, and became part of the local landscape.

Over time, all these plants have completely transformed California's ecosystem. Southern California's landscape today is a world apart from what it was a few centuries ago. While foraging and doing research for this book, I've even found seeds and grains my own ancestors used—plants that have traveled from Europe and Asia and are now common here too.

California's rich diversity offers endless opportunities for discovery. I've gathered over 90 types of edible wild seeds and grains here, with each year revealing exciting new finds. So far, I've identified around 120 plants with edible seeds and grains, though many remain academic knowledge, as I haven't yet located all of them in the wild. While numerous species are non-native, venturing farther from urban areas uncovers highly nutritious native seeds. These native plants were essential food sources for Native Californian tribes and continue to play a vital role in the landscape today.

When it comes to foraging native seeds and grains, I feel it's important to be respectful. The environment is already under pressure from all the new, fast-spreading plants, so I try to focus on gathering non-native plants and do my part to help native ones grow by planting seeds of those I use often. Foraging isn't just about collecting food—it's also about taking care of the land and keeping its balance wherever you are located. This applies to any location in the world.

Here are what I call the "Big Four" most common native edible seeds and grains in my immediate area:

Thistle sage (***Salvia carduacea***)**:** Thistle sage has purple flowers and produces seeds that can be ground into flour. These seeds are rich in protein and healthy fats.

Golden chia (***Salvia columbariae***)**:** Golden chia seeds are tiny and packed with protein, traditionally used by Native peoples. Similar to store-bought chia.

Indian ricegrass (***Eriocoma hymenoides***)**:** Indian ricegrass grows well in dry areas, and its seeds, high in fiber, were a staple food in the Southwest.

California buckwheat (***Eriogonum fasciculatum***)**:** California buckwheat has small seeds that are easy to collect and can be made into a coarse flour.

Let's take a closer look at each of them.

Thistle Sage

SALVIA CARDUACEA

Thistle sage is one of the most striking wild sages, with bright purple-blue flowers and spiky, silvery leaves that catch the eye in the local desert landscape. The long spines on its leaves resemble those of a thistle—hence its name. Native to California, this sage prefers sunny, open areas with sandy soil. It has adapted exceptionally well to these tough conditions, thriving in spots with plenty of sun and minimal water.

When it blooms, thistle sage is truly eye-catching. Thistle sage grows upright with stalks that can reach over 1 foot (30 cm) tall, each crowned with clusters of beautiful and vivid purple flowers surrounded by spiky bracts. These blooms are like bursts of color against the dry, muted backdrop, making them easy to spot even from a distance. Though it's not as widespread as some other sage species, thistle sage can be locally abundant when conditions align with its preferences.

Extraction

My Native friends still collect thistle sage seeds using a "seed beater basket" for efficient gathering. This traditional method involves using a paddle or a scoop-shaped beater to hit the mature flower heads, knocking the ripe seeds directly into a large, open-mouthed basket held below. You can achieve a similar effect with a gloved hand and a box—just give the flower heads a good tap and the seeds will fall right in. The glove keeps your hand safe from the plant's spiky bits, and the box catches the seeds. It's an easy and efficient way to collect plenty of seeds for cooking or storing, but you'll need some thick gloves.

When your seeds are dry, store them in a cool, dry place. Use paper bags or jars with tight-fitting lids. Label them with the date and type of seed for future reference (see Drying and Storage, page 18).

Culinary Uses

Thistle sage has long been valued as a food source, especially by Native peoples. Its round seeds are packed with protein and healthy fats, making them a nutritious component of traditional diets. Historically, these seeds were often ground into a coarse flour or meal, which could then be mixed with water to make a porridge-like mush. This meal is easy to store, transport, and prepare, providing a reliable, energy-rich food perfect for life in arid regions.

Roasting the seeds over an open fire was another common preparation method, intensifying their nutty taste and adding a touch of smokiness. The roasted seeds could then be sprinkled over food to contribute an earthy, rustic flavor. Today, a quick toasting of the seeds in a skillet can bring out this rich, smoky flavor, perfect for topping roasted vegetables or as a crunchy salad addition. In my opinion, toasted thistle sage seeds taste better than toasted sesame seeds.

Ground thistle sage seeds can be mixed with other grains to add depth and richness to sourdough and similar wild ferments. They can also be blended into smoothies or soaked to make a refreshing drink, with a texture similar to chia.

Thistle sage also has a place in desserts and sweet treats. The seeds' nutty flavor pairs well with honey, maple syrup, and warm spices like cinnamon or cardamom, making them ideal for energy bars and granola.

Modern recipes for savory snacks have also embraced thistle sage seeds. The whole or crushed seeds can be mixed with salt and herbs to make a flavorful coating for grilled meats and fish.

Golden Chia

SALVIA COLUMBARIAE

Golden chia, also called desert chia or chia sage, is a type of sage in the mint family (Lamiaceae). This hardy little plant grows well in dry areas across the southwestern United States and parts of Mexico. It's usually found at elevations below 8,200 feet (2,500 m), especially in deserts like the Mojave and Sonoran. It is well suited to drought and thrives in sandy, sunny places.

Golden chia grows up to 1 foot (30 cm) tall, with thick, wrinkled leaves near the ground. Its bright blue-purple flowers bloom in round clusters on thin stems, standing out against the desert's muted colors. These flowers attract bees, hummingbirds, and other pollinators, which help the plant produce seeds.

Extraction

Golden chia seeds are relatively easy to extract; once the flowers dry, the seed heads become brittle and can be harvested by gently shaking or tapping them. Hold a container, like a paper bag or shallow box, directly beneath the seed heads. For efficient collection, I like to use a method similar to the one I use for thistle sage seeds. I use a gloved hand to "spank" the seed heads into a large bowl, which helps release more seeds with minimal time and effort. After collection, the seeds can be sifted to remove any remaining plant debris, making them ready for culinary use or storage.

Once dry, store the seeds in a cool, dry place. Use paper bags or jars with tight-fitting lids. Label them with the date and type of seed for future reference (see Drying and Storage, page 18).

Culinary Uses

Golden chia seeds are a traditional and nutritious food among Indigenous communities, who still gather and use them today. The seeds are often ground into flour and mixed with water to make a filling porridge or drink or to thicken soups and stews. You can also use the whole seeds. The seeds swell when soaked in water, creating a gel-like consistency that makes them useful in many recipes.

For modern foragers, golden chia seeds are popular additions to smoothies, baked goods, and puddings, where their thickening properties add texture. I also like to use golden chia seeds in my raw cracker recipe, blending them with other wild seeds. The gel quality of chia helps hold the crackers together (see “Mary’s Gone Wild” Crackers, page 245).

In terms of nutrition, chia seeds are exceptionally rich in omega-3 fats, fiber, calcium, and magnesium, making them a powerhouse of essential nutrients. Below is the nutritional breakdown per 100 grams of chia seeds, along with the percentage of the daily recommended value they provide:

Calories: 24%
Protein: 33%
Fat: 47%
Omega-3 Fats: Over 1,000%
Omega-6 Fats: 48%
Carbohydrates: 14%
Fiber: 123%
Calcium: 63%
Magnesium: 84%
Phosphorus: 123%
Potassium: 9%
Iron: 43%
Zinc: 42%
Vitamin B1 (Thiamine): 52%
Vitamin B3 (Niacin): 55%
Vitamin E: 3%

Indian Ricegrass

ERIOCOMA HYMENOIDES

Indian ricegrass is a tough, long-lasting bunchgrass that grows widely across North America, especially in dry and semi-dry areas like the Great Basin, Mojave Desert, and parts of the Rocky Mountains. Indian ricegrass thrives in sandy soils and on rocky slopes, where few other plants can grow. Its resilience allows it to flourish at various elevations, from low valleys to high mountains, easily withstanding drought, cold, and poor soils. On a trip from Southern California to Idaho to visit my daughter, I was struck by the way this grass covered the Great Basin, stretching all the way to the horizon.

Indian ricegrass grows in clumps, often forming dense patches. The leaves are thin and can feel rough to the touch due to tiny hairs. The plant is typically pale green or grayish, blending into dry landscapes. During its

flowering stage, it produces delicate, open clusters of small seeds at the tips of tall, thin stems, giving it a light, airy appearance. The seeds are dark brown or black and are encased in papery, cream-colored coverings.

Collection and Extraction

Harvesting Indian ricegrass seeds requires patience and specific techniques, as the seeds are small and can sometimes be sparse. One approach I use is the Comb Threshing method (page 37). It's best to let the cut grass dry for a few weeks (or months), allowing the seeds to fully mature and detach more easily. I then comb the mature seed heads into a container. After collection, I winnow the seeds to remove any debris. For large quantities, I use a traditional method of beating the stalks inside a large bowl (see page 34) or over a tarp using a stick. The Flame Winnowing method (page 42) also works well, as does the Vitamix Threshing method (page 47).

Once dry, store the seeds in a cool, dry place. Use paper bags or jars with tight-fitting lids. Label them with the date and type of seed for future reference (see Drying and Storage, page 18)

Culinary Uses

For a long time, I was perplexed about how to use Indian ricegrass seeds, since they're kind of tough and even look "empty" inside, but they're really meant to be processed into flour. The seeds have long been used as a gluten-free food, rich in protein and fiber. They are traditionally ground into flour using stone tools, and this flour is mixed with water to make simple bread or porridge. Indian ricegrass flour can be blended with other flours to create foods like pancakes, flatbreads, or muffins, adding a faintly nutty flavor. Pan-roasting the seeds prior to making the flour makes it quite delicious. Some online resources will tell you that the seeds can also be cooked like rice or quinoa for 45 minutes, but I doubt they've actually done it—the end result is less than spectacular and quite fibrous. I think flour is the way to go.

Of course, if you don't have a stone grinder, you can use a Vitamix or similar food processor at high speed to make the flour.

California Buckwheat

ERIOGONUM FASCICULATUM

California buckwheat is a native species that thrives on dry, rocky slopes and in coastal sage scrub across California and parts of the southwestern United States. It prefers well-drained sandy or rocky soils and is typically found in chaparral, coastal scrub, and desert landscapes. Drought-tolerant and sun-loving, this very abundant plant is well suited to arid, open environments.

California buckwheat is a small, bushy shrub that reaches up to 3 feet (90 cm) in height, with slender, gray-green leaves clustered along its stems. The plant is most noticeable from late spring through summer, when it displays clusters of tiny white-to-pale-pink flowers that deepen to a reddish-brown as they age. The rounded flower heads eventually produce small, pinkish seeds that mature and dry by late summer. Its narrow, sometimes rolled leaves give California buckwheat a distinct appearance in arid landscapes, and my students often mistake it for rosemary.

Collection and Extraction

To gather California buckwheat, wait until the flower heads have dried on the plant. Remove the dried flower heads with your fingers and collect them in a container. Although some people do it, there's no need to separate the seeds from the chaff; the entire dried cluster, seeds and chaff together, can be used.

To make a coarse flour from California buckwheat, take a handful of the dried flower heads, and rub them firmly between your palms. This motion crushes the clusters, breaking down the seeds and chaff together into a coarse, textured, whole-plant flour that requires no further separation.

Once the flowers are properly dried, store them in a cool, dry place if not processing immediately. Use paper bags or jars with tight-fitting lids. Label them with the date and type of seed for future reference (see Drying and Storage, page 18).

Culinary Uses

This is an interesting one . . . While you'll find mentions of California buckwheat seeds being used for food on various websites and even in videos, I can't locate any documented traditional culinary uses in ethnobotanical records. The only references I've found involve medicinal uses, such as

decoctions and infusions for various ailments. Unless I missed something, it's possible that using the seeds as a food source is a more recent adaptation.

I've experimented with removing the seeds from the flower heads and incorporating them into cereals or granola, but I didn't have much success. The seeds remain quite fibrous even when cooked, and they retain an unpalatable, rough texture. My main use for California buckwheat is to add the coarse flour to other flours for making flatbreads, breads, crackers, and pancakes. It adds fluffiness to these baked goods. This flour is also visually appealing, especially in crackers and bread. I suspect it's mostly composed of fiber, with limited nutritional value.

Beyond the "Big Four"

How many more edible seeds and grains are there in my local environment? So many more! To give you an idea, I decided to write a list of edible wild seeds and grains, both native and non-native, that you can find in California and much of the Southwest (though it's always incomplete, as I keep finding more!). This list comes from my own research along with several other sources, which I've included at the end.

This should give you an idea of what you can expect in terms of numbers in your own terroir. Just a quick note: you should still verify the edibility of any plant/seed listed here through your own research. I always do this, even if I see a plant listed as edible in a book or a reputable source. You gain more knowledge and peace of mind that way.

I have removed three "edible" seeds from my personal list for this book. The first two are called Menzies' fiddleneck (*Amsinckia menziesii*) and tarweed fiddleneck (*Amsinckia lycopsoides*), and though some sources list these seeds as edible, my research shows that the seeds contain pyrrolizidine alkaloids, which can be toxic to the liver in larger amounts or over a prolonged period. Traditional preparation methods like parching, fermenting, or soaking might reduce these risks, and it's definitely something I want to explore further. Similarly, California buttercup (*Ranunculus californicus*) is known to be toxic if eaten raw. Traditional uses of the seeds involve cooking and/or parching them, but I also need to investigate this one more thoroughly to make sure it's safe.

Achyrachaena mollis (Blow wives)
Aegilops triuncialis (Barbed goatgrass)
Amaranthus albus (Tumble pigweed)
Amaranthus blitoides (Prostrate pigweed)
Amaranthus retroflexus (Redroot amaranth)
Amaranthus palmeri (Palmer amaranth)
Anethum graveolens (Dill weed)
Artemisia dracunculus (Wild tarragon)
Avena barbata (Slender oat)
Avena fatua (Wild oat)
Bouteloua gracilis (Blue grama)
Brassica nigra (Black mustard)
Brassica rapa (Field mustard)
Bromus carinatus (California brome)
Bromus diandrus (Great brome)
Bromus hordeaceus (Soft brome)
Bromus marginatus (Mountain brome)
Bromus tectorum (Cheatgrass)
Calandrinia ciliata (Fringed redmaids)
Capsella bursa-pastoris (Shepherd's-purse)
Chenopodium album (Lamb's-quarters)
Chenopodium murale (Nettleleaf goosefoot)
Clarkia biloba (Two lobe clarkia)
Clarkia purpurea (Winecup clarkia)
Clarkia rhomboidei (Diamond clarkia)
Clarkia unguiculata (Elegant clarkia)
Claytonia perfoliate (Miner's lettuce)
Cleomella serrulata (Rocky mountain beeplant)
Cyclospermum leptophyllum (Wild celery)
Cyperus esculentus (Yellow nutsedge)
Danthonia californica (California oatgrass)

Daucus carota (Wild carrot)
Descurainia incana (Mountain tansymustard)
Descurainia sophia (Flixweed)
Dicoria canescens (Desert twinbugs)
Digitaria sanguinalis (Hairy crabgrass)
Echinochloa colona (Junglerice)
Echinochloa crus-galli (Barnyard millet)
Eleusine indica (Goosegrass)
Elymus canadensis (Canada wildrye)
Elytrigia repens (Quackgrass)
Epilobium densiflorum (Denseflower willowherb)
Epilobium torreyi (Torrey's willowherb)
Eriocoma hymenoides (Indian ricegrass)
Eriogonum fasciculatum (California buckwheat)
Foeniculum vulgare (Wild fennel)
Galium aparine (Catchweed bedstraw)
Helianthus annuus (Common sunflower)
Hemizonia congesta (Hayfield tarweed)
Hirschfeldia incana (Shortpod mustard)
Hordeum jubatum (Foxtail barley)
Hordeum murinum (Hare barley)
Hordeum spontaneum (Wild barley)
Layia chrysanthemoides (Smooth tidytips)
Lepidium nitidum (Shining pepperweed)
Lepidium perfoliatum (Clasping pepperwort)
Lolium perenne (Italian ryegrass)
Lolium temulentum (Darnel ryegrass)
Lomatium (Biscuitroot)
Lomatium dissectum (Fernleaf biscuitroot)
Madia elegans (Elegant madia)
Madia elegans (Common madia)
Madia glomerata (Mountain tarweed)
Madia sativa (Coast tarweed)
Malva sylvestris (Common mallow)
Mentzelia albicaulis (Whitestem blazingstar)
Mentzelia dispersa (Nevada blazingstar)
Nasturtium officinale (Watercress)
Nuphar lutea (Rocky Mountain pond-lily)
Oenothera biennis (Evening primrose)
Oloptum miliaceum (Smilograss)
Papaver somniferum (Breadseed poppy)
Perideridia gairdneri (Gairdner's yampah)
Perideridia kelloggii (Kellogg's yampah)
Plagiobothrys fulvus (Fulvous popcornflower)
Plagiobothrys nothofulvus (Rusty popcornflower)
Plantago major (Broadleaf plantain)
Plectritis congesta (Shortspur seablush)
Pleuropogon spp. (Semaphoregrass)
Pleuropogon californicus (Davy's semaphoregrass)
Polygonum convolvulus (Wild buckwheat)
Polygonum douglasii (Douglas' knotweed)
Polygonum persicaria (Ladysthumb)
Raphanus raphanistrum (Wild radish)
Rumex aquaticus (Western dock)
Rumex crispus (Curly dock)
Rumex hymenosepalus (Canaigre dock)
Rumex paucifolius (Alpine sheep sorrel)
Rumex salicifolius (Willow dock)
Salvia apiana (White sage)
Salvia carduacea (Thistle sage)
Salvia columbariae (Chia)
Salvia mellifera (Black sage)
Scirpus californicus (California bullrush)
Setaria pumila (Yellow foxtail)
Silybum marianum (Milk thistle)
Sinapis arvensis (Field mustard)
Sisymbrium altissimum (Tumbleweed mustard)
Sisymbrium irio (London rocket)
Sorghum halepense (Johnsongrass)
Stellaria media (Chickweed)
Torreyochloa pallida (Pale false mannagrass)
Tropaeolum majus (Nasturtium)
Urtica urens (Small nettle)

Wyethia angustifolia (California compassplant)

Wyethia glabra (Coast Range mule-ears)

Wyethia mollis (Woolly mule-ears)

Bibliography

Anderson, M. Kat, Jim Effenberger, Don Joley, and Deborah J. Lionakis Meyer. *Edible Seeds and Grains of California Tribes and the Klamath Tribe of Oregon in the Phoebe Apperson Hearst Museum of Anthropology Collections, University of California Berkeley*. Davis, CA: Natural Resources Conservation Service, 2012.

Asingh, Pauline, and Niels Lynnerup, eds. *Grauballe Man: An Iron Age Bog Body Revisited*. Aarhus, Denmark: Jutland Archaeological Society, 2007.

Bouby, Laurent, Gilbert Fages, and Jean Michel Treffort. "Food Storage in Two Late Bronze Age Caves of Southern France: Palaeoethnobotanical and Social Implications." *Vegetation History and Archaeobotany* 14 (2005): 313–28. https://doi.org/10.1007/s00334-005-0079-6.

Colledge, Sue, and James Conolly. "Wild Plant Use in European Neolithic Subsistence Economies: A Formal Assessment of Preservation Bias in Archaeobotanical Assemblages and the Implications for Understanding Changes in Plant Diet Breadth." *Quaternary Science Reviews* 101 (October 2014): 193–206. https://doi.org/10.1016/j.quascirev.2014.07.013.

Goodrich, Jennie, Claudia Lawson, and Vana Parrish Lawson. *Kashaya Pomo Plants* (American Indian Studies Center, 1996).

Kabukcu, Ceren. "The Real Paleo Diet: New Archaeological Evidence Changes What We Thought About How Ancient Humans Prepared Food." *The Conversation*, November 23, 2022. https://theconversation.com/the-real-paleo-diet-new-archaeological-evidence-changes-what-we-thought-about-how-ancient-humans-prepared-food-195127.

Nielsen, Nina H., Peter Steen Henriksen, Morten Fischer Mortensen, Renée Enevold, Martin N. Mortensen, Carsten Scavenius, and Jan J. Enghild. "The Last Meal of Tollund Man: New Analyses of His Gut Content." *Antiquity* 95, no. 383 (October 2021): 1195–1212. https://doi.org/10.15184/aqy.2021.98

Stead, I. M., J. B. Bourke, and Don Brothwell. *Lindow Man: The Body in the Bog*. Guild Publishing, 1986.

CHAPTER 6

Sprouts and Microgreens

Years ago, when I first started gathering wild seeds and grains, my focus was mostly on using them in recipes for bread, crackers, porridges, and so on. But as I gained more experience, I realized there were so many creative culinary possibilities. I began mixing the seeds and grains I harvested with ferments, using them as spices, making tasty condiments like pickled seeds and homemade "Dijon mustard," and even roasting them to add flavor to my plant-based cheeses.

Then, in the winter of 2022, while I was living in an RV and stuck in the mountains for weeks due to heavy snow, I ran out of fresh salad greens and couldn't drive to the store. That's when I decided to try sprouting some of my wild seeds and grains.

It took some trial and error, but I learned a lot along the way. I started by sprouting a few commercial seeds and grains I'd been gifted a few months earlier. It wasn't much, but it helped me get the hang of the techniques. Once I felt confident growing sprouts and microgreens from commercial seeds, I began experimenting with the wild seeds I'd harvested, which turned out to be a great way to compare the results.

Commercial seeds and grains are typically chosen for sprouting based on factors like high germination rates, good taste and texture, and affordability. Seeds that produce a lot of sprouts with minimal resources (such as water, space, and effort) are preferred for commercial use, especially for businesses aiming at efficiency and profitability. But there are plenty of other reasons to grow your own sprouts or microgreens beyond these practical considerations:

Nutritional benefits: Sprouts and microgreens are rich in vitamins, minerals, antioxidants, and enzymes, often surpassing their mature counterparts in nutrient density, which makes them a powerful addition to your diet for boosting your intake of essential nutrients. For instance, broccoli microgreens can contain up to forty times more nutrients than mature broccoli.

Convenience: Sprouts and microgreens are easily cultivated indoors and require minimal space. This is great for people who have limited gardening space, live in urban environments, or like me, get stuck in an RV in the mountains for weeks due to snow.

Year-round availability: They can be grown indoors anytime, providing fresh greens even during winter.

Quick growth: Sprouts are ready in days, and microgreens typically mature in 1 to 3 weeks, depending on the variety.

Quality: Growing your own food ensures that it is organic and free from pesticides or herbicides.

Flavor and texture: Sprouts and microgreens add unique flavors and textures to salads, sandwiches, smoothies, and other dishes.

Cost savings: Growing your own sprouts and microgreens can be more affordable than buying them, especially if you consume them regularly. Microgreens are actually quite expensive—close to 5 dollars for a small tray at the local supermarket (though there are good reasons for that higher price compared to regular greens). While living at high altitude in the mountains of Southern California during the winters of 2023 and 2024 and growing my own microgreens, I also saved quite a bit of money because I didn't have to drive an hour roundtrip to the nearest supermarket for fresh greens.

But why grow sprouts or microgreens from wild seeds and grains? It's an interesting question. The practice is not common because it requires knowledge about the edibility of these seeds and grains, and collecting wild grains and seeds for sprouting is far more time-consuming than placing an order online. Plus, it's not necessarily easier than cultivating commercial seeds—in fact, I often achieve higher yields with commercial organic sprouting seeds and grains. Here are my personal reasons for growing sprouts and microgreens from foraged edibles:

Spending time outdoors: Foraging for wild seeds and grains connects you with nature. It's a chance to explore natural habitats, learn plant identification, and engage in sustainable harvesting practices.

Helping the environment: Most of the seeds and grains I collect in Southern California are non-native and sometimes invasive. (Interestingly, some invasives are crops in other countries.) Removing them helps local flora and fauna. For example, I've been able to reduce black mustard—a highly invasive plant—in some areas over the years by foraging the seeds. When I work with native seeds or grains, I always plant more than I take.

Nutritional diversity: Grocery stores offer only a fraction of what's out there. I can gather over 90 edible wild seeds and grains locally, none of which are available in stores. Wild varieties might also provide a broader range of nutrients than their commercial counterparts.

It's free: Buying organic commercial seeds and grains or shopping for organic sprouts and microgreens in the grocery store can be quite expensive, while wild food is free.

Flavor and variety: Sprouts and microgreens offer a wide variety of flavors, from spicy and peppery to sweet and nutty, enhancing the taste profile of meals without adding significant calories. This is especially true if you use wild seeds, which can produce some really potent flavors.

Sprouting and growing wild microgreens has also taught me about timing for collection and seed storage. For instance, harvesting at the right time is critical. Last year, I collected black mustard seeds over a month too late, which led to poor sprouting success. The intense California sun likely didn't help either.

Sprouts Versus Microgreens

Sprouts are the tender, edible shoots that emerge from germinated seeds of various plants. The process of sprouting involves soaking seeds in a container (usually a jar) for a specific amount of time, then rinsing them a couple of times daily. This process allows them to germinate and grow for a short period, typically a few days. During this time, the seeds develop into young plants with tiny roots, shoots, and often the first set of leaves, called cotyledons, which are part of the seed and provide the plant with nutrients to grow.

Seeds that are germinated on wet paper towels or similar surfaces, such as grow mats made of jute, felt, or coconuts fibers, are also typically, but not always, referred to as sprouts. Once they develop tiny roots and shoots, they are considered sprouts. However, some sprouting kits sold online refer to this end product as microgreens. It's a blurry line.

Sprouts are harvested at an early stage of growth, usually within 4 to 7 days after germination when you're using commercial seeds. They are known for their crisp texture, mild flavor, and high nutritional content. Sprouts are commonly used as side dishes or in salads, ferments, sandwiches, wraps, and other culinary applications, adding a fresh and crunchy element to dishes.

Microgreens are young, tender edible plants that are harvested at an early stage of growth, after the emergence of the first true leaves. These true leaves are the second set of leaves to appear when the plant sprouts, after the cotyledons emerge. Unlike the cotyledons, they resemble the mature plant's foliage and so are the first indication of its identity. For example, the first two leaves of many plants in the brassica family, such as black mustard and wild radish, are heart shaped. The second set of leaves resembles the leaves of the mature plant.

Microgreens are more mature than sprouts but still in the early stages of development compared to fully grown plants. Commercial microgreens are typically harvested when the plants are 1 to 2 weeks old, depending on the specific variety. Microgreens are valued for their intense flavors, vibrant colors, and high nutritional content.

What to Know When Growing Wild Sprouts and Microgreens

If you have cultivated sprouts or microgreens using the typical seeds and grains available online, one of the first things you'll notice when sprouting wild seeds and grains is that it takes longer, sometimes much longer.

Most commercial seeds will sprout in 3 to 7 days, although this range can vary based on factors such as temperature, humidity, and the freshness of the seeds. Here are some examples of common commercial seeds/grains, their flavor profiles, and their typical sprouting times when they're grown in a jar (of course, microgreens take even longer):

Alfalfa seeds; 5 to 7 days: One of the most popular sprouting seeds due to rich nutrient content, ease of sprouting, and crisp, fresh flavor.

Wild arugula microgreens after 3 weeks.

Broccoli seeds; 3 to 5 days: Highly valued for their health benefits and, of course, they taste like . . . broccoli. Quite a few types of wild mustard and wild radish seeds have an identical flavor.

Mung beans; 3 to 5 days: A staple in Asian cuisines, known for their crunchy texture and slightly sweet taste.

Radish seeds; 5 to 7 days: A spicy flavor, similar to mature radishes, adding a nice kick to salads and sandwiches. Wild radish seeds have a similar, albeit even stronger flavor.

Salad mix; 5 to 7 days: Usually a mix of alfalfa, radish, broccoli, and clover seeds. Perfect as a topping for soups or an addition to salads, sandwiches, wraps, smoothies, and juices.

Chickpeas (garbanzo beans); 2 to 3 days: These sprouts have a slightly nutty flavor and are great in salads or as a crunchy snack.

Clover seeds; 4 to 6 days: Similar to alfalfa sprouts in taste and appearance.

Wild sprouts and microgreens tend to take longer than their civilized counterparts. It's not uncommon for sprouting to take 1 to 2 weeks and for microgreens to take even more time, although there are exceptions.

Wild seeds or grains often take longer to sprout for several reasons. Many come from plants that have adapted to tough or unpredictable environments. These seeds may have hard outer shells or need specific conditions, like steady moisture or changes in temperature, to start sprouting. This helps them survive in nature by preventing them from sprouting at the wrong time. And unlike commercial seeds and grains, wild ones haven't been bred for quick growth or high yields. Commercial seeds and grains are designed to germinate fast and easily, but wild ones focus on survival, not speed. Many have even adapted for a survival technique called dormancy. This means they might have hard shells or natural chemicals that stop them from sprouting until the environment is just right for the sprout's success. If conditions aren't perfect, it can take longer for the seeds to germinate.

Even though they take more time, sprouting and growing microgreens from wild seeds and grains is worth it. Not only do they have unique flavors, textures, and nutrients that you won't find in store-bought options, but growing them gives you a chance to connect with nature and learn about a variety of plants. Furthermore, you're sparing your wallet and getting free organic greens out of the process.

Cultivating Wilder Sprouts

There are several methods for sprouting, each with its own advantages depending on the type of seeds or grains and your preferences. Sprouting in a jar is my favorite method, though, because it's not too complicated. It involves soaking your seeds or grains in water for a specific amount of time to initiate germination, then draining and rinsing them regularly through a sprouting lid to provide moisture and prevent mold growth. The jar is typically kept at an angle to ensure proper drainage and airflow, promoting the seeds' growth into sprouts. After a few days of this process, depending on the type of seeds or grains, the sprouts are ready to eat, offering a nutritious addition to meals.

Note that not all seeds can be sprouted in jars. Many wild mustard seeds, for instance, are so small that they slip through the mesh of a sprouting lid. Additionally, certain seeds produce a mucilaginous coating when wet, complicating the sprouting process. Examples include the native golden chia, some varieties of stinging nettles, broadleaf plantain, and certain mustard seeds. If you can't sprout your seeds in jars, there are alternative methods available, such as using paper towels (see Sprouting on Paper Towels, page 212), specialized sprouting mats, or even soil (see Cultivating Wilder Microgreens, page 215). There are also such things as sprouting bags, which serve as an alternative to jars, but I haven't experimented with this method.

Finally, it is important to understand that sprouting isn't always the optimal approach. For instance, cultivating tumbleweed mustard or stinging nettles as microgreens in soil proves to be a far better method than attempting to sprout them.

Sprouting wild seeds and grains is highly experimental, and the time it takes to sprout the ones you find in your location will vary immensely. When I started, resources on the process were scarce to nonexistent. Should you decide to explore sprouting with your local wild seeds, brace yourself for results that might defy usual expectations. For example, my wild arugula seeds sprouted at the same speed as the regular commercial arugula seeds, but curly dock or lamb's-quarter seeds took much longer. The record went to my black mustard seeds, which took 12 days! After a week, I was about to throw them out when I noticed a few seeds starting to sprout.

SPROUTING IN JARS

Using a glass jar, my favorite method for sprouting wild seeds and grains, is an easy and efficient way to cultivate fresh, nutritious sprouts at home. Start with small batches to find the right quantities for your needs.

Equipment

1–2 tablespoons seeds or grains
Clean, wide-mouth glass pint (500 ml) jar
Cold water
Sprouting lid or cheesecloth and a rubber band

Soaking Time Guidelines

Drawing from my modest sprouting experiences, I adhere to a simple guideline that should also help your journey into the world of wild sprouts: soak small seeds for about 4 to 6 hours, and soak larger seeds overnight, approximately 8 hours.

Examples of small seeds include lamb's-quarter, shortpod mustard, wild amaranth, tumble-weed and tansy mustard, among others. For large seeds, examples include black or brown mustard, wild fennel, chia, curly dock, stinging nettles, and the like.

Method

1. Choose seeds and grains from your wild pantry that are suitable for sprouting or experimentation, such as black mustard, arugula, or wild radish.
2. Add the seeds to your jar and cover them with cold water. Place the sprouting lid or cheesecloth on top.
3. Soak the seeds at room temperature and out of direct sunlight, overnight or for the recommended period for your specific type (see Soaking Time Guidelines).
4. After soaking, drain the water through the lid or cheesecloth. Rinse 2 or 3 times by adding fresh water, swirling it around the jar, and draining again. Afterward, invert the jar at an angle in a bowl or dish rack to allow complete drainage and airflow. Keep the jar at room temperature and out of direct sunlight. Rinse and drain at least twice daily. After each rinse, invert the jar again.
5. Most wild seeds and grains begin to sprout within a week and are typically ready to eat in 7 to 10 days, although some of them might take longer. To green up your sprouts, place the jar near a window during the last day of sprouting, but avoid direct sunlight.
6. Once your sprouts reach the desired length, give them a final rinse and remove any unsprouted seeds or hulls, if possible. While not strictly necessary, removing hulls improves texture.
7. After the final rinse, drain thoroughly. I like to use a salad spinner for this.
8. Refrigerate sprouts in a clean, closed container. A plastic bag with a damp paper towel works well. Sprouts should last about a week, but always check for signsof spoilage before eating.

Place seeds in a clean jar and cover with cool water. Place the sprouting lid on top. Soak the seeds overnight or for the soaking period recommended for your specific type of seeds.

Drain, then turn the jar upside down and let it rest at an angle to allow for drainage and airflow.

Continue to rinse and drain the seeds at least twice a day.

While the seeds are sprouting, keep the jar at room temperature out of direct sunlight.

Once the sprouts have reached the desired length, drain them well after a final rinse. Remove any unsprouted seeds or hulls if you can.

Refrigerate the sprouts in a clean closed container.

Seed-Specific Notes

Wild mustard seeds: Mustard seeds come in various sizes. Many of them are very tiny, so I avoid sprouting those in jars. Instead, I use the paper towel method (page 212) or grow them as microgreens in soil. Larger mustard seeds, such as black or brown mustard, wild radish, or field mustard, work very well in jars. I soak these larger mustard seeds for 8 hours, then proceed with the usual sprouting procedure of draining and rinsing.

While commercial seeds from the brassica family—such as radish, arugula, or broccoli—sprout within 3 to 5 days, black or brown mustard seeds take up to 12 days to be ready for harvest. My local wild arugula took 5 days—just a tad longer than commercial seeds.

Wild amaranth seeds: Despite their small size, I successfully sprouted wild amaranth seeds in a jar because they tend to clump together, so the seeds didn't pass through the sprouting lid mesh.

I soaked the seeds for 6 hours before following the standard sprouting process of draining and rinsing. The sprouts were ready to harvest in 7 days. The flavor profile is quite amazing—they taste like beets.

Lamb's-quarter seeds: Although these seeds are also tiny, I managed to sprout them in a jar, and not too many escaped through the fine mesh. I soaked them for 6 hours before following the standard sprouting process of draining and rinsing.

The sprouts were ready to harvest in 7 days. They had an absolutely beautiful reddish-purple color, even more pronounced than the amaranth sprouts.

Wild fennel: These took longer than I thought they would—around 10 days to sprout. Many of the seeds didn't sprout, and I suspect I should have collected them earlier. They're usually ready at the end of summer. Quite delicious, though.

Example: Sprouting Curly Dock Seeds

Curly dock offers a good example of dealing with more unusual seeds and grains. At first, I didn't think I would be able to sprout these seeds at all due to their strange papery, winged casings (see page 97), but the jar method ended up working quite nicely.

Attempting to separate the seeds from the casings proved challenging, so I opted to sprout them as they were—papery seed casings and all—and see what happened. I placed the seeds inside a jar, soaked them in water for 8 hours, and then drained them.

The soaking and draining process took longer than I expected. After 7 days, I still couldn't see any signs of sprouting and began to wonder if I had a batch of bad seeds. Nevertheless, I continued with the process and—eureka!—in a few days I caught a glimpse of the first sprout. Although I'd learned through experimentation that some wild seeds take quite a while to sprout, this was the first time I'd observed the process take 12 days, which seems to be the norm for dock seeds.

Separating the casings from the sprouted seeds turned out to be fairly easy. Once the sprouts reached the desired stage, the key was to transfer them to a bowl of water and stir them vigorously with my hand to detach the sprouts from the chaff. The seed casings floated to the surface, and I then used a small strainer to remove them.

Put the seeds in a clean jar and cover them with cold water. Secure the sprouting lid on top and soak the seeds overnight.

Drain and place the jar upside down at an angle to allow for drainage and airflow. Continue to rinse and drain the seeds at least twice a day.

A few casings remained on the sprouts and took a few minutes to pick off by hand. The result was a harvest of delicious lemony sprouts, perfect for adding to a salad, soup, or sandwich.

Once the sprouts reach the desired stage, vigorously stir them in water with your hand to separate the sprouts from the chaff.

Use a small strainer or similar utensil to remove the casings.

Remove any lingering casings by hand. It's not too difficult and takes only a few minutes.

The result is delicious lemony sprouts, which are a perfect addition to a salad, soup, or sandwich.

SPROUTING ON PAPER TOWELS

Most of the time I use the jar system to sprout my seeds and grains, but some seeds are so small they would pass through the mesh sprouting lid and go down the drain. This is the case with many of the mustard seeds I harvest locally, such as tansy or tumbleweed mustard, as well as other seeds such as lamb's-quarter, chickweed, and stinging nettle.

Paper towels are an inexpensive medium for germinating small seeds and cultivating sprouts. While regular paper towels work, I prefer to use unbleached ones, which can be found in some supermarkets. You may wonder, how is it possible to grow a plant on paper alone, which has no nutritional value? The solution resides in the seed, which contains all the nutrients necessary for its initial sprouting and growth. Water and light are all we need to provide. Keep in mind that while paper towels work well for small-scale or temporary setups, they may not be the best medium for growing sprouts, as they lack the nutrients needed for long-term growth.

Equipment

Paper towels
Spray bottle
Cold water
Shallow dish, plate, or storage container
Seeds
Plastic wrap or lid

Method

1. Take 3 sheets of paper towel and fold them in half once. If necessary, cut them with scissors to fit your container.
2. Spray the paper towels with water until they are damp but not soaked, and place them in the container.
3. Sprinkle the seeds evenly across the surface of the paper towel, making sure to spread them out so they have enough space to grow. Mist the seeds until damp.
4. Cover the container loosely with plastic wrap or a lid. It doesn't need to be airtight. In fact, if you are using a tight lid, you may want to poke a few holes in it.
5. Place the container in a somewhat warm area out of direct sunlight. The idea is to maintain moisture and create a favorable environment for germination. Seeds don't need light at this stage of the process, and I often place a towel on top of the container to keep it dark until the seeds sprout.
6. Check the paper towels regularly to ensure they remain moist. If they start to dry out, mist lightly with water.
7. A couple of days before you plan to harvest, move the container outside or close to a window to give the sprouts some sun. This enhances their flavor, texture, and color. Note that the ideal temperature for sprouting is between 65 and 85°F (18–29°C). The sprouts are ready to harvest when they reach your desired size, usually within 7 to 12 days. After this point, the seeds will deplete their nutrient reserves and the greens will wither.

Sprinkle the seeds evenly across the surface of a damp paper towel inside a container.

Mist the seeds and make sure they are damp as well.

Cover the container loosely with plastic wrap or a lid. It doesn't need to be airtight.

Seeds don't need light in the beginning of the process; place away from sunlight or cover.

When the sprouts show up, place the container in an area with natural light, such as a windowsill.

Ensure the sprouts remain moist. Once they have reached the desired size, they can be harvested.

Once you've mastered the basics, it's fine to bend the rules a little. I usually skip covering with plastic wrap; instead, after preparing the paper towels as usual and spreading the seeds on top, give the seeds an extra spray of water. Without a cover, you'll need to water more frequently due to increased evaporation, which requires some discipline. I check my sprouts a couple times a day, usually spraying them in the morning and again before bed. In hot Southern California weather, I often pour water directly over the sprouts and then tilt the container to drain off any excess before setting it back down. I might check and add more water midday, then repeat my routine before bedtime. I like simplicity, it really works!

Sprouted shortpod mustard seeds.

Suggested Seeds

Seeds that grow well on paper towels include:

Lamb's-quarter
Wild mustards, such as black mustard, shortpod mustard, and tumbleweed mustard
Stinging nettle
Wild arugula
Various amaranths, such as Palmer amaranth (*Amaranthus palmeri*), redroot pigweed (*Amaranthus retroflexus*), and prostrate pigweed (*Amaranthus blitoides*)

Dehydrating Sprouts

Dehydrated sprouts are absolutely delicious. Very often, their flavors are enhanced by the dehydration process. They're a nice addition to soups or can be used as garnish for your dishes.

Dehydrate sprouts at 125 to 135°F (52–57°C) for 6 to 12 hours until completely dry and brittle. Then store them in a closed container, like a jar.

Cultivating Wilder Microgreens

One of my favorite uses for wild seeds is growing tasty microgreens, which can be used in a multitude of dishes, including salads, sandwiches, and wraps, or as garnishes on soups, pastas, and other entrees. Their versatility makes them an easy nutritional boost to a wide array of meals, wild or not. The great thing about microgreens is that you can eat them at any stage of growth. For example, I often harvest my black mustard microgreens as soon as the first set of true leaves appears—they're barely bigger than sprouts, but the flavor is amazing. Just don't plant too many seeds at once. It's easy to overcrowd and "suffocate" them with sheer quantity.

Seeds from plants in the brassica family are perfect for growing microgreens. In Southern California, there are over 10 different types of mustard that I use. My favorite is wild arugula, or should I say "feral" arugula, which is plentiful in the local hills. Black mustard and wild radish seeds also make for very tasty microgreens.

Yet the brassica family isn't the only option. I've successfully grown microgreens from lamb's-quarter, various wild amaranths (including *Amaranthus hybridus*, *A. retroflexus*, *A. palmeri*, *A. viridis*, and others), stinging nettles, curly dock, chickweed, and wild fennel, among others. This diversity provides ample opportunity for experimentation in your microgreen cultivation.

The variety of mediums available for growing plants, including microgreens, caters to different gardening preferences and systems, ranging from traditional soil-based growing to mats made of various materials to modern hydroponic setups. Some gardeners also use artificial lights to grow microgreens indoors. In this book, we'll keep things simple, using natural light and utensils and materials you can find in your home. The key to successful growth without artificial light is ensuring your microgreens receive enough natural sunlight and are kept in a suitable environment. During shorter days or in regions

Wild amaranth microgreens—redroot pigweed.

with less natural sunlight, however, you might need to supplement with artificial light if you cannot find a location that maximizes available light.

Originally, I thought pretty much any soil could work to grow microgreens, but I've learned a lot over the last two years! Although many edible "weeds" are quite adaptable to various soil types, starting with good soil often increases the size of your harvest. Use a light, organic potting mix that allows for good drainage, or forage your own (see Foraging and Sterilizing Soil, page 221).

Equipment

Growing trays or containers with drainage holes
Potting mix
Seeds or seedpods
Spray bottle
Plastic lid or wrap
Scissors

Method

1. Select a spot in your home that receives plenty of natural sunlight and choose the seeds you want to use.
2. Fill trays or containers with 2 to 3 inches (5–7.5 cm) of a quality organic potting mix.
3. Sprinkle the seeds evenly across the soil surface, then add around ¼ inch (0.5 cm) of soil on top. There's no need to bury them deeply; a light covering of soil is enough. You can press the surface gently so the soil makes good contact with the buried seeds.
4. Initially, water to moisten the soil without disturbing the seeds. A spray bottle is ideal for this. Keep the soil consistently moist but not waterlogged throughout the growth period.
5. Covering the trays with a clear plastic lid or another tray helps keep moisture in and aid germination. Just be sure to remove the cover as soon as the seeds have sprouted to prevent mold growth.
6. Place your trays near a light source. If the light comes from a window, you may need to rotate your trays daily to ensure even growth, as microgreens tend to lean toward the light source. Another solution, which I use during fall and winter, is to place the tray outside during the day if it's not freezing and bring them inside at night. The ideal temperature for growing microgreens varies, but a general guideline is between 65 and 75°F (18–24°C).
7. Continue to keep the soil moist with a spray bottle.
8. Most wild microgreens are ready to harvest in around 2 to 4 weeks. When the first true leaves begin to emerge (this is the second set of leaves you'll see, following the cotyledons), it's time to harvest.

Use an organic potting mix that is light and allows for good drainage, or forage your own soil.

Fill the tray with the potting mix, moisten the soil, then sprinkle the seeds evenly across the soil surface.

Cover the seeds with around ¼ inch (0.5 cm) of soil. Press on the soil gently to ensure it makes good contact with the buried seeds.

Moisten the soil without disturbing the seeds, ideally using a spray bottle. Throughout the growth period, keep the soil consistently moist but not waterlogged.

Cover the tray with a clear plastic lid or wrap to keep moisture in. Remove the cover as soon as the seeds have sprouted, then place the tray near a light source.

Most microgreens are ready to harvest in 3 to 4 weeks. Use clean, sharp scissors to cut the microgreens just above the soil line.

Use clean, sharp scissors to cut the microgreens just above the soil line. After harvesting, you can compost the soil and roots.

Notes on Growing Wilder Microgreens

"There are no rules." This is one of my favorite sayings and it applies pretty well to wild microgreens, which can grow at unpredictable rates, depending on the time of year, the quality of light they get, and the temperature. While most wild microgreens typically grow in 3 to 4 weeks, there are exceptions, and patience is often required. A few times, mine just stopped growing altogether and ended up as glorified sprouts.

For reference, regular microgreens typically take 7 to 21 days to grow, depending on the variety:

Fast-growing varieties (7 to 10 days): radish, mustard, arugula, broccoli.
Medium-growing varieties (10 to 14 days): kale, cabbage, Swiss chard.
Slower-growing varieties (14 to 21 days): basil, cilantro, parsley, beets.

Wild plants usually take longer. Based on my experience, and factoring in climate variations, here's what you might expect:

Brassica family plants (2 to 4 weeks): wild radish, wild mustards.
Common wild edibles (4 to 6 weeks): nettles, amaranth, chickweed, miner's lettuce, curly dock, lamb's quarter, etc.

Some feral plants, like wild arugula, might be ready in as little as 2 weeks. On the other hand, more exotic savory plants like wild fennel, yampah, and wild carrot can take over 5 weeks.

You might be thinking, is growing wild microgreens even worth the effort and uncertainty? Absolutely! Experimenting with local wild plants is so much fun, and having access to unique, fresh flavors at any time of year is priceless. I once enjoyed chickweed microgreens during a harsh mountain winter—they were like tiny bursts of spring and pure soul therapy! Plus, growing them teaches you to recognize how edible wild plants look at different stages of growth.

Wild microgreens at week 3. From top left: Dwarf nettle (*Urtica urens*), chickweed (*Stellaria media*), Palmer amaranth (*Amaranthus palmeri*), black mustard (*Brassica nigra*), and two types of miner's lettuce (*Claytonia perfoliata* and *Claytonia parviflora*).

GROWING MICROGREENS FROM SEED PODS

When handling wild seeds that are difficult to extract from their seedpods, such as wild radish, planting the whole pod in soil and growing microgreens is a useful alternative. Locally, some mustard seeds, such as London rocket, are so tiny that growing microgreens straight from the small seedpods can be a worthwhile option. It's a straightforward process, and, similar to growing from seeds, it allows you to enjoy fresh greens in just a few weeks. Note that the specific steps may vary slightly based on the type of seedpods you're using.

Equipment

Growing tray or container with drainage holes
Organic potting soil
Seedpods (wild radish or other varieties)
Spray bottle or watering can
Plastic lid or wrap
Scissors

Method

1. Fill your tray or container with 2 to 3 inches (5–7.5 cm) of quality organic potting soil that is light and allows for good drainage.
2. Sprinkle the seedpods evenly across the soil surface, then add ¼ to ½ inch (0.5–1 cm) of soil on top. For wild radish pods, I usually use ½ inch. You can gently press the soil surface so it makes good contact with the buried seedpods.
3. Water to moisten the soil. A spray bottle is ideal for this. Keep the soil consistently moist but not waterlogged throughout the growth period.
4. Covering the tray with a clear plastic lid or another tray can help retain moisture and aid germination. Just be sure to remove the cover as soon as the seeds have sprouted to prevent mold growth.
5. Place your trays near a light source. The ideal temperature for growing microgreens varies, but a general guideline is between 65 and 75°F (18–24°C). Continue to keep the soil moist until harvest time, usually 2 to 4 weeks.

Growing microgreens from wild radish pods.

Foraging and Sterilizing Soil

At the beginning of my experiments, I bought regular organic potting mix to grow my microgreens, but eventually I switched to foraging soil. My friend has a property in the Angeles National Forest, with a very old oak forest growing on part of it. I've always been in love with the earthy smell of the soil there; over countless years, lots of leaves and other organic matter have slowly composted and created a very rich mixture that, in my opinion, rivals any store-bought organic potting mix.

A lightweight and porous medium is essential for the delicate roots of microgreens to penetrate easily and access water and nutrients without being waterlogged. One of my first steps is to strain my foraged soil to remove twigs, small rocks, and other debris—another good reason to collect all kinds of strainers of different sizes.

Most commercial potting mixes are somewhat sterile, but soil used for growing microgreens doesn't necessarily have to be. However, it should be free from pathogens, other "weed" seeds, and pests—including their eggs or larvae—to reduce the risk of infestations that could damage your microgreens. Sterilizing your soil is especially important if you're reusing soil previously used for other gardening projects. I once reused soil that I had used to grow mustard microgreens in order to grow amaranth microgreens, and I ended up with a mess when some of the mustard seeds that didn't germinate the first time around decided to finally sprout.

Sterilization is not a "must," and, frankly, I never touch the beautiful soil I get from my friend's place. But should you choose to do it, here are two simple methods for sterilizing soil at home, both utilizing heat treatment through baking or steaming. Note that both methods can produce strong, earthy odors. I like it, personally, but if it's not your thing, ensure good ventilation in your kitchen or wherever you're sterilizing the soil. There are other methods of sterilization that require expensive equipment or professional facilities, so I stick to the two methods described here.

Remember, there is no need to be extreme with foraging soil. If you live in a large city and can't find good soil nearby, purchasing a pre-sterilized, high-quality potting mix designed for seed starting is the way to go. And it's totally okay to have fun, grab some good-looking soil from somewhere, skip the sterilizing, and experiment with growing microgreens. That's exactly what I did in the beginning, and I learned so much along the way.

THE OVEN METHOD

Materials

Foraged soil
Spray bottle
Metal tray or glass baking dish, or another oven-safe container
Aluminum foil
Cooking thermometer

Method

1. Preheat your oven to 180°F (82°C).
2. Moisten the soil slightly so it's damp but not soggy. This helps to conduct heat more evenly during the sterilization process.
3. Spread the soil evenly in an oven-safe container. The soil layer should be no more than 2 to 4 inches (5–10 cm) deep for even heating.
4. Cover the container tightly with aluminum foil to help retain moisture and ensure even heating.
5. Place the container in the preheated oven. Use a thermometer to monitor the soil's temperature. The goal is to get it up to 180°F (82°C) and hold it there for 30 minutes. Overheating the soil can destroy beneficial organisms and alter the soil structure, making it less suitable for plant growth. Don't go above 200°F (93°C) in the oven.
6. After sterilization, allow the soil to cool completely before removing the foil. Watch out for steam that might escape when uncovering.

THE STEAMING METHOD

Steaming is an effective alternative to the oven method. I've done this in the past by using the rack of my water bath canner and placing the soil in a cheesecloth.

Materials

Foraged soil
Cheesecloth or heat-resistant container
Steamer basket or rack
Large pot with lid or foil cover
Cooking thermometer

Method

1. Place the soil in a heat-resistant container or cheesecloth, then put the container in a steamer basket or on a rack above a pot of boiling water. Cover the setup with a lid or foil to trap the steam.
2. Allow the soil to reach at least 180°F (82°C), and ensure it remains there for 30 minutes.
3. Allow the soil to cool completely before using it for planting.

CALCULATING YOUR SOIL PH

If you forage soil for growing microgreens, it's important to know its acidity. The acidity of soil is measured by its pH level, which tells us if the soil is acidic, neutral, or alkaline. For microgreens, the soil's pH is important because it affects how well these tiny plants can absorb nutrients from the soil. Most microgreens prefer a slightly acidic to neutral soil pH (around 6.0 to 7.0) to thrive and be healthy. It's good to check the acidity of foraged soil in order to give your microgreens the best chance. For example, the soil from my local pine forest turned out to be too acidic to be used for many microgreens, but the soil from the oak forest on my friend's property is perfect.

You can calculate the pH of your soil by using a test strip (available in garden centers or online) or a digital pH tester (available online) and the following instructions.

Materials

Foraged soil
Measuring cup
Clean container and spoon
Distilled water
Soil pH test strips or digital pH tester

Method

1. Take a small sample of the soil to be tested. It's best to collect soil 1 to 2 inches (2–5 cm) below the surface to avoid any contaminants that might be on the surface.
2. Place about ½ cup (118 mg) of soil into the clean container and slowly add ½ cup (118 ml) distilled water to the soil, mixing as you go, until you have a muddy consistency. Allow the soil-water mixture to settle for a few minutes so the solids can separate from the liquid.
3. Once the mixture has settled, dip the pH test strip (or digital pH tester) into the liquid portion of your soil slurry for a few seconds. If you're using pH test strips, remove the strip and shake off any excess liquid. Compare the color of the strip to the color chart provided with your pH test strips. This will give you the pH level of your soil. If you're using a digital pH tester, check the reading. The pH scale ranges from 0 to 14, with 7 being neutral. Numbers below 7 indicate acidity, while numbers above 7 indicate alkalinity. If the pH is too low, you may wish to find another soil.

It is possible to lower soil pH (make it more acidic) by adding substances like sulfur or peat moss, or to raise soil pH (make it more alkaline) by adding lime or wood ash, but such techniques are beyond the scope of this book.

CHAPTER 7

Culinary Fun

When most people think of seeds and grains, they picture the basics: bread, rice, oats—staples that make up our everyday meals. Wheat, the cornerstone of bread, finds its way onto almost every table. Rice follows closely, appearing as a simple side dish or in everything from hearty stews, pilafs, and casseroles to sweet, sticky desserts. Breakfast often comes to mind, too: a warming bowl of oatmeal, crunchy granola, or maybe a savory porridge made from rice or quinoa. Even if you're not much of a cook, these comforting meals are quick and satisfying classics that everyone knows, the kind of food that feels like a hug on a chilly morning.

Seeds and grains also make effortless snacks and garnishes. Who hasn't grabbed a handful of sunflower seeds, pumpkin seeds, or popcorn for a quick bite? Or noticed how sesame and poppy seeds elevate breads and salads with their subtle texture and flavor? These are the easy wins—seeds and grains sneak a variety of nutrients and tasty pleasures into our diets without us even trying.

But let's step beyond the basics. Wild seeds and grains offer something different, something untamed. They're not just ingredients; they're stars, and I've found that they shine brightest when you let them take the lead. These foods—unavailable in your average store—remind us of what it feels like to live more freely, to eat in ways deeply connected to nature and our ancestors, and to step outside the confines of industrialized food. On their own, they bring history and terroir to your plate, turning a simple meal into something unforgettable.

Sprout them for vibrant salads or grow microgreens that burst with flavor. Ferment them into something extraordinary—imagine kimchi-style

Wild grains and seeds can be wonderful additions to familiar preparations such as salsa, pesto, salads, guacamole, yogurt, hummus, and much more, adding variety, nutrition, and flavors.

ferments or tangy sauerkraut. Toasted grains can become flavorful infusions or transform into drinks thanks to a bit of fermentation magic. And aromatic seeds like mustard, fennel, or carrot? They're powerhouses, adding bold flavors to condiments, sauces, and hearty dishes.

This is just the start of an adventure with wild seeds and grains. Let's dive in and explore the incredible ways they can transform how we cook and eat.

WILD GRAINS TEA

Grains are not just for eating—you can also drink them! Around the world, grains like brown rice, corn, rye, wheat, sorghum, and barley are roasted and steeped in water to create unique, traditional teas. Barley tea, for instance, is a popular beverage in East Asian countries such as Japan (*mugicha*), Korea (*boricha*), and China (*dàmài chá*), where it's enjoyed for its pleasant taste and potential health benefits. It's also caffeine-free, making it suitable for any time of the day. Other traditional roasted-grain beverages, ranging from Japanese *genmaicha* (green tea with popped brown rice) to Korean corn tea (*oksusu cha*), Russian rye tea, and Italian *caffè d'orzo*, offer a variety of flavors, from nutty to sweet.

Of course, because we're more feral, we have to use wild grains. And yes, there are no rules—you can mix and match with what you forage. For the tea in the photograph, I used a mix of wild barley and oats.

Ingredients

2–3 tablespoons foraged grains or store-bought roasted barley grains

Method

1. Preheat a dry skillet over medium heat. Add the grains and stir continuously for about 10 minutes, or until they turn a rich brown color and emit a nutty aroma. Be careful not to burn them. Skip this step if you're using store-bought roasted barley grains.
2. In a large pot, bring 1 quart (1 L) of water to a boil.
3. Add the roasted grains to the boiling water. Reduce the heat to low and let it simmer uncovered for 20 to 30 minutes. The longer you simmer, the stronger the tea.
4. Use a fine-mesh strainer to strain the grains from the tea. Serve hot, or let it cool and serve chilled. The tea will have a light brown color and a mild, nutty flavor.
5. Any leftover tea can be refrigerated for a few days. It's delicious both cold and reheated.

Note: *You can adjust the amount of grain or the brewing time to make the tea stronger or weaker according to your preference. Feel free to add honey, maple syrup, or sugar to taste.*

PRICKLY PEAR AND CHIA SEED JUICE

Making this juice is simpler than you might think, and results in a refreshing, nutritious drink. Locally, I forage fruits from the coastal prickly pear cactus (*Opuntia littoralis*), but in both North and South America, you can often find prickly pears at supermarkets. These are often nopal prickly pear cactus (*Opuntia ficus-indica*) and are usually larger than my foraging finds. It is possible to find prickly pears in Europe, too, especially in Spain, where the cacti are quite common. There are many varieties of prickly pear, each offering unique flavors. This simple yet delicious drink offers the unique tartness of cactus pears paired with the smooth texture of chia seeds.

Ingredients

30 prickly pear cactus fruits or 14 larger nopal cactus fruits
2 tablespoons (about 20 g) chia seeds

Note: *You can make similar drinks with any kind of homemade or store-bought juice. Use a ratio of 1 tablespoon (about 10 g) of chia seeds for every 2 cups (480 ml) of juice.*

Method

1. If foraging, use dry twigs to brush off the glochids (tiny spines) before handling the fruits; make sure to work upwind to avoid getting pricked. Once most of the spines are removed, twist off the fruits with your hands or kitchen tongs and store them in a paper bag or bucket.
2. Soak the cactus pears in cold water for about an hour. This softens any remaining glochids, making the fruits easier to handle.
3. Cut the fruits in half and scoop out the juicy, seed-filled pulp with a spoon, placing it into a blender.
4. Add 1½ cups (360 ml) of water to the fruit pulp and blend on low speed for a few seconds. Alternatively, you can crush the pulp by hand if you enjoy a more traditional approach.
5. Pour the blended mixture through a strainer over a clean bowl and press the juice through with a spoon to remove the seeds. You'll now have a beautiful, thick, carmine-colored juice.
6. Slowly stir in the chia seeds, adding the them gradually to prevent clumping. Keep stirring for about a minute, then let the juice stand for 10 minutes to allow the seeds to expand and thicken the drink.
7. Once ready, pour the juice into a bottle and refrigerate.

WILD YEAST STARTER

A couple of pages ago, we made a grain tea (Wild Grains Tea, page 227). Now, let's get ready to take it to the next level and ferment the tea into a sort of beer. For this, we'll need yeast.

While you can use store-bought brewer's yeast, foraging wild yeast is very easy. That white bloom you see on many berries and fruits like grapes, elderberries, juniper berries, blueberries, apples, and plums isn't just for looks—it's packed with wild yeast. This protective layer is perfect for kick-starting natural fermentation. To harness it, simply soak the fruit in sugar water, and you've got yourself a wild yeast starter.

The goal of a yeast starter is to multiply yeast cells by feeding them sugar, ensuring a robust fermentation when you add it to your brew.

Method

1. Mix 10 percent sugar (by weight) with 90 percent water. Avoid tap water, as chlorine may inhibit fermentation. You can use the same ratio of honey or maple syrup instead of sugar.
2. Pour the sweetened water into a clean jar or bottle with a well-fitted top, leaving enough room for the fruits or berries.
3. Add fruits or berries with a visible white bloom, filling roughly 30 percent of the container's volume. The remaining 70 percent should be liquid.
4. Seal the lid and shake the container 2 to 3 times a day. After shaking, loosen the lid slightly to release built-up fermentation gases (a process known as burping).
5. Within 3 to 5 days (or sooner in warm weather), you should see bubbling—a sign that fermentation is active. Smell the starter to ensure it doesn't have a foul odor; it should smell pleasantly yeasty or fruity.
6. To use the starter, strain out the fruit and add ¼ to ½ cup (90–120 ml) of the starter to 1 quart (1 L) of a brew. Fermentation should begin within 2 to 3 days.

> **Note:** *If your starter doesn't bubble or smells off, discard it and try again. This method is highly reliable and works great for various types of brews. For more in-depth information and recipes, refer to my book* The Wildcrafting Brewer.

Pick wild berries or fruits that have a nice waxy bloom, which contains a lot of yeast.

Mix 10 percent sugar (or honey or maple syrup) and 90 percent water (not from the tap) together in a jar.

Add the fruits or berries until they are roughly 30 percent of the container's volume. Close the lid and shake, then burp the container 2 to 3 times daily.

Around 3 to 5 days later (sooner in hot weather) you will notice some bubbling in the solution. Congratulations, your fermentation is active!

WILD GRAINS "BEER"

I've always wanted to try making a kind of beer with local wild grains. For this batch, I gathered grains from wild oats, cheatgrass, and wild barley. It might be better to call it a "brew," because it's not quite like your typical beer or brewing process. Usually, beer is made by malting, whereby grains (commonly barley) are soaked in water, germinated, and then dried in a kiln to convert starches into fermentable sugars. Here, I skip the malting step, make a tea of pan-roasted grains, and simply add brown sugar. Yet, if I had to place it in a category, I'd say it fits well with beer thanks to its unique taste. It has a mix of interesting flavors—bitter, sour lemon, and earthy tones—and a slightly boozy kick.

Ingredients

2–3 tablespoons (30–45 g) wild grains
1 quart (1 L) filtered water
Couple of mugwort leaves; other herbs like hops or yarrow are also good options for flavoring
3 tablespoons (36 g) brown sugar
Juice of ½ lemon (approximately 20 ml)
¼–½ cup (90–120 ml) Wild Yeast Starter (page 230) or commercial beer yeast

Method

1. Heat a skillet over medium heat and roast the wild grains to your liking. Transfer the grains to a pot, add the water, and bring to a boil. Reduce the heat, cover, and simmer for around 20 minutes.
2. Add the mugwort, sugar, and lemon juice and simmer another 2 minutes before taking the pot off the heat. Let the mixture steep for another 3 minutes to infuse the herbs.
3. Strain the liquid, transfer to a container with an airlock (bottle, jar, or crock), and let it cool.

Heat a skillet over medium heat and roast the wild grains to your liking.

I like my grains to be quite dark. In this case I used wild oats, wild barley, and cheatgrass, but you can make this type of drink with other wild or commercial grains.

4. Add the wild yeast starter or commercial beer yeast and ferment for 2 to 3 days, then transfer to a swing-top bottle. Keep in mind, wild yeast might need a little more time to work its magic. The key sign you're looking for is active fermentation, which you can spot by the bubbles passing through the airlock.

5. Remove the airlock, close the top, and continue the alcoholic fermentation process for another day or two in the closed bottle. Check the carbonation by gently opening the top once a day, then move the bottle to the fridge to halt fermentation once you are satisfied. I usually drink this type of brew within a week. It tastes like a lemony, low-alcohol bitter beer. Quite refreshing!

Transfer the grains to a pot, add water, and bring it to a boil. Reduce the heat and simmer for 10 minutes.

Add the mugwort, sugar, and lemon juice 2 minutes before taking it off the heat. After removing from heat, let it steep for another 5 to 10 minutes to infuse the herbs.

Strain the liquid, transfer to a container with an airlock, and let it cool. Add yeast and ferment for 2 to 3 days, then transfer to a swing-top bottle.

I often use the same bottle during the fermentation process. After 2 to 3 days, I remove the airlock and close the bottle. Check the carbonation by gently opening the top. Place in the fridge when you are satisfied.

KHAKSHIR-INSPIRED DRINK

Khakshir is a traditional Persian drink made with the seeds of tansy mustard, also called flixweed, a member of the mustard family (Brassicaceae). Popular in Iran, this refreshing drink is perfect for hot days and is prized for its health benefits. Similar to a chia seed drink, the seeds form a gel when mixed with liquid. The flavor is nutty, with subtle hints of hazelnuts and beets. Seeds from other plants in the same family can provide a similar taste and texture. Locally, I often use seeds from tumbleweed mustard and London rocket, but flixweed is especially abundant—and invasive—in my area.

Ingredients

1 tablespoon (14 g) flixweed, tumbleweed mustard, or London rocket seeds
1–2 teaspoons (5–10 g) sugar (or sweetener of your choice)
1–2 teaspoons (5–10 ml) freshly squeezed lemon or lime juice, or a few drops of rose water (optional)
Ice cubes, for serving

Method

1. Combine the seeds and 1 cup (250 ml) of cold water in a glass.
2. Add the sugar and stir until dissolved.
3. Add the lemon or lime juice or rose water, if desired.
4. Add ice cubes and stir well.

ANCESTRAL SOUP WITH WILD GRAINS, SEEDS, AND GREENS

You can do a lot of experimentation with this basic recipe, using what you collect from your local terroir, and it's a great example of why foraging grains and seeds is a worthwhile activity. I started extracting and processing the various grains at nine o'clock, and by noon, this delicious, hearty, and nutritious soup was ready.

Eating it was a surreal experience as I realized this kind of gastronomic encounter has likely been absent from most Western palates since the dawn of agriculture. This is a true hunter-gatherer soup, crafted from ingredients untouched by cultivation and unbridled by civilization. You're not just savoring a meal, but truly tasting a long-lost, forgotten era when humanity's sustenance relied on the untamed abundance of the wild.

Ingredients

¼ cup (around 30 g) wild grains and seeds. I used:

- 1 tablespoon (7 g) wild barley grains
- 1 tablespoon (7 g) wild oat grains
- 1 teaspoon (3 g) feral barley
- 1 teaspoon (3 g) foraged millet
- 1 teaspoon (4 g) wild radish seeds
- 1 teaspoon (3 g) great brome grains
- 1 teaspoon (3 g) field mustard seeds

½ teaspoon (2.5 g) salt
2 teaspoons (10 ml) mammoth fat … or olive oil
A couple of mushrooms (wild or commercial), sliced
1 garlic clove, minced
1 cup (236 ml) vegetable or chicken stock (I used homemade wild stock)
1½ ounces (42 g) mixed wild greens (I used lamb's-quarter, wild amaranth, mustard, and wild radish leaves), chopped
1 tender cattail stalk, chopped
2 teaspoons (10 ml) soy sauce (optional)
2 teaspoons (10 ml) apple cider vinegar (optional)

Method

1. Rinse the grains and seeds thoroughly, then place them in a medium-sized pot. Add the salt and enough water to generously cover the grains.
2. Bring the pot to a boil, then reduce the heat to medium-low for a gentle simmer. Cook the grains until tender to the bite, which will vary based on the grains you're using. In this case, it took about 50 minutes. Taste periodically to check doneness. Once cooked, drain and set aside.
3. Heat the olive oil in another medium-sized pot over medium-high heat. Sauté the mushrooms, stirring frequently, until cooked. Add the garlic and stir together with the mushrooms.
4. Add the stock to the pot, then add the cooked grains. Bring the mixture close to a boil. (Stopping short of a boil will help keep the grains intact.)
5. Stir in the wild greens and cattail. Cook for 2 to 3 minutes, or until the greens are wilted and tender. If you're choosing to include them, stir in the soy sauce and apple cider vinegar.
6. Serve the soup warm.

NETTLE SOUP WITH SEEDS

Nettle soup is fantastic for you because it's packed with nutrients—including vitamins A and C, iron, and protein—which can help boost your immune system and improve overall health. It was a popular dish in late winter or early spring in the old days due to the abundance and accessibility of nettles in the wild. Wear gloves while picking and washing the nettles to avoid getting stung.

Ingredients

4 cups (400 g) fresh nettle leaves, washed and tough stems removed
1 tablespoon (15 ml) olive oil or butter
1 onion, finely chopped
1 garlic clove, minced
1 celery stalk, chopped
1 potato, peeled and chopped
1 quart (1 L) vegetable or chicken stock
Salt and pepper, to taste
A splash of cream or yogurt, for serving (optional)
Nettle seeds or roasted sesame seeds, for serving (optional)

Method

1. Blanch the nettles in a pot of boiling water for 1 to 2 minutes to remove the sting. Drain and rinse with cold water to stop the cooking process. Squeeze out excess water and set aside.
2. In a large pot, heat the olive oil or butter over medium heat. Add the onion and garlic, sautéing until the onion is translucent. Add the celery and potato and cook for a couple more minutes, until the vegetables start to soften.
3. Pour in the stock and bring the mixture to a boil. Reduce the heat to a simmer, cover, and let it cook until the potato and celery are tender, about 15 minutes.
4. Add the blanched nettles to the pot just before you are ready to blend the soup. Let them warm in the hot soup for a minute.
5. Using an immersion blender, blend the soup directly in the pot until smooth. Alternatively, you can transfer the soup in batches to a blender, blend it, and then return it to the pot. Season with salt and pepper.
6. If desired, add a splash of cream or yogurt for extra creaminess, and garnish with a pinch of nettle seeds.

HUMBLE SOUTHERN CALIFORNIA BREAKFAST

There are so many culinary applications for wild grains and seeds, but I have to say that one of my favorites is to use them in my morning breakfast cereals.

I usually wake up early, just before sunrise, so I can get outside and admire the start of a new day. It's my meditation time in the mountains. I reflect on the day to come and plan the tasks I want to accomplish.

My first meal is meditative, humble, and an ode to the land, using local ingredients in simple ways. You can easily do something similar wherever you live by adding your own wild seeds and grains, such as nettle or broadleaf plantain seeds, common flax seeds, local pine or maple syrup, foraged fruits and berries, and so on. This breakfast is more than a meal; it's a moment of peace and connection with nature. Enjoy it slowly, appreciating the simplicity and nourishment it provides.

Ingredients

½ organic apple
½ cup (50 g) organic quick oats
1 teaspoon (4 g) dehydrated elderberries
2 teaspoons (6 g) wild chia seeds
1 teaspoon (3 g) roasted thistle sage seeds
1 tablespoon (10 g) boiled wild barley grains
Pinecone syrup (or maple syrup), to taste

Method

1. In a pot, bring ¾ cup (177 ml) of water to a boil. This is the unconventional part of my method, as I find that boiling the water separately ensures the oats and other ingredients meld perfectly.
2. While the water is heating, chop the apple and place it in a bowl along with the quick oats, elderberries, wild chia seeds, roasted thistle sage seeds, and boiled wild barley grains. Pour the boiling water into the bowl over the dry ingredients. Stir gently to combine.
3. Allow the mixture to sit for 5 to 7 minutes. This allows the oats to soften and absorb the flavors and the temperature to reach the perfect level for eating. Drizzle pinecone or maple syrup over the top, to taste.

Note: *Raw elderberries are unsafe for consumption and must be cooked before being eaten. My method for drying elderberries is to first dehydrate the berries at 200°F (93°C) for 30 minutes, then reduce the temperature to 160°F (71°C) and continue dehydrating until they are fully dried. This is my personal method and has not been scientifically tested.*

IRON AGE PORRIDGE EXPLORATION

In my ongoing journey with edible wild grains and seeds, I've come across some fascinating research and discoveries. One of my most meaningful takeaways has been a new understanding of the "invention" of agriculture. The more I learn, the more I realize it wasn't some sudden breakthrough, as we're often taught in school or history books, but rather a gradual shift over time. I can imagine early hunter-gatherers slowly incorporating grains like rye, barley, and einkorn into their diets while foraging.

This got me thinking: what did my European ancestors actually eat? I decided to recreate an Iron Age meal, using ingredients as close as possible to what they might have used. It's based on archaeological studies of ancient human remains like the Tollund Man (circa 400 BCE), Ötzi the Iceman (circa 3000 BCE), and the Grauballe Man (circa 200 BCE) and the analyses of their stomach contents (see chapter 5).

This research has revealed that in some regions and time periods, porridge wasn't just made with cultivated grains—it often included a wide range of wild seeds and grains, and in some cases, it was entirely wild. In fact, blending cultivated grains with wild seeds and grains seemed to be a common practice, though this idea confused some archaeologists at first. It's likely because modern agriculture has imposed a divide between "weeds" and "crops." Back then, those "weeds" were simply an additional source of nutrition—what we'd now call "wild food."

This porridge "recipe" is inspired by what might have been eaten in the European Iron Age. The base, about 80 percent of the meal, is barley, to which I add wild oats, wild barley, brome grains, field mustard seeds, lamb's-quarter seeds, acorn flour, and greens like stinging nettles, chickweed, and orache. To start, I crush the barley with a stone grinder, combine it with water (4 parts water to 1 part barley) in a pot, and simmer it for about 50 minutes. While the barley cooks, I add wild ingredients at appropriate intervals for each to cook properly. For example, lamb's-quarter seeds need about 25 minutes of cooking after proper rinsing. (See chapter 4 for cooking guidelines for other wild grains and seeds.) For sweetness, I add dried elderberries, blueberries, and a drizzle of pinyon pine–flavored honey to the cooked porridge.

This type of porridge gets easier with practice and really highlights how much nutritional variety has been lost in today's processed breakfast cereals. Taste as you go, and add water if needed to get the consistency you like. In no time, you'll become a Neolithic porridge pro.

DEHYDRATED WILD SEED CRACKERS (NO COOKING REQUIRED)

I'd been wanting to make crackers entirely from wild ingredients for a long time, and now I have! These crackers make a great snack, and the process couldn't be easier.

The base ingredient is chia seeds. I'm fortunate to have plenty growing around my pottery studio here in Southern California, but if you don't have wild chia available, you can use store-bought chia seeds. You can also mix wild and regular seeds, and experiment with flavors like miso, nutritional yeast, or herb blends like herbes de Provence or Italian seasoning—the possibilities are endless. I kept my recipe simple to highlight the natural flavors of the wild seeds, although I toasted the thistle sage seeds to give the crackers a slightly nutty, sweet flavor and an extra crunch. If you don't have thistle sage seeds you can use toasted sesame seeds.

Ingredients (for around 20 crackers)

¼ cup (40 g) chia seeds
4 teaspoons (10 g) toasted thistle sage seeds
2 teaspoons (3 g) nettle seeds
2 teaspoons (6 g) tumbleweed mustard seeds
1 teaspoon (3 g) tansy mustard seeds
1 teaspoon (3 g) toasted sesame seeds (optional)
½ teaspoon (2.5 g) salt

Method

1. Put the chia seeds in a bowl and whisk in 1 cup (236 ml) of water. Let the chia seeds absorb the water for 30 minutes, then add the rest of the seeds and the salt. Whisk again to combine.
2. Cover the bowl with plastic wrap and refrigerate for 6 to 8 hours.
3. Using a spatula, evenly spread the mixture, which will have become thick and gelatinous, on parchment paper, to about 2 mm thickness.
4. Place in a dehydrator at 140°F (60°C) until crispy, which should take a couple of hours.
5. Break the sheet into smaller cracker pieces. Let them cool, then store in a glass jar. They keep well for up to a month, but I tend to finish them much sooner!

"MARY'S GONE WILD" CRACKERS

I love tasty, crunchy crackers, so I decided to play around with a recipe loosely based on Mary's Gone Crackers, a brand found in some American supermarkets. Although in this case, "Mary's Gone Wild."

The result is super tasty, but it's still a work in progress. Nevertheless, this is a good base for making wilder crackers, and you can use your own foraged seeds and grains. Of course, you can simplify the recipe, too.

Ingredients

1 cup (200 g) cooked brown rice
1 cup (185 g) cooked quinoa
1½ tablespoons (22 ml) soy sauce
2 teaspoons (6 g) garlic powder
2 teaspoons (4 g) wild spice blend or Italian herbs
2 teaspoons (5 g) tumbleweed mustard seeds
2 teaspoons (5 g) tansy mustard seeds
2 teaspoons (5 g) golden chia seeds
1 teaspoon (2 g) black sage seeds
2 teaspoons (6 g) flax seeds
2 teaspoons (6 g) roasted sesame seeds
½ teaspoon (1.5 g) sedge seeds
1 teaspoon (5 g) cooked lamb's-quarter seeds

Method

1. Preheat the oven to 350°F (175°C) and line a baking sheet with parchment paper.
2. Make a paste with the cooked rice and quinoa in a stone grinder or blender, then transfer to a bowl.
3. Add the remaining ingredients, and mix well to make a thick, sticky dough. Add water if necessary.
4. Roll small pieces of dough into 1-inch (2.5 cm) balls and place them on the parchment paper about 3 inches (7.5 cm) apart.
5. Cut a small square out of a separate sheet of parchment paper and brush one side lightly with olive oil. Working one by one, place the paper (oil side down) on top of each ball and, using a jar top or something similar, press down to flatten until the ball is around 2¼ inches (4 cm) in diameter.
6. Bake the crackers for around 15 minutes. I often rotate the tray after the first 10 minutes.
7. Let cool before eating.

SAVORY FLATBREADS

This recipe is a simple, fun way to make flavorful flatbreads using local wild seeds and grains. It's adapted from my first book, *The New Wildcrafted Cuisine* (page 334). The basic mix of flour, olive oil, water, and salt is super versatile and easy to adapt to your foraged ingredients. Like the "Mary's Gone Wild" crackers (page 245), you can experiment with local ingredients. For example, instead of California buckwheat flour, try wild oat flour, barley flour, or flour made from your local wild grains and seeds. Have fun with it!

Ingredients

¼ cup (32 g) curly dock seed flour
1½ cups (180 g) einkorn flour or bread flour
¼ cup (30 g) California buckwheat flour
2 teaspoons (11 g) sea salt
⅓ cup (80 ml) olive oil
About ¾ cup (180 ml) warm water (adjust as needed)
2 teaspoons (3 g) Italian seasoning, herbes de Provence, or other herbs of your choice

Method

1. Preheat the oven to 400°F (200°C) and line a baking sheet with parchment paper.
2. Mix all the flours and the sea salt in a bowl. Add the olive oil and mix with your hands while slowly adding the warm water until the dough forms a solid consistency. Adjust with more flour if needed.
3. Knead the dough for about 5 minutes, then shape it into a ball, cover with plastic wrap, and let it rest for 30 minutes.
4. Using a rolling pin, roll the dough into flatbreads. Brush with olive oil and sprinkle with your toppings of choice. Roll lightly one more time to press the toppings into the dough, then brush with more olive oil.
5. Bake for 8 to 12 minutes, keeping an eye on the flatbreads to avoid overcooking.

Note: *You can get creative with toppings! I like using garlic powder, herb powders like chickweed or chervil, chili flakes, salt, or savory herbs such as sage. Store-bought herb blends like Italian seasoning or za'atar also work great.*

WILD FLOURS BREAD

This is a project I've been wanting to do for ages—making bread with flours from wild grains, including some of my area's most invasive local plants. For this loaf, I used flours made from wild oats, wild barley/foxtail, cheatgrass, curly dock, and smilo grass. I also grew some einkorn (wild wheat) on my property, which gave me a great harvest. The bread turned out a bit denser than regular bread, which is to be expected since it's made with coarse, stone-ground flour from ancient grains with lower gluten content. It has a nutty, rustic flavor and really brings out the unique tastes of wild grains.

Ingredients

- 2 cups (240 g) einkorn flour (or substitute bread or all-purpose flour)
- ¾ cup (120 g) wild grain flour mix (wild oats, wild barley, smilo grass, Indian ricegrass)
- ⅓ cup (15 g) curly dock or California buckwheat flour
- 1½ teaspoons (8 g) salt
- 1 tablespoon (15 g) sugar, maple syrup, or honey
- 1 packet (2¼ teaspoons) RapidRise yeast (or similar)
- ¾ cup (180 ml) warm water (120°–130°F [49°–54°C])
- 2 tablespoons (30 ml) olive oil

Method

1. In a large bowl, mix all the flours with the salt, sugar, and yeast.
2. Slowly add the warm water and olive oil to the dry ingredients, mixing until the dough comes together and feels slightly sticky. Add more water if needed.
3. Knead the dough on a lightly floured surface for 4 to 6 minutes, until smooth. Shape into a loaf or rolls and place in a greased bread pan or on a baking sheet.
4. Cover the dough with a damp cloth or plastic wrap and let it rise in a warm spot for 30 minutes, or until it doubles in size. Preheat the oven to 375°F (190°C) while the dough is rising.
5. Bake for 30 to 35 minutes. The bread is done when it sounds hollow when tapped or the internal temperature reaches 190° to 200°F (88°–93°C). I usually don't check anything and just bake for 30 minutes—it comes out perfect in my oven.
6. Let the bread cool completely on a wire rack before slicing. This bread is delicate when warm, so be patient before cutting into it.

Fermentation with Wild Grains and Seeds

Fermentation has always been my thing. If you've read my other books, you'll know it's a big part of my work. I even wrote an entire book about fermenting wild foods: *Wildcrafted Fermentation*. Naturally, my obsession has led me to explore how grains and seeds can be used in all kinds of ferments.

Grains and seeds have been a big part of fermentation for ages. A classic example is beer. It all starts with grains like barley, which are soaked in water to sprout—a step called malting. This process turns the starches in the grains into sugars, which are dissolved in water to make a sweet liquid called wort. Then, yeast is added to the wort, and it eats the sugars, turning them into alcohol. Along the way, fermentation creates those awesome flavors and aromas we love in beer. Depending on the type of beer, this can take anywhere from a few days to weeks.

But beer is just one example, and fermented grains and seeds are everywhere in our daily lives. Take a trip to the supermarket, and you'll spot fermented products like soy sauce, rice vinegar, malt vinegar, miso, vegan cheeses made with nuts and seeds, and more. Even bread and pastries rely on fermentation, and seed-based yogurts—made from flax, sunflower, or pumpkin seeds—are becoming super popular.

In terms of wild grains and seeds, you could go all out and make complex ferments, like beer, soy sauce, or miso. But honestly, my favorite way to use them is in simple lacto-ferments, where they will add texture and sometimes even a little extra flavor.

For example, great brome grains might be too chewy to eat when they're simply cooked due to their tough skin (bran), but once they're in a ferment, that chewiness becomes a fun feature. Seeds from plants like tumbleweed mustard, Sahara mustard, and tansy mustard bring nutty, earthy notes to the mix. Wild grains like oats, barley, and rye are also fantastic additions. My go-to method is to soak them overnight and then add them raw to the ferment. This way, they stay whole and don't turn mushy.

Toasted seeds are another great way to elevate your ferments when serving them. Instead of the usual roasted sesame seeds, I like to use roasted thistle sage seeds. They have a similar flavor but with a bit of a unique twist.

On the next few pages, you'll find more examples and ideas. Fermented grains and seeds offer endless possibilities for flavor and texture—perfect for experimenting and adding your own creative touch.

FERMENTED GRAINS AND SPROUTS

This is one of my favorite condiments—it's like a mix between a chunky hot sauce and a flavorful side dish. You can throw it on top of fish or eat it as is. The recipe is super flexible, so swap in your own local seeds and grains, or mix regular and wild ingredients. Don't hesitate to play around with this one.

Ingredients for a pint (500 ml) jar

2 tablespoons (26 g) dried wild or regular oats
2 tablespoons (26 g) dried wild or regular barley grains
1 teaspoon (about 3 g) great brome grains
7 ounces (170 g) sprouts (salad mix sprouts or mix of wild brassica sprouts)
1 large jalapeño or 2 medium ones, minced
5 small Thai chili, cayenne, or serrano peppers, minced
3 garlic cloves, minced
1 teaspoon (about 3 g) tumbleweed mustard seeds
1 tablespoon (6 g) grated ginger
2 teaspoons (5 g) gochugaru powder
1 tablespoon (about 8 g) gochugaru flakes
1 ounce (28 g) cilantro, minced
1½ teaspoons (8 g) salt

Method

1. Prepare the grains. Soak the oats and barley overnight and drain well. Cook the great brome for 60 minutes (see page 90).
2. In a bowl, combine all the ingredients. Mix well to evenly distribute the salt and spices. Transfer the mixture to a clean pint (500 ml) jar. Press it down to remove air pockets; the jar should end up ¾ full.
3. Close the jar and place it in a shaded spot at room temperature, away from direct sunlight.
4. Burp the jar twice daily by briefly opening the lid to release the fermentation gases. Press down or stir the mixture to distribute the acidity and remove gas pockets, then close the jar again.
5. After 5 to 7 days, fermentation activity will slow, and the mixture will develop a tangy flavor. The exact fermentation time will depend on room temperature. You can then transfer the jar to the refrigerator.
6. The fermented condiment is best eaten within 2 months for optimal flavor and texture.

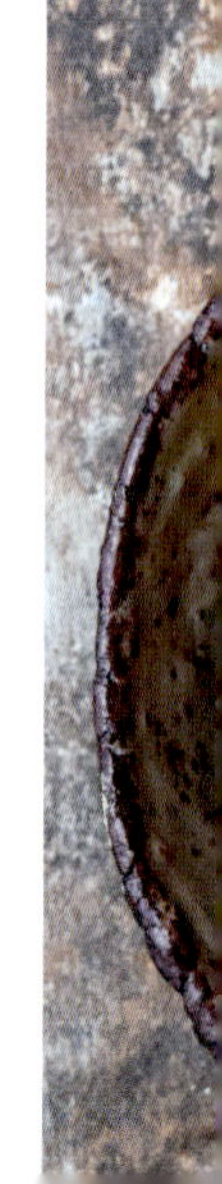

WILDER KIMCHI WITH BOK CHOY, WILD GRAINS, AND MUSTARD LEAVES

This is my go-to kimchi for my foraging classes in Los Angeles—my students really like it. I've tweaked the ingredients over time.

Ingredients for a pint (500 ml) jar

12 ounces (340 g) baby bok choy
2–3 teaspoons (10–15 g) salt (for salting the bok choy leaves)
1 ounce (28 g) wild radish or mustard leaves, chopped or chiffonade cut

Ingredients for the paste

2–3 garlic cloves, minced
1-inch piece (2.5 cm) ginger, minced
2 teaspoons (4 g) gochugaru flakes
2 teaspoons (4 g) gochugaru powder
3 teaspoons (15 ml) fish sauce
½ teaspoon (2.5 g) salt or 2 teaspoons (10 g) shrimp paste
1 tablespoon (15 g) chopped red onion
2 tablespoons (30 g) soaked or cooked wild grains and seeds (e.g., wild barley, great brome, wild oats)

Method

1. Separate the leaves of the baby bok choy and rinse them briefly in cold water, then drain. Place the leaves in a bowl and sprinkle them with salt. Gently massage the salt into the leaves and let them sit for a couple of hours to draw out moisture. Rinse the bok choy leaves twice in cold water to remove excess salt and drain.
2. In a bowl, combine the garlic, ginger, gochugaru flakes, gochugaru powder, fish sauce, salt (or shrimp paste), and chopped red onion; add 3 tablespoons (60 ml) of water and mix into a smooth paste.
3. Stir in the soaked or cooked wild grains and seeds.
4. Add the prepared bok choy leaves and the wild radish (or mustard) leaves to the paste. Mix thoroughly, ensuring all of the leaves are evenly coated with the paste. Cover the bowl and let the mixture stand at room temperature for 2 to 3 hours, which will make it easier to pack into a jar.
5. Transfer the mixture to a clean jar. Press down firmly to remove air pockets, leaving about 1 inch (2.5 cm) of space below the jar's rim. Close the jar and place it in a shaded spot at room temperature, away from direct sunlight.
6. Burp the jar twice daily by opening the lid to release fermentation gases and quickly pressing down on the mixture with a clean spoon to bring the acidic brine to the surface and remove excessive gas pockets; then close the jar again. Allow the kimchi to ferment at room temperature for 2 to 3 days, tasting daily until it's reached your desired tanginess. Once it's ready, refrigerate to slow the fermentation.

SPICY FERMENTED MEDLEY WITH WILD GRAINS AND SEEDS

This is a very tasty but spicy condiment. I keep changing the ingredients slightly, and they're always a hit in my foraging workshops and tastings. If it's too hot, use more bell peppers and fewer habaneros or Thai chilis.

As a forager, think of it as a concept recipe. In this recipe, I'm using a lot of local wild grains and seeds, but they are mostly from invasive plants that are found pretty much all over the world, so you should be able to replicate it somewhat easily. Instead of tumble mustard seeds, you can use local wild mustard seeds. Enjoy it with fish, tacos, and various other dishes, adding a unique and spicy kick.

Ingredients for a pint (500 ml) jar

1 ounce (30 g) wild oat grains
0.5 ounce (15 g) wild barley grains
0.3 ounce (7 g) great brome grains
3 ounces (90 g) chopped/sliced Thai peppers
1.5 ounces (45 g) chopped habaneros
1 ounce (30 g) wild radish sprouts
1.5 ounces (45 g) red bell pepper, chopped
0.5 ounce (15 g) red onions, chopped
1 teaspoon (5 g) tumbleweed mustard seeds
0.5 ounce (15 g) fresh ginger, grated
1 teaspoon (5 g) smoked jalapeño (chile morita) flakes
1 teaspoon (5 g) gochugaru powder
½ teaspoon (2.5 g) curry powder
0.5 ounce (15 g) cilantro, chopped
5 tablespoons (75 ml) sauerkraut juice
1½ teaspoons (7.5 g) sea salt
1 tablespoon (15 ml) fish sauce

Method

1. Prepare the wild oats and barley by soaking overnight. Prepare the great brome by cooking for 60 minutes (see page 90).
2. Mix everything together in a bowl, then transfer it to a clean pint jar, pressing the mixture down to remove air pockets.
3. Close the lid tightly. Burp the jar twice a day by loosening the lid to let the gases escape and gently stirring the contents each time.
4. After 10 days of fermentation, move the jar to the refrigerator to slow down the process and allow the flavors to develop further. Let it age in the fridge for at least a couple of weeks. The spiciness will mellow out over time, but it will remain a hot and flavorful condiment. Use within a few months for best flavor.

SPICY FERMENTED GRAINS AND GREENS SALSA

This is another one of my favorite condiments, and it can be made with a variety of wild greens. Instead of cilantro, you can use chopped or minced chickweed, wild chervil, miner's lettuce, or other savory wild greens. Try it!

Ingredients for a pint (500 ml) jar

1.5 ounces (45 g) mixed wild or regular grains (barley, great brome, etc.)
2 ounces (60 g) wild or regular oats
4 ounces (120 g) jalapeños, chopped
1.5 ounces (45 g) cilantro or savory wild greens, minced
1 ounce (30 g) onions, minced
2 ounces (60 g) red or yellow pepper, chopped
4 garlic cloves, minced
1 teaspoon (5 g) salt
2 tablespoons (30 ml) fish sauce

Method

1. Prepare the grains and oats by soaking them overnight or cooking them if necessary (e.g., great brome grains should be cooked for 60 minutes—see page 90).
2. Combine all of the ingredients in a bowl and mix thoroughly.
3. Transfer the mixture to a clean pint (500 ml) jar, pressing it down firmly to eliminate air pockets.
4. Close the lid and place the jar in a shaded spot at room temperature, away from direct sunlight.
5. Burp the jar twice daily by briefly opening the lid to release the fermentation gases. Press down or stir the mixture to distribute the acidity and remove gas pockets, then close the jar again.
6. After 5 to 7 days, fermentation activity will slow, and the mixture will develop a tangy flavor. The exact fermentation time will depend on room temperature. Transfer the jar to the refrigerator once fermentation is complete.
7. The salsa is best enjoyed within 2 months for optimal flavor and texture.

FERMENTED WILD GRAINS PORRIDGE: AN ANCIENT STAPLE

No matter where you look on the map, people have been fermenting grains into porridge for generations, way before probiotics were considered fancy. Our ancestors across Europe, Africa, and Asia figured out that soaking and fermenting grains not only made them easier to digest but also added flavor. This innovation was a survival food, a healing food, and a daily staple.

In Europe, folks in the Middle Ages made sour porridges from oats, barley, or rye. The Scots had *sowans*, a tangy oat porridge made by fermenting oat husks in water. In Russia and Eastern Europe, people used buckwheat and rye to make porridge with a natural sour kick.

In Africa, fermented porridge is still a staple. You've got *uji* in Kenya, *mahewu* in southern Africa, and *ogi* in Nigeria—all made from millet, sorghum, or maize. These porridges are thick, slightly sour, and packed with nutrition.

In China, people have been fermenting rice porridge for centuries, sometimes adding herbs for extra health benefits. Korea has *sikhye*, a sweet, lightly fermented rice drink that's been around forever.

Today, fermented porridges are making a comeback for all the right reasons—flavor, nutrition, and those gut-friendly probiotics. Of course, I had to take this in a wilder direction, but you can easily make this with commercial grains, too.

Ingredients for a ½ pint (125 ml) jar

1 ounce (28 g) great brome grains
1 tablespoon (7 g) wild barley grains
1 teaspoon (2.5 g) crabgrass
Around 3 ounces (85 g) wild oat grains
1–2 tbsp (15–30 ml) sauerkraut or kimchi juice (optional)
¼ tsp (2 g) salt

Method

1. Cook the great brome grains for 60 minutes (see page 90).
2. Grind the wild barley, crabgrass, and wild oats roughly in a stone grinder, then transfer to a jar. A food processor on low speed works, too.
3. Add the prepared great brome grains. (Don't grind the boiled grains.) These cooked grains are a little chewy, but they enhance the porridge's texture.
3. Add ¼ cup (60 ml) of water and the sauerkraut or kimchi juice (if using).
4. Add the salt, mix well, close the jar, and let ferment for 2 to 3 days at room temperature. Shake and burp the jar by briefly opening the lid at least once daily to release the fermentation gases. If the porridge is too thick, add a little water.

> ***Note:*** *The porridge develops a nice tangy flavor—sour but balanced, like a touch of lemony vinegar with a hint of cheese-like richness. When serving, you can emphasize the cheesy notes by adding nutritional yeast or miso to taste. If you're feeling creative, try mixing in roasted seeds (like sesame), spices, herbs, or even soy sauce. I often serve a small spoonful on acorn crackers at my wild food tasting events, and it always gets a great reaction!*

My trusty stone grinder is perfect for roughly grinding wild grains.

STONE-GROUND (OR NOT) DIJON-STYLE MUSTARD

Making your own mustard condiment from wild or commercial mustard seeds at home is not complicated. You can use either a stone grinder or a food processor or blender for the process. For a classic "Dijon" flavor, opt for black or brown mustard seeds. You can forage them or buy them at your local Middle Eastern, Indian, or Hispanic market.

Ingredients

¾ cup (130 g) black or brown mustard seeds

Around ⅔ cup (160 ml) red wine vinegar or apple cider vinegar

1 teaspoon (5 g) salt

1 tablespoon (15 g) honey, maple syrup, or sugar (optional)

Method

1. Place the mustard seeds in a small bowl or jar and add the vinegar. Note that you may end up needing a bit more vinegar later on; my recent batch, which used very dry seeds, required close to ¾ cup of vinegar.
2. Cover and allow the seeds to soak for a couple of days. This softens them, helps develop their pungency, and makes your job easier.
3. Transfer the soaked seeds to a stone grinder, blender, or food processor, and add the salt and sweetener (if using). Grind or blend the mixture until it reaches your desired consistency. If the mustard is too thick, add a little more vinegar to thin it out.
4. Taste your mustard and adjust the seasoning or sweetness according to your preference.
5. Transfer the mustard to a jar or container and seal it tightly. Refrigerate the mustard for at least a week before using. Freshly made mustard tastes somewhat bitter, so this waiting period allows the flavor to mellow. This condiment will keep for up to 6 months in the refrigerator.

Note: *Instead of using only a single vinegar, you can blend 2 parts apple cider vinegar and 1 part red wine vinegar. Sometimes I use 2 parts vinegar and 1 part wine or beer.*

GREEN CATTAIL CATKINS IN WILD SEEDS VINAIGRETTE

Once, when out foraging for my weekly class, I found some unripe cattail catkins. They were smaller than usual, but still perfect for making this tasty dish. The idea came from my mother, who used to serve artichoke leaves with vinaigrette—a simple but delicious favorite. I wanted to recreate that experience with wild ingredients, and cattail catkins turned out to be a great substitute.

Green cattail catkins are completely edible—both the male part (on top) and the female part (below). The male part eventually sheds its pollen and disappears, while the female part matures, turning brown and fluffy later in the year, at which point it is no longer edible. This recipe uses the female parts while they're still green and tender.

I normally boil green catkins for about 20 minutes, but since these were on the smaller side, I cut that down to 10 minutes. They ended up with a nice corn-like flavor.

I then served them with my go-to homemade wild seed vinaigrette, which I always have in the fridge. The recipe changes a little each time, but the base stays the same. I make a fresh batch (about ½ cup) every week for my daily salads, and it worked perfectly with the catkins.

Ingredients

Several cattail catkins
1 ounce (28 g) red onion or shallots, chopped
½ jalapeño or similar pepper, chopped
2 teaspoons (10 g) Pickled Wild Seeds (page 262)
1 tablespoon (15 g) Stone-Ground Dijon-Style Mustard (page 259) or store-bought
½ teaspoon (2.5 g) garlic powder
1 teaspoon (1.5 g) Italian herbs (I use my own wild spice blend)
3 tablespoons (45 ml) elderberry wine vinegar or red wine vinegar
1–2 tablespoons (60 ml) olive oil
Salt, to taste

Method

1. Boil the green cattail catkins for about 10 minutes, or until tender. Drain and set aside.
2. In a jar, combine the remaining ingredients with 2 tablespoons (30 ml) of water. Seal the jar and shake well.
3. Drizzle the vinaigrette over the boiled catkins or use as a dip.

PICKLED WILD SEEDS

This is easily one of my top five favorite condiments. I use it all the time—in potato salads, ferments, sandwiches, you name it. It's a must-have in my wild food classes because it's salty, sweet, and bold, and it works with so many recipes.

The method is quite direct—just soak wild seeds in a mix of vinegar, salt, and a bit of sugar. I usually go with black mustard seeds as the base because they bring that classic mustardy flavor with a little spicy kick.

The exact seeds I use change with the seasons. Below is a recipe for a batch I made during the fall.

Ingredients for a pint (500 ml) jar

⅓ cup (60 g) yellow mustard seeds
⅓ cup (60 g) black mustard seeds
1 tablespoon (6 g) nettle seeds
2 teaspoons (7 g) wild chia seeds
1 tablespoon (10 g) tumbleweed mustard seeds
1 tablespoon (10 g) tansy mustard seeds
1 teaspoon (7 g) broadleaf plantain seeds
1 teaspoon (7 g) poppy seeds
1 teaspoon (7 g) wild watercress seeds
1 teaspoon (7 g) wild arugula seeds
1 cup (250 ml) apple cider vinegar
3 tablespoons (45 ml) maple syrup
1½ teaspoons salt

Method

1. Place all the seeds in a pint jar—it should be about half full. Add the vinegar, maple syrup, and salt.
2. Seal the jar and let it stand in a cool, shady spot for a couple of weeks, stirring daily during the first week. At first, it might taste pretty bitter, but with time, the flavors mellow out.
3. Depending on the seeds, you might need to adjust the vinegar or seed amounts to get the consistency you like. After 2 weeks, move the jar to the fridge. It'll keep for at least a year!

WILD DIJON POTATO SALAD

This potato salad is an easy no-fuss dish to throw together, but it's packed with flavor and works with whatever wild greens are in season. In early spring, I might use chickweed or wild chervil, while later in the year, wild arugula is a great addition. If foraging isn't an option, you can easily swap in store-bought herbs like parsley, chives, or cilantro.

Ingredients

2.25 pounds (1 kg) baby red potatoes
2–3 teaspoons (5 g) salt, divided
2 tablespoons (30 g) Stone-Ground Dijon-Style Mustard (page 259)
1 tablespoon (15 g) Pickled Wild Seeds (page 262, optional)
¼ cup (60 ml) red wine vinegar
2 teaspoons (4 g) herbes de Provence or Italian herbs
2 teaspoons (4 g) garlic powder
2 tablespoons (15 ml) olive oil (optional)
4 ounces (115 g) red onion, chopped (along with a few slices, for garnish)
1–2 ounces (30–60 g) wild greens (e.g., chickweed, arugula, wild chervil), chopped

Method

1. Scrub the potatoes well and cut them in half. Put them in a large pot, cover with cold water, and add 1 to 2 teaspoons of salt. Bring to a boil, then reduce the heat, cover, and let them simmer until fork-tender, about 15 to 20 minutes. Drain and set aside to cool slightly.
2. In a small bowl, whisk together the mustard, pickled wild seeds, red wine vinegar, herbs, garlic powder, remaining 1 teaspoon salt, and olive oil, if using.
3. Once the potatoes have cooled a bit, transfer them to a large bowl. Add the chopped red onion along with the wild greens. Pour the dressing over the top and gently fold it into the salad.
4. Taste and adjust the seasoning if needed. Allow 15 to 20 minutes for the flavors to come together before serving.
5. Garnish with the onion slices and serve at room temperature or chilled.

LAMB'S-QUARTER "QUINOA" AND WILD RICE

This wild rice dish pairs perfectly with Lamb's-Quarter "Quinoa" (page 106) since both ingredients take about the same time to cook. You could even throw them in the same pot to make things easier.

It's a hearty side for two, made mostly with foraged greens and wild seeds or grains. I don't forage wild rice, but instead of using the commercially grown kind, I always go for hand-harvested rice from tribal members. Supporting tribal harvests helps protect their land, culture, and traditional economy.

Ingredients

5 tablespoons (40 g) wild rice
2 tablespoons (15 g) lamb's-quarter seeds
½ teaspoon (1 g) tumbleweed mustard seeds
2 teaspoons (5 g) minced onion
1–2 teaspoons (5–10 g) minced jalapeños
1½ tablespoons (22 ml) seasoned rice vinegar
2–3 mushrooms, wild or store-bought (I used wild oyster mushrooms), cooked and sliced
1 teaspoon (1 g) minced dill weed, chickweed, or wild chervil

Method

1. Rinse the wild rice and lamb's-quarter seeds (see page 106), then place them in a small pot and add roughly double their volume in water. Bring to a boil, then reduce the heat, cover, and let them simmer for about 25 minutes, or until tender. Drain any excess water.
2. Transfer the cooked grains to a bowl and add the mustard seeds, onion, jalapeños, vinegar, and mushrooms. Mix everything together and let it sit for a few minutes so the flavors meld.
3. Mix or sprinkle with the fresh dill, chickweed, or wild chervil before serving.

VEGETARIAN MEATBALLS WITH WILD FLOURS, SEEDS, AND GRAINS

I've always thought that the grains and seeds I collect from the environment would make a great addition to vegetarian or vegan meatballs or burger patties. It took me a while to put a recipe together, as I wanted people to also be able to use regular ingredients. But I have to tell you, the wild flavors are so much better. Feel free to experiment with this recipe and add your own ingredients—make it your own!

Ingredients for 9 medium-size meatballs

2 tablespoons (20 g) wild grains (e.g., wild oats, great brome, wild barley)
1 tablespoon olive oil
½ large onion (150 g), finely chopped
2 garlic cloves, minced
1 cup (150 g) finely chopped mushrooms (cremini, baby bella or wild oyster mushrooms)
5 tablespoons (60 g) breadcrumbs
2 tablespoons (15 g) wild flour
¼ cup (27 g) nutritional yeast
2 teaspoons (6 g) wild or store-bought chia seeds
1 teaspoon (3 g) tumbleweed mustard seeds (optional)
½ teaspoon (1.5 g) smoked paprika
2 teaspoons (2.5 g) herbes de Provence or Italian herbs
1 teaspoon ground cumin
2 teaspoons (10 ml) Worcestershire sauce (vegetarian)
1 teaspoon salt, or to taste
1 egg

Method

1. Soak the wild grains overnight or cook as necessary (in the case of great brome, which should be boiled for 60 minutes—see page 90). Drain thoroughly.
2. Heat the oil in a skillet over medium heat. Sauté the onion until translucent, about 5 minutes. Add the garlic and cook for another minute. Remove from the heat and let cool completely.
3. Preheat the oven to 375°F (190°C). Grease or line a baking sheet with parchment.
4. In a large bowl, combine the chopped mushrooms, cooled onion and garlic mixture, breadcrumbs, wild flour, nutritional yeast, wild grains, chia seeds, tumbleweed mustard seeds (if using), smoked paprika, herbes de Provence, cumin, Worcestershire sauce, and salt.
5. Add the egg and mix well. Adjust the consistency with additional breadcrumbs or a splash of water if needed.
6. Form the mixture into 9 golf ball–size meatballs.
7. Place the meatballs on the baking sheet. Bake for 15 minutes, turning halfway through for even browning.
8. Serve warm with your favorite sauce, paired with pasta, rice, or salad.

Note: *For the wild flour, I used a blend of 50 percent wild oat and wild barley flour, combined with 50 percent cold-leached acorn flour. You can use organic whole wheat flour if you prefer. The wild grains can be replaced with store-bought grains such as wheat, barley, or oats.*

Marinara Sauce

For the meatball preparation in the photo, I made a simple marinara sauce.

Ingredients

2 tablespoons (30 ml) olive oil
3 garlic cloves, minced
1 can (28 oz / 800 g) crushed tomatoes
1 teaspoon dried oregano
½ teaspoon (3 g) salt
¼ teaspoon (0.5 g) black pepper
¼ teaspoon (0.5 g) red pepper flakes (optional)
1 teaspoon (7 g) honey or maple syrup (optional)
2 tablespoons (5 g) fresh basil, chopped (optional)

Instructions

1. Heat the olive oil in a saucepan over medium heat.
2. Add the garlic and sauté for about 1 minute, until fragrant.
3. Stir in the crushed tomatoes, oregano, salt, black pepper, and red pepper flakes, if using.
4. Reduce the heat to low and simmer uncovered for 15 to 20 minutes, stirring occasionally.
5. Taste and adjust the seasoning, adding honey or maple syrup if the sauce is too acidic.
6. Stir in the fresh basil (if using) before serving warm with the vegetarian meatballs.

POWER BALLS

I used to make power bars, a kind of raw energy bar, with this method, but this time, I decided to roll them into bite-size power balls. They're fun to plate and easy to snack on, and make an eye-catching treat.

This is more of a method than a strict recipe, and it's a great way to experiment with bold flavors. The base is simple—date paste and seeds—but you can get creative with additions. Play around with flavors and textures by mixing in ingredients like chocolate powder, coffee, vanilla extract, black sage powder, roasted bay nut powder, pine or fir sugar, wild carrot seed powder, poppy seeds, or wild dill seeds. Or see the spices section of this book (page 150) for more flavorful ideas. There's no limit to what you can create!

For extra texture and crunch, roll the balls in toasted seeds, cocoa powder, dark chocolate shavings, pine pollen, black sage powder, and so on.

Ingredients

1½ cups (300 g) date paste
½ cup (150 g) mixed seeds and flavorful ingredients (e.g., chia, flixweed, flax, sesame, etc.)
Toppings of choice for coating

Method

1. Mash the date paste with the seeds and other flavorful ingredients in a bowl, kneading the mixture with your hands until everything is well combined. If you have a stone grinder, you can use it to create a smoother paste and better incorporate the ingredients.
2. If the mixture feels too soft to roll into balls, spread it onto a parchment-lined dish or tray and refrigerate for 1 to 2 hours until it firms up. If it already holds its shape, skip this step.
3. Once firm, scoop small portions and then use your hands to roll them into bite-size balls.
4. Coat each ball in your chosen topping—fennel powder, black sage powder mixed with cocoa, toasted seeds, or any other flavorful dusting.
5. Refrigerate in an airtight container for up to 2 weeks.

Power balls with various toppings: native chia seeds, tansy mustard seeds, lerps sugar (a crunchy insect honeydew), and cattail pollen.

RUSTIC WILD FLOURS PASTA

This is such a fun and delicious project! I use some of my wild flours to create this unique pasta, featuring non-native, and often invasive, wild seeds and grains from Southern California, like wild barley, oats, smilo grass, and curly dock. The cooked pasta has a perfect texture, with wonderfully nutty flavors from the toasted acorn flour. It's surprisingly easy to make, too!

Ingredients

1¼ cups (150 g) einkorn flour or all-purpose flour
¼ cup (30 g) acorn flour, cold-leached and toasted
¼ cup (30 g) curly dock flour
¼ cup (30 g) mixed wild flours (such as wild oats, wild barley, or smilo grass)
1 teaspoon (5.5 g) salt, plus more for boiling the pasta
3 eggs
1 tablespoon (15 ml) olive oil

Method

1. In a bowl or on a clean surface, combine all of the flours with the salt. Create a well in the center.
2. Crack the eggs into the well and add the olive oil. Use a fork to whisk the eggs and oil, gradually pulling in flour from the edges until a dough forms.
3. Knead by hand on a clean surface for 8 to 10 minutes, until smooth and elastic. Wrap the dough in plastic wrap or cover it with a damp towel and let it rest for 30 minutes.
4. Divide the dough into smaller portions. Roll out each portion with a rolling pin on a lightly floured surface until thin (about 1 mm). Use a knife or pizza cutter to cut the dough into your desired pasta shape.
5. Bring a pot of water to a boil and add salt. Boil the pasta until tender, about 2–4 minutes, depending on thickness. Toss with your preferred sauce.

Note: *To store fresh pasta in the fridge, lightly coat the pasta with flour to prevent sticking and divide into portions for easier use. Place the pasta in an airtight container or resealable bag. Store in the fridge for up to 2 days. For longer storage, consider freezing; fresh pasta freezes well and lasts for 1 to 2 months.*

Combine the flours and salt in a bowl or on a clean surface. Create a well in the center. Crack the eggs into the well and add olive oil.

Use a fork to whisk the eggs and oil, gradually pulling in flour from the edges until a dough forms.

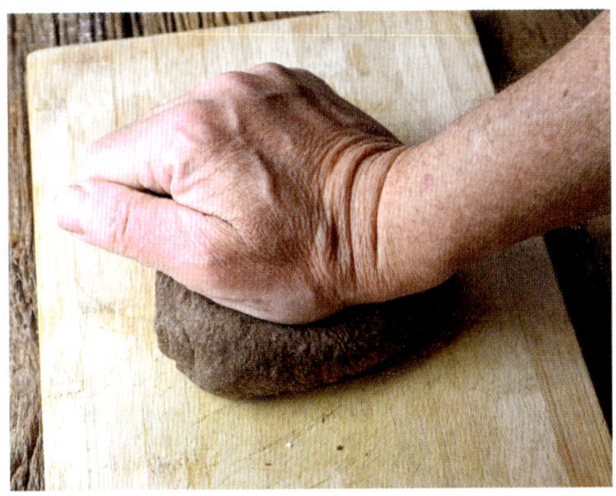

Knead by hand on a clean surface for 8 to 10 minutes, until smooth and elastic.

Wrap the dough in plastic wrap or cover it with a damp towel and let it rest for 30 minutes.

Divide the dough into smaller portions. Roll each portion out with a rolling pin on a lightly floured surface until thin (about 1 mm).

Use a knife or pizza cutter to cut into your desired pasta shape. Boil in salted water for 2 to 4 minutes, depending on thickness.

SAVORY SPROUTED WILD GRAIN AND SEED PANCAKES

This dish highlights local grains and seeds that, while not native to Southern California, thrive in the region. I use wild oats, barley, and tumbleweed mustard seeds for their nutty flavors. The grains were sprouted in jars (see page 207). I serve mine with Greek yogurt, smoked salmon, dill, and wild mustard flowers.

Ingredients (Makes about eight small pancakes, 2.5 inches / 6 cm)

2 tablespoons (16 g) wild barley grains
½ cup (70 g) sprouted grains (I used einkorn)
2 tablespoons (16 g) sprouted wild oats
1 teaspoon (2.5 g) tumbleweed mustard seeds
4 ounces (40 g) minced jalapeños
0.7 ounce (20 g) minced red onion
0.35 ounce (10 g) radish sprouts
½ teaspoon (2.5 g) salt
½ garlic clove, minced
1 tablespoon (15 ml) Dijon mustard (commercial or homemade, see page 259)
1 teaspoon (2 g) herbes de Provence (or Italian herbs)
2 eggs
3 tablespoons (24 g) whole wheat flour

Method

1. Boil the wild barley grains for 30 to 40 minutes.
2. In a bowl, combine the prepared wild barley, sprouted grains, wild oats, mustard seeds, jalapeños, onion, radish sprouts, salt, garlic, mustard, and herbs and mix well.
3. In a separate bowl, beat the eggs and gradually whisk in the flour until smooth.
4. Add about 3 to 4 tablespoons (45–60 ml) of batter to the sprouted grain blend and mix well.
5. Heat a skillet greased with olive oil over medium heat. Scoop small portions onto the skillet, flatten slightly with a spatula, and cook until golden brown on both sides.
6. Set the cooked pancakes on a paper towel–lined plate to remove any excess oil.
7. Serve hot.

WILD BERRY AND SEED FRUIT PASTE COOKIES

I call these "cookies" because of the way they look, but they're really fruit leather made the old-fashioned way—using a stone grinder.

Anyone can make these with a bit of foraging knowledge and whatever ingredients are available. I used local wild berries and edible seeds, but you can easily swap in store-bought options like blueberries, grapes, chia, and sesame seeds. The method is simple, and the result is delicious—nutty, fruity, sweet, and packed with nutrition!

For this batch, I used blackberries, manzanita berries, tumbleweed mustard seeds, wild chia seeds, and thistle sage seeds. The manzanita berries (with their apple-like flavor) were ground into powder, and the thistle sage seeds were lightly roasted. The tumbleweed mustard seeds have a hazelnut-like taste. When I was in Colorado, I did something similar with Oregon grapes and feral apples as a base. Endless creative possibilities!

Ingredients (makes 10 cookies)

1 cup (150 g) blackberries, blueberries, or grapes (wild or not)
2 teaspoons (4 g) manzanita berry powder
2 teaspoons (6 g) chia seeds (wild or commercial)
1 teaspoon (3 g) roasted thistle sage seeds (or roasted sesame seeds)
1 teaspoon (4 g) tumbleweed mustard seeds (optional)

Method

1. Mash everything together in a stone grinder, like a molcajete, or a food processor.
2. Shape the mixture into small balls and place them on parchment paper. Gently press them flat with a fork and let them dehydrate in the sun. Or, set a dehydrator to 115°F (46°C) and dry until firm but still slightly chewy, about 12 to 24 hours, depending on humidity.
3. These cookies keep in the fridge for at least a month and can be frozen for up to a year.

WILD INFUSED OIL

Did you know that combining toasted wild seeds and grains can add deep, complex flavors to infused oils? A mix of ingredients like sesame seeds, thistle sage seeds, and wild grains like oats and barley creates a rich, nutty, and aromatic oil—perfect for drizzling over salads, roasted vegetables, or soups and adding depth to sauces.

Ingredients

¼ cup (30 g) sesame seeds
2 teaspoons (6 g) thistle sage seeds (or other aromatic seeds)
2 teaspoons (6 g) wild barley or wild oat grains
1 cup (240 ml) avocado oil (or another neutral oil)

Method

1. Start by toasting the sesame seeds, thistle sage seeds, and wild barley separately in a dry pan over low heat until fragrant. Toasting each seed or grain separately will give you more control over the result.
2. Once toasted, use a mortar and pestle to gently crush the seeds and grains. The goal is to break them up slightly, not turn them into powder.
3. Place the crushed seeds and grains in a clean, dry jar and pour in the oil, making sure the seeds and grains are fully submerged.
4. Cover the jar and let it stand in a warm spot out of direct sunlight for 1 to 2 weeks. Shake the jar gently once a day to help blend the flavors.
5. When the infusion is ready, strain the oil through a fine sieve or cheesecloth to remove the solids. Store the finished oil in a clean, airtight bottle.

Note: *You can also make infused oils with wild seeds like caraway, fennel, or mustard. Other great additions include herbs and spices like basil, garlic, oregano, and rosemary.*

RESOURCES

Plants for a Future (PFAF) Database

Provides information on over 7,000 useful plants worldwide, including plants with edible seeds.

www.pfaf.org

Native American Ethnobotany Database

A comprehensive resource documenting the use of plants by Native American tribes, including seeds for food, medicine, and more.

http://naeb.brit.org

USDA PLANTS Database

Offers detailed botanical information on plants native to the U.S., including species with edible seeds.

https://plants.usda.gov

Seed Savers Exchange

While primarily a resource for preserving heirloom seeds, the database offers insights into edible seed varieties.

www.seedsavers.org

Literature

Edible Seeds and Grains of California Tribes and the Klamath Tribe of Oregon in the Phoebe Apperson Hearst Museum of Anthropology Collections by M. Kat Anderson, Jim Effenberger, Don Joley, and Deborah J. Lionakis Meyer (Davis, CA: Natural Resources Conservation Service, 2012).

This report is available online through multiple sources and can be found with a quick search of its title.

INDEX

Note: Page numbers in *italics* indicate photographs.

C

D

G

H

I

J

K

Q

R

S

T

U

V

W

Y

Z

ABOUT THE AUTHOR

Pascal Baudar is the author of four previous books: *Wildcrafted Vinegars* (2022), *Wildcrafted Fermentation* (2020), *The Wildcrafting Brewer* (2018), and *The New Wildcrafted Cuisine* (2016). A self-described "culinary alchemist," he leads classes in traditional food preservation techniques. Through his business, Urban Outdoor Skills, he has introduced thousands of home cooks, celebrity chefs, and foodies to the flavors offered by their wild landscapes. Baudar was named one of the most influential local tastemakers by *Los Angeles Magazine*.